Technology-enhanced Learning

in the Early Years Foundation Stage

KT-514-580

EARLY YEARS

You might also like the following books from Critical Publishing.

The Critical Years: Early Years Development from Conception to Five
By Tim Gully
978-1-909330-73-3

Developing as a Reflective Early Years Professional: A Thematic Approach, Second Edition
By Carol Hayes, Jayne Daly, Mandy Duncan, Ruth Gill and Anne Whitehouse
978-1-911106-22-7

Early Years Placements
By Jackie Musgrave and Nicola Stobbs
978-1-909682-65-8

Early Years Policy and Practice: A Critical Alliance
By Pat Tomlinson
978-1-909330-61-0

Global Childhoods
By Monica Edwards, edited by Chelle Davison
978-1-909682-69-6

Language, Literacy and Communication in the Early Years
By Carol Hayes
978-1-910391-54-9

Learning through Movement in the Early Years
By Sharon Tredgett
978-1-909682-81-8

Studying for your Early Years Degree
Edited by Jackie Musgrave, Maggi Savin-Baden and Nicola Stobbs
978-1-911106-42-5

Well-being in the Early Years
By Caroline Bligh, Sue Chambers, Chelle Davison, Ian Lloyd, Jackie Musgrave, June O'Sullivan and Susan Waltham
978-1-909330-65-8

Our titles are also available in a range of electronic formats. To order please go to our website www.criticalpublishing.com or contact our distributor, NBN International, 10 Thornbury Road, Plymouth PL6 7PP, telephone 01752 202301 or email orders@nbninternational.com.

Technology-enhanced Learning

in the Early Years Foundation Stage

MOIRA SAVAGE & ANTHONY BARNETT

EARLY
YEARS

First published in 2017 by Critical Publishing Ltd

All rights reserved. No part of this publication may be reproduced, stored in a retrieval system, or transmitted in any form or by any means, electronic, mechanical, photocopying, recording or otherwise, without prior permission in writing from the publisher.

The authors have made every effort to ensure the accuracy of information contained in this publication, but assume no responsibility for any errors, inaccuracies, inconsistencies and omissions. Likewise every effort has been made to contact copyright holders. If any copyright material has been reproduced unwittingly and without permission the Publisher will gladly receive information enabling them to rectify any error or omission in subsequent editions.

Copyright © 2017 Moira Savage and Anthony Barnett.
Chapter 7 written with Michelle Rogers

British Library Cataloguing in Publication Data
A CIP record for this book is available from the British Library

ISBN: 978-1-911106-18-0

This book is also available in the following e-book formats:

MOBI: 978-1-911106-19-7
EPUB: 978-1-911106-20-3
Adobe e-book reader: 978-1-911106-21-0

The rights of Moira Savage and Anthony Barnett to be identified as the authors of this work have been asserted by them in accordance with the Copyright, Design and Patents Act 1988.

Cover design by Out of House Limited
Text design by Greensplash Limited
Project management by Out of House Publishing
Printed and bound in Great Britain by TJ International, Padstow, Cornwall

Critical Publishing
3 Connaught Road
St Albans
AL3 5RX

www.criticalpublishing.com

MIX
Paper from responsible sources
FSC® C013056
www.fsc.org

SHREWSBURY COLLEGE LIBRARY
Inv No. 1862204   Date 9/8/18
Ord No. 4700 5137   Date
Class No. 371.33 SAV
Price £22.99   Checked
082421

Contents

Acknowledgements

The publishers would like to thank the following companies for permission to include images from their products in this book:

2Simple, Figures 10.3, 10.4, 10.5 and 10.6 (pp 126, 127 and 130)

Barefoot, Figure 4.2 and 4.3 (pp 44 and 45)

codeSpark, Figure 4.11 (p 58)

Crick Software, Figure 11.5 (p 144)

DrTechniko, Figure 4.5 (p 51)

Inclusive Technology, Figures 11.1, 11.2, 11.3, 11.4 (pp 136, 137, 141 and 142)

Jolly Learning Ltd, Figures 8.1, 8.2 and 8.3 (pp 101 and 102)

Kinderlab, Figure 4.10 (p 56)

National Literacy Trust, Figure 2.1 (p 11)

New Zealand Government, Figure 7.1 (p 91)

Primo Toys, Figure 4.9 (p 55)

Scratchjr, Figure 4.4 (p 48)

Widgit Software, Figure 5.1 (p 63)

Wonder Workshop, Figure 4.6 (p 52)

The authors would like to thank Michelle Rogers for her contribution to Chapter 7, and in particular for the case study and discussion.

Meet the authors

Moira Savage is a technology-enhanced learning leader and subject leader for primary computing at the University of Worcester. Her research focuses on technology and learning, from early childhood to higher education. She previously worked in primary schools and co-ordinated information and communication technology (ICT) across several schools.

Anthony Barnett works at the University of Worcester where his teaching role includes primary design and technology, creativity in foundation subject teaching and educational studies modules focusing on issues in ICT. He has a particular interest in the early years and supports undergraduate and PGCE students in their research projects focusing on the early years.

1 Overview of chapters

Introduction

Discussing technologies in relation to early childhood (birth to five years of age) education can provoke a wide range of passionate responses from sceptics to enthusiasts. This book will detail and discuss the issues in a neutral and research-informed manner. The book aims to help early years professionals confidently unpick complex issues; understand the scope of technology available; explore the interplay between learning and specific technologies; and create a vision for a technology-enabled learning environment that is child-centred, playful, creative and interactive.

Throughout the book there will be a strong emphasis on the children themselves selecting, exploring and using technologies in an enabling and empowering way across indoor and outdoor learning spaces. The book's approach goes beyond where *technology* is typically referred to within the confines of *understanding of the world* and challenges professionals to consider *if* and *when* technologies may make a wider contribution. The suggestions for selecting and deploying technologies will embrace the characteristics of effective learning as detailed in the Early Years Foundation Stage (EYFS) framework. The approaches suggested within the book always have children centre stage; recognising their natural curiosity, desire to explore and play. It is argued that these factors should be the driver in determining the choice and availability of technology in settings and not vice versa.

Who will benefit from reading this book?

The book is written to appeal and be relevant to a range of educators working in the early years. You may be in training or an experienced professional wishing to explore your use of technology and undertake continued professional development. The book acknowledges that you may fall under a number of professional titles including; early years practitioner, someone with Early Years Teacher Status (EYTS) or a graduate with Qualified Teacher Status (QTS) working in early years (three to seven) in a school setting; typically in reception or attached kindergarten. This book is also appropriate for both undergraduate and postgraduate students on Education, Early Childhood and Initial Teacher Training courses in the UK and internationally. The text may also appeal to allied professionals (eg health visitors) and interested parents who want to make informed decisions about their children's use of technology at home.

Chapter features

Technologies evolve constantly, become more portable and less expensive with higher levels of functionality – this can be daunting for both new and experienced professionals. In this book you will be introduced to familiar and newer technologies that can be deployed purposefully to enhance learning. Examples of devices and applications are suggested throughout. However, rather than providing an exhaustive list of the latest *must-have app*, you are prompted to think critically and analytically about the interrelationship between pedagogy and functionality. This level of criticality will help inspire you to explore and discover other technologies and applications over time. This approach will help to foster confidence in those educators nervous about using technology and will motivate confident technology users to think outside the box and innovate.

Each chapter begins with a section outlining the contents and identifying the professional links in relation to statutory guidance. Care is taken to explore how the areas of learning and specific Early Learning Goals can be interpreted to include technology. You are encouraged to embrace your existing pedagogical and experiential knowledge rather than abandon it because it doesn't explicitly make reference to technology. The authors will guide you to make the links as to how technology can enhance learning within these theoretical models and principles of effective practice. Embedded within each chapter are carefully selected *critical questions*. These questions are intended to give you the opportunity to pause and reflect, make links to your current practice and robustly consider your current beliefs and ideas about technology-enhanced learning. Different readers may come to slightly different conclusions in response to the questions; it is your unique journey with technology and that is fine.

Additionally, you will encounter illustrative case studies detailing examples from across the age range. Each case study is followed by a *commentary*, which unpicks pedagogical points and analyses how the technology is scaffolding learning. These are intended to help you both visualise potential activities or consider how you could re-interpret similar scenarios you may have encountered. Where appropriate, sections are included that focus on *international perspectives*, exploring practices and initiatives across the globe and encouraging you to consider the position of your culturally situated practices with technology. Finally, each chapter will suggest some recommended reading should you wish to explore a particular topic in more depth.

Chapter 2: What is technology-enhanced learning?

This chapter explores a holistic definition of what can be considered *technology* and what is meant by *technology-enhanced learning*. Is it the same as learning with technology?

You will be asked to be critical and focus on *how* and *when* the technology is bringing about enhancement. Time is spent deconstructing the facets and implications of the phrase *technology-enhanced learning*. Although these constructs really apply across all phases of learning (even higher education), care is taken to explore them in relation to early years education. This deepened understanding will enable you to consider the extent to which functionality is exploited to its full potential and to consider *who* typically has control of these technologies – the children or the adult? In your setting, who gets to choose *what*, *when* and *how* children play and explore with technology? Furthermore, how does this contradict or complement the children's learning using technology at home?

Chapter 3: Key debates and research evidence

A range of people will pick up this book; you will be somewhere along the spectrum in your attitude and disposition to technology based on your prior experiences. Some of you may be very resistant to technology and believe it shouldn't really have a place in early childhood education. Others might feel they lack confidence and capability but ought to learn about this topic. And there will also be those of you who may already be educational technology evangelists who want more ideas! It is acknowledged that not all technology solutions are effective or deployed well and a critical stance is maintained in discussion. Developing this criticality is the essence of this chapter – *where is the evidence?* should become your mantra.

As an early years educator you often have to face a baffling array of fact and fiction claims about both the benefits and dangers of technology use with young children. The deliberate approach taken in this chapter is to articulate these common beliefs, fears and/or claims. You will probably have encountered headlines and parenting guides suggesting technology use can harm children's physical and mental well-being; or that technology leads to childhood obesity from hours sat staring at a screen; that technology causes anti-social behaviour and isolation etc. The factors underlying these claims will be highlighted and you will be guided through some of the emerging research to reinforce or debunk these populist statements about technology. Often, all technologies are packaged together as *technology* and the full account as to whether they are passive or interactive, self-selected and initiated or adult-directed is ignored. A picture of digital childhoods will be examined and notions of *digital natives* challenged, ie that today's young learners do not need to be 'taught' how to use technology.

Chapter 4: Understanding the world: technology

When first glancing at this book, you probably wondered whether the entire book was going to be about this sub-area of *Understanding the world: technology*. Hopefully you have realised already that it has a much wider focus than that. This area of learning is discussed early on in the book as it also gives a holistic sense of why technology-enhanced learning is so relevant in today's world. The EYFS framework statement, '*children recognise that a range of technology is used in places such as homes and schools. They select and use technology for particular purposes*', begins to suggest the possibilities that this chapter explores at length. Here the components of this strand are categorised into the three themes adopted in the national curriculum computing programmes of study: *Computer Science*, *Digital Literacy* and *Information Technology* (DfE, 2014). The chapter is not about primary computing but the analysis given explores how the seeds of these concepts, attitudes and capabilities are evident in early years practice. Many of the practices you employ to foster problem-solving and thinking critically resonate with aspects developed later in relation to *computational thinking*. The characteristics of effective learning are explored through the lens of approaches needed for computational thinking; *tinkering*, *creating*, *debugging* (fixing mistakes), *persevering* and *collaborating*. The chapter highlights how these approaches manifest in common early years practice and it is argued that these kindergarten, playful pedagogic approaches should also be adopted further on in education. Global trends are reflected upon and we review the educational/toy manufacturers' innovative responses to introducing young children to coding (programming).

The chapter dedicates an important section to discussing digital childhood and what growing up as a digital citizen might entail. Importantly, you are encouraged to explore a stance that embodies scaffolding children to understand and empower themselves in a digital word; ie to become digitally literate.

Chapter 5: Communication and language

The chapter will review the exemplification of the area of learning and development – *Communication and Language*; specifically *listening and attention*, *understanding* and *speaking* (DfE, 2014). You will explore how technologies can be utilised for developing children's speaking and listening skills. Audio recording and playback functionality can empower young children to give detailed verbal accounts of their unique perspective. Young children have the opportunity to hear back the sounds and language they are using. Multimodal and interactive texts can naturally support attentive listening in individual or group contexts. The chapter will show how you can scaffold experiences for children by recording simple instructions (with talking boxes, or recordable clipboards) that children can play back at their own pace, repeating when necessary, to foster independence.

Chapter 6: Physical development

This chapter asks you to consider the potential role of technology in relation to the *physical development* (DfE, 2014, p 7) area of learning, encompassing both fine and gross motor skills and physical exercise. The EYFS framework states that children must have the opportunity to learn how to '*handle equipment and tools effectively*' and this chapter will ask you to consider what this means within the wider notion of object affordances (DfE, 2014, p 10). iPads and tablet devices are revisited and the notion of *digital skill development* considered. The chapter ends by looking into the future and at what advances in technology might mean for psychomotor capability. *Exergaming* and *gamification* are considered in terms of motivation, enjoyment and tracking accomplishments and activity levels.

Chapter 7: Personal, social and emotional development

This chapter examines technology-enhanced learning in relation to the *'prime area of personal, social and emotional development'* (DfE, 2014, p 7). Pertinent questions from Chapter 3 are revisited in relation to technology and social interaction. Prompted by the popular Mosaic Approach, you are encouraged to consider how simple technologies can be used to empower children to articulate and express their unique voices. Technologies can provide opportunities for young learners to gain a sense of themselves by exploring their *image, motion* and *sound* via photos, video and audio. These can contribute developmentally to their sense of *self* from *internal* and *external* perspectives. When this is extended to include digital artefacts of friends and family, positive relationships can be reinforced. How can digital technology contribute to active learning through play? Hughes' (2002) taxonomy of play types, *socio dramatic, imaginative, fantasy* and *role play* are explored – for example, children acting out scenarios with a microwave oven or swiping a card cash register in the role-play area set up as a cafe.

Chapter 8: Literacy

The EYFS framework defines the development of literacy as involving *'encouraging children to link sounds and letters and to begin to read and write'*(DfE, 2014, p 8). Therefore, this chapter will explore how technologies can support early mark-making, letter recognition and introduce synthetic phonics. Also, *'children must be given access to a wide range of reading materials (books, poems, and other written materials) to ignite their interest'*(DfE, 2014, p 8). The chapter will illustrate how technology can play an important role in the reading and writing process even when the product may be in a traditional form; for example, in relation to planning and sequencing. A range of multimodal tools are available to foster enjoyment and scaffolding of children's narrative or recount. Multimodal texts, including ebooks, combine aural, visual and textual modes and provide inclusive and stimulating opportunities for young children to express ideas. The chapter will consider the potential of technology to enhance children's learning in literacy – for example, digital reading and writing. It will exemplify characteristics of effective learning through technology by evaluating strategies for enabling children to enjoy their favourite stories, poems and songs, for linking sounds and letters, for writing during role play and for book making.

Savage and Barnett (2015) asked whether the nature of literacy has changed now that a great deal of information and content is digitised and characterised by cultural nuances (eg an emoticon/emoji) (p 7). This chapter will respond further to this topic by tackling the controversial question of what it means to become 'literate' in the modern world. Facer (2009) recognised that the *'process of writing is inevitably changing with technological developments'* and children today engage in extensive on-screen reading and writing (p 101). If your definition of literacy is about being able to access information and communicate, then these non-traditional forms should not be disregarded but viewed as an a extension of genres which reflect an acute awareness of their purpose and audience.

Chapter 9: Mathematics

This chapter begins by highlighting challenges related to maths teaching and use of digital technology. You're asked to reflect on your own feelings about maths teaching and the value of cultivating a growth mindset. Bruner's stages of cognitive representation are referred to in the context of digital technology. This is followed by a focus on child development and mathematical knowledge related to the Early Learning Goals. Autonomy, capability, creativity, quality and scope are exemplified through control technology, iPad apps, open-ended digital technology and exemplars.

Chapter 10: Expressive arts and design

This chapter considers how technologies can be utilised to empower young children to express themselves and create a unique voice in their chosen medium (which can include digital mediums). Again, technology use is explored both in the *process* and/or *product* of creative expression. You will be guided through digital tools and approaches to foster '*being imaginative*' and '*exploring and using media and materials*' (DfE, 2014, p 12). The question is posed as to whether children should be *producers* as well as *consumers* of digital content (games, music, audio, graphics, animations, films etc). Time is spent exploring the affordances of technology in relation to the creative process. Does the power of the 'undo' (eg provisionality affordance) button encourage risk taking and experimentation? To give an international perspective, similarities are explored between the Reggio approach of creating *ateliers* (workshops) and the *MakerMovement*. Examples of current research in the Reggio tradition view digital forms as adding to the many *languages* with which children have to express themselves. The chapter concludes that working in different and varied expressive forms is very powerful for children and can create rich channels for self expression.

Chapter 11: Technologies for inclusion

Many of the technologies and deployment strategies which have been raised are reconsidered from the perspective of inclusion. How can technologies enable young children, including those with special educational needs and disabilities, to both *access* the curriculum and express the *output* of that engagement with the curriculum? The role technology can play in creating an autonomous, enabling environment will be explored and ideas for additional input/output devices will be provided. It is acknowledged that any contextual response needs to be driven by individual learning needs, whether this is to access, support or extend learning.

Chapter 12: Safeguarding and welfare

This important chapter gives a comprehensive overview and explanation of professional safeguarding issues when technology is deployed in an early years setting. These issues include the collection of, storage of and access to information about children and the data protection legal implications. The rights of the child, safeguarding and confidentiality protocols are paramount. Recommended protocols and requirements of key bodies including Ofsted (2016), National Crime Agency, Local Safeguarding Children Board and NDNA are reviewed in addition to the provision requirements of the EYFS framework and the Teachers' Standards. An overview will be given about the rights and responsibilities of children, practitioners, outside agencies, parents and guardians in relation to artefacts held digitally across devices and cloud services utilised (eg *Tapestry*). You will be supported in comprehensively reviewing your personal online professional reputation; and will be given common-sense advice on how to differentiate between personal and professional digital personas in order to maintain this. The 2016 Ofsted inspection framework for safeguarding makes reference to online bullying (p 5), online safety (p 6) and e-safety education (p 11), the robustness of systems in place to protect children from being exposed to harmful online material (p 12) and awareness of reporting strategies.

Chapter 13: Conclusion

In this chapter, a review of the journey through the book will be provided and questions posed for the future.

References

Department for Education (DfE) (2014) Statutory framework for the Early Years Foundation Stage: setting the standards for learning, development and care for children from birth to five. [online] Available at: www.gov.uk/government/uploads/system/uploads/attachment_data/file/335504/EYFS_framework_from_1_September_2014__with_clarification_note.pdf (accessed 1 March 2017).

Facer, K (2009) Educational, social and technological futures: a report from the beyond current horizons programme. [online] Available at: http://blogfolio.org.uk/sites/default/files/1/images/facer_2009_pdf_11027.pdf (accessed 1 March 2017).

Hughes, B (2002) *A Playworker's Taxonomy of Play Types*. London: Play Education.

Office for Standards in Education, Children's Services and Skills (Ofsted) (2016) Inspecting safeguarding in early years, education and skills settings: guidance for inspectors undertaking inspection under the common inspection framework. [online] Available at: www.gov.uk/government/uploads/system/uploads/attachment_data/file/547327/Inspecting_safeguarding_in_early_years_education_and_skills_settings.pdf (accessed 1 March 2017).

Savage, M and Barnett, A (2015) *Digital Literacy for Primary Teachers*. Northwich: Critical Publishing.

2 What is technology-enhanced learning?

CHAPTER OUTLINE AND PROFESSIONAL LINKS

This chapter will help you to reach a broad and context-specific understanding of what is meant by the term *technology-enhanced learning*. You will be guided through which technologies are relevant in a contemporary early years context; supported to return to what you already know about children's learning and to consider how the integration of technologies can have a constructive impact. You will be introduced to a simple framework for categorising technologies according to functionality and age-appropriate versions will be suggested. You will be prompted to consider the extent to which functionality is exploited to its full potential. Importantly, you will be challenged to think about who is in control when you deploy technologies in your setting; *you* as the practitioner or the *child(ren)* as the learners? How does this contradict or complement the children's learning at home? In your setting, who gets to choose what, when and how children play with and explore technology?

Within the *understanding the world* strand, Early Learning Goal 15 relates directly to technology:

> *Children recognise that a range of technology is used in places such as homes and schools. They select and use technology for particular purposes.*
>
> (Standards and Testing Agency, 2014, p 1)

Chapter 4 focuses on unpicking the components of this Early Learning Goal (ELG) in greater depth. Part of creating the necessary *enabling environment* is reflecting what children are encountering in their wider familial and societal contexts where technology is relatively ubiquitous.

Technologies

The first thing for you as a practitioner to decide upon is what you are defining as technology. You may think of the iPad you use to record observations and assessments of the children or the interactive whiteboard at the front of your room, but what else could be included?

Technologies are engineered devices that can be employed by humans for practical and particular purposes. These technologies may have a scientific or computer science component. Learning technologies can be understood as technologies that in some way support learning and learning processes. Learning can be viewed as the acquisition and assimilation of knowledge, understanding, skills, aptitudes and attitudes. Your studies and experiences as a practitioner to date will already have generated your view that learning can take many forms, is complex and not always linear, and can vary greatly for individuals. The interpretation presented here is intentionally simplistic in that you should broaden your conception of learning technologies beyond those mentioned to include any engineered device that can be used by a learner/learners), in a multitude of contexts, to perform a task.

CASE STUDY

Amelia and Jake are absorbed playing with the remote-control car on the floor. They have worked out how to turn the car on and spend several minutes pressing the central lever on the handset to see what happens. There is some disagreement about who holds the handset but this is mainly excited chatter about what to do.

Commentary on case study

Are Amelia and Jake actively learning anything? Is the remote-control car facilitating that learning? Is this toy a learning technology? You could argue *yes* to all of the above. From a primary computing curriculum perspective, the foundations of programming are being laid. The children recognise and acknowledge that their actions are controlling what the car does. The car is not operating by magical forces; their manipulation of the remote control (input device) is directly leading to a physical movement (output) in the car. Their experimentation (trial and error) leads to the refinement of procedures; to move the car forwards, the lever must be moved forwards.

Typology of learning technologies in an early years setting

There is no universally agreed-upon definition of what falls under the heading *learning technology* in an early years context any more than there is in higher education. Your next challenge is to be able to process the possibilities in a simple logical manner. A recommended approach is for you to focus upon the functionality offered by the technologies and/or the purpose they can fulfil in the learning context.

When you think about technologies in this wider conceptualisation it is easier to look around your early years setting and see where technologies are (or can be) embedded in everyday learning. More detailed exemplars are explored in subsequent chapters relating to specific areas of learning but the list below organises typical technologies into a simple typology according to functionality.

- *Replicating and imitating real-world technologies.*
    - Home domestic technologies (eg microwave, dishwasher, washing machine, etc).
    - Public domestic technologies (eg cashpoint, tills, information points, traffic lights, car park barriers, street lights, conveyor belts etc).
- *Programmable or controllable toys* (eg cars, electronic pets, Bee-Bots, Constructa-Bot etc).
- *Visual playback or exploration* (eg television, video, DVD, torches, light boxes and tables, microscopes etc).
- *Audio playback* (eg radio, MP3 player, CD player, etc).
- *Communication with others* (eg mobile phone, email, walkie talkies, FaceTime, Skype etc).
- *Recording devices* (eg video recorder, recordable microphone, sound pegs etc).
- *Games and games-based applications* (eg PlayStation, Xbox, WII, etc).
- *Computer technology* (eg desktop computers, laptops, tablets, photocopiers etc).

iPads in the early years

The use of tablets, especially iPads, is growing in popularity and it is worth spending time to consider their potential in greater detail. You will no doubt know young children with fine motor skills which include the *pinch* and *swipe* gestures required to interact with the interface on a iPad. There is something very intuitive about a device with only one button that appeals to most ages and abilities. The research on iPads is critically reviewed in Chapter 3.

What do we know about how iPads are being used in early years settings? Study the wordle illustration by the National Literacy Trust (Formby, 2014) reproduced in Figure 2.1. If you are unfamiliar with wordles, the larger the text, the greater the frequency of a word or phrase.

Figure 2.1 *Activities on tablet computers. (Formby, 2014, p 7; reproduced by permission of the National Literacy Trust)*

Susie Formby of the National Literacy Trust (Formby, 2014, p iv) highlighted that touch-screen technology offered new opportunities for young learners:

> with the introduction of technologies that are more suitable for use by children than ever before, there have been considerable changes in the way children's language and communication skills may be supported. This is particularly the case for children in the early years for whom touch-screen technology and tablet computers in particular have enabled them to communicate with the world using technology.

The National Literacy Trust continued to expand on how early years practitioners in their study used tablets, '*categorising the types of activities as creative activities, accessing resources, interactive activities and class activities*' (Formby, 2014, pp 7–8).

Table 2.1 *Overview of how early years practitioners used iPads extracted from Formby (2014)*

Percentage of practitioners who used tablet technology to:			
67% **creative activities**	Includes 35% who used the tablet for taking photos	Includes 35% who made reference to mark making	Includes 30% who used a tablet for filmmaking
59% **accessing resources**	Includes 43% using the tablet to research topics	Includes 35% who went on to visit apps and websites with links to songs and rhymes	Includes 22% using apps for stories

National Literacy Trust (Formby, 2014, pp 7–8)

Theoretical perspectives and pedagogy

Rather than trying to find new theory to justify your use of technology in the early years, you are encouraged to recall the pedagogy and theories of learning you already know well. Technology has not changed the essential ingredients of the learning process. You can also probably recall examples from practice when technology has in fact hindered learning. This brings us to the second and third words of the book's title – *enhanced learning*. What you need to consider here is when (and if) learning processes are being enhanced, how are they enhancing that process and to what extent?

Enhancing learning with technology

Eady and Lockyer (2013, p 74) state that there is a general assertion that one of the reasons for using technology in the early years is to '*keep pace with society and prepare students for their roles in society*'. McPake (2011, p 2) similarly recalled how during her studies '*children's play activities incorporated technologies in ways which demonstrated that they saw technological tools as part of their everyday environment and understood their purposes*'. Eady and Lockyer continued by summarising that '*educators and researchers point to the potential of technology to increase motivation and engagement of learners, cater for different learning styles and improve learning outcomes*' (2013, p 74).

Critical question

» *Eady and Lockyer (2013) reported four claims about learner responses when technology is used:* increased learner motivation and engagement, *the potential to* cater for different learning styles *and* improved learning outcomes. *Based on your experiences to date as a developing practitioner, to what extent do you agree with these claims? Can you think of examples that concur with or contradict these statements?*

Affordances of technology

Savage and Barnett (2015) refer to the widely accepted affordances of digital technology to support practitioners in making rational decisions about the use of technology in teaching (p 78). These are based on the Department for Education and Employment (DfEE, 1998) affordances of digital technology and include *provisionality*, *speed and automatic functions*, *capacity*, *range* and *interactivity*.

CASE STUDY

The National Literacy Trust (Formby, 2014, p 7) also included an example of how the functionality of the iPad enabled them to create a multimodal story.

> We retold a story, then innovated the story and made it our own, then voice-recorded on the iPad; we then created the scenes from the story and photographed the scenes. We edited the pictures as necessary, for example the children used a drawing programme to add flames to one picture. Then I put their work together as a 'movie'.

Commentary on case study

Utilising the DfEE (1998) framework, the *provisionality* affordance of the technology allowed for the editing, reworking and revising of content. The *multimodal* affordance of technology enabled the learners to combine graphics, text, sound and animation. The iPad technology was capable of performing the required tasks *quickly* and efficiently.

Fisher, Higgins and Loveless (2006) devised a useful categorisation of *purposeful activity with digital technology* (p 20). Table 2.2 is a reproduction of their table.

Table 2.2 *Clusters of purposeful activity with digital technologies (reproduced from Fisher, Higgins and Loveless, 2006, p 20: Table 1)*

Knowledge building	• adapting and developing ideas • modelling • representing understanding in multimodal and dynamic ways
Distributed cognition	• accessing resources • finding things out • writing, composing and presenting with mediating artefacts and tools
Community and communication	• exchanging and sharing communication • extending the context of activity • extending the participating community at local and global levels
Engagement	• exploring and playing • acknowledging risk and uncertainty • working with different dimensions of interactivity • responding to immediacy

The categorisation above by Fisher, Higgins and Loveless (2006) remains relevant and can also be successfully applied in an early years context.

Critical question

» *Recall a planned technology activity you have initiated in your setting recently. Using the categorisation suggested in Table 2.2, consider how the technology used enhanced the learning.*

Indoor and outdoor technologies

Many of the concerns and criticisms of technology relate to a static model of passive learner use via a desktop computer or television screen. However, this is a self-limiting view of the potential of mobile and interactive technologies. Technology does not always need to be indoors and boring!

Imagine an outdoor learning space rich in embedded technology for playing, exploring, interacting and capturing data. All the technology is free for the children to engage with as and when they choose. In the *Recordable Talking Garden* there are stepping stones that play pre-recorded messages or music and sparkling butterflies that play back messages recorded by children. Handheld microscopes are available to peer closely at treasured finds. Intrepid explorers could use their *See and Speak Recordable Binoculars* to document their wildlife discoveries. Imagine the fascination and fun children could experience using a waterproof bendy microscope to poke down holes, crevices and into ponds. All of these technologies are readily available via TTS – you can find more details of each of the items described in this section at www.tts-group.co.uk.

Locus of control: who has their hand on the mouse?

You may have already noticed that the technologies illustrated in the above outdoor learning scenario are designed to be utilised by children. Children's natural curiosity, supported as necessary by practitioners, the simplicity of the devices and robust construction mean that these technologies appeal to children. Often practitioners *restrict* the use of technologies in the sense that they are retrieved from the locked cupboard for occasional planned activities by the adult. How does this contradict your practitioner pedagogical stance of independent and playful learning? Perhaps, instead, envision a scenario where children can access and choose to use technologies when they feel it will assist their learning and having fun. Would this also replicate their access to technologies beyond your setting?

Critical question

» *Reflect on how accessible and mobile the technologies truly are in your setting. Do procedures in place constrain children's technology-enhanced learning? Which technologies would you feel comfortable about always being accessible to children?*

International perspective

You will not be surprised to read that early years practitioners around the globe are also tackling the complexities about which technologies to use to enhance learning. The International Society for Technology in Education (ISTE) has created a list of technology-related standards for teachers that can be accessed at www.iste.org/docs/pdfs/20-14_ISTE_Standards-T_PDF.pdf. The ISTE Standards also have relevance for practitioners in early years settings within the UK and can be a useful tool to reflect on your professional practice and development needs. The Standards *'Design and develop digital age learning experiences'* and *'modelling digital age work and learning'* resonate with much that you have considered when reading this chapter.

The Erikson TEC Center: Technology in Early Childhood is an American organisation aspiring to:

> *empower early childhood educators to make informed decisions about the appropriate use of technology with children from birth to age 8. Through carefully selected resources and real-world examples, the Center strengthens educators' digital literacy and their ability to intentionally select, use, integrate, and evaluate technology in the classroom and other early childhood settings.*
>
> (2016, accessed at http://teccenter.erikson.edu)

Conclusion

An aim of this chapter was to provide you with an accessible understanding of what technology-enhanced learning means in an early years setting. You have considered a wide range of technologies in terms of functionality, locus of control and purposeful learning activity. The technologies themselves will continue to evolve. However, this may not be as daunting for you as practitioner as you first thought. Learning processes and typical functionality will always resonate with what has gone before. A playful approach to exploring new technologies is just as important for you as a professional as it is for the young learners in your care. The following chapter explores in some depth the research findings to date in response to some commonly articulated concerns. The purpose is to increase your confidence in decision-making and communicating your rationale for technology use to fellow practitioners and parents.

Recommended further reading

- Donohue, C (ed) (2015) *Technology and Digital Media in the Early Years*, 'provides strategies, theoretical frameworks, links to research evidence, demonstrations and descriptions of best practices, and resources to develop essential digital media literacy attitudes, knowledge, experiences and competencies for the digital age' (2015, http://teccenter.erikson.edu/tech-in-the-early-years/).

- The National Association for the Education of Young Children (2008) have produced a useful read entitled *Meaningful Technology Integration in Early Learning Environments* that can be accessed online at www.naeyc.org/files/yc/file/200809/OnOurMinds.pdf.

- A final recommended read is from New Zealand and was produced by the Ministry of Education in 2004: *The Role and Potential of ICT in Early Childhood Education: A Review of New Zealand and International Literature*, which can be accessed online at www.nzcer.org.nz/system/files/ictinecefinal.pdf.

References

Department for Education (DfE) (2014) Statutory framework for the Early Years Foundation Stage: setting the standards for learning, development and care for children from birth to five. [online] Available at: www.gov.uk/government/uploads/system/uploads/attachment_data/file/335504/EYFS_framework_from_1_September_2014__with_clarification_note.pdf (accessed 1 March 2017).

Department for Education and Employment (DfEE) (1998) *Initial Teacher Training National Curriculum for the Use of Information and Communications Technology in Subject Teaching, Circular 4/98 Annex B.* London: Department for Education and Employment.

Donohue, C (2015) *Technology and Digital Media in the Early Years: Tools for Teaching and Learning.* Abingdon: Routledge.

Eady, M J and Lockyer, L (2013) Tools for Learning: Technology and Teaching Strategies, in *Learning to Teach in the Primary School.* Brisbane: Queensland University of Technology. [online] Available at: http://ro.uow.edu.au/cgi/viewcontent.cgi?article=1413&context=asdpapers (accessed 1 March 2017).

Fisher, T, Higgins, C and Loveless, A (2006) *Report 14: Teachers Learning with Digital Technologies: A Review of Research and Projects.* Futurelab. [online] Available at: www.nfer.ac.uk/publications/FUTL67/FUTL67.pdf (accessed 1 March 2017).

Formby, S (2014) Practitioner perspectives: children's use of technology in the early years. [online] Available at: www.literacytrust.org.uk/assets/0002/1135/Early_years_practitioner_report.pdf (accessed 1 March 2017).

McPake, J (2011) *Rethinking Young Children Creating and Communicating. Research Briefing 3 for Digital Childhoods.* Glasgow: Scottish Universities Insight Institute.

National Association for the Education of Young Children (2008) Meaningful technology integration in early learning environments. [online] Available at: www.naeyc.org/files/yc/file/200809/OnOurMinds.pdf (accessed 1 March 2017).

Savage, M and Barnett, A (2015) *Digital Literacy for Primary Teachers.* Northwich: Critical Publishing.

Standards and Testing Agency (2014). EYFS profile exemplification for the level of learning and development expected at the end of the EYFS. Understanding the world. ELG16 – technology. [online] Available at: www.gov.uk/government/uploads/system/uploads/attachment_data/file/360542/ELG15___Technology.pdf (accessed 1 March 2017).

3 Key debates and research evidence

CHAPTER OUTLINE AND PROFESSIONAL LINKS

As a practitioner you may feel that you are faced with a baffling array of contradictory messages in the popular media about technology use with children between birth and five years old. As a result it can be a real challenge to unravel fact from fiction in claims about both the benefits and dangers of technology use in early childhood. You will no doubt have some mixed opinions yourself and you may have read many headlines and parenting guides suggesting that technology is harming our children. For example:

- 'Tablets and smartphones may affect social and emotional development, scientists speculate' (The Guardian, 2015);

- 'Children spend six hours or more a day on screens' (BBC, 2015);

- 'Over-use of iPads, iPhones and smart screens hurting kids' (CBC, 2015).

Any parent or practitioner is understandably going to be concerned when reading and listening to news reports. Can using technology harm the physical and mental well-being of the young learners in your care? Is technology responsible for childhood obesity, anti-social behaviour, ADHD, overstimulation and isolation? Should screen time for under twos be banned?

Critical question

» *Before reading this chapter further, write down three concerns you have, or have heard parents and colleagues say, about using technology in the early years. Try to describe the problem or concern in as much detail as possible. What benefits do you think there are to using technology to support early learning? What evidence is there to support these claims (for and against) that you are aware of?*

In Chapter 2 you were encouraged to explore the meaning of the term *technology-enhanced learning* and how this actually relates to an array of technologies that can be employed in a variety of learning contexts by children. The word *enhanced* is particularly important to the key questions this chapter explores and you should look for ways in which technology is adding to (or updating), not replacing or harming, processes for learning. The purpose of this chapter is to discuss common beliefs, fears or claims, identify the underlying factors and look to the research to reinforce or debunk statements about technology.

Discussing technologies in relation to early childhood and learning can provoke a wide range of passionate responses from sceptics to enthusiasts. This chapter seeks to detail and discuss the issues in a neutral and research- and pedagogy-informed manner.

Professional engagement with research evidence

As a practitioner you have a professional responsibility to ensure that learning opportunities in your classroom are varied, developmental and inclusive. The National College for Teaching and Leadership (2013) states that an early years teacher should have a depth of knowledge about '*early development, keep their knowledge and skills up-to-date*' and be '*self-critical*' (p 2). As a developing professional it is essential to unpick the complex issues presented here; understand the scope of technology available; explore the interplay between learning and specific technologies; and more broadly, create a vision for a technology-enabled learning environment that is child-centred, playful, creative and interactive.

In line with the Teachers' Standards (early years) 2013, classroom approaches should have the child centre stage, fostering their natural curiosity and their desire to explore and play. For example, standard 4.2 requires that you '*plan balanced and flexible activities and educational programmes that take into account the stage of development, circumstances and interests of children*'. Standard 4.3 emphasises the importance of promoting a '*love of learning and stimulate children's intellectual curiosity in partnership with parents and/or carers*' (p 3). Standard 7 requires that you '*safeguard and promote the welfare of children, and provide a safe learning environment*', which means the concerns raised earlier need to be robustly addressed (p 4).

The characteristics of effective teaching and learning, as articulated in the EYFS Framework, are a valid and useful way to analyse some of these questions and concerns. Table 3.1 suggests some questions you may have, which this book will try to answer.

Critical question

»   *Using the tabular framework suggested in Table 3.1, note down any questions or concerns you have about technology and its uses in your setting.*

Table 3.1 *A possible framework based on the* 'characteristics of effective learning' *for reflecting on the research evidence relating to technology (DfE, 2014, p 9)*

Characteristic of effective learning	Playing and exploring • Finding out, investigating and exploring • Playing with what they know • Being willing to 'have a go'	Active learning • Being involved and concentrating • Keeping trying – persevering • Enjoying achieving what they set out to do	Creating and thinking critically • Developing their own ideas • Making links • Choosing ways to do things – developing strategies
	How can technologies be deployed to promote playful learning?	How might technologies foster self-regulated learning?	Can technologies support children's unique voice and means of expression?
	How can technology foster curiosity?	Can putting technologies in the control of children support their sense of agency?	Can the multimodal affordances of technology scaffold children making links?
	Does technology offer low-risk exploration and experimentation?	Can the gamification model foster perseverance?	Can technology support creativity?

Reviewing the evidence for key questions

In Table 3.1 questions were deliberately phrased in a neutral or positive manner; however, this is not normally the case with alarmist headlines. In this section we will explore the literature and research to answer some of the commonly articulated statements of concern including:

- *We don't need to teach this generation to use technology; it comes naturally to them – they are 'digital natives'.*

- *Children nowadays are overweight and inactive because they spend too long staring at screens.*

- *Technology is damaging children's social skills.*

- *Traditional educational skills are being lost because of technology (eg handwriting, spelling, reading etc).*

- *Today's kids are over-stimulated by technology and as a result cannot concentrate or suffer from ADHD.*

- *Technologies stop children from being creative and imaginative.*

Challenging the *digital natives* concept

In a world increasingly saturated with digital technology, it's reasonable to regard those being born into this world as *digital natives*, learning to *speak digital as their first language* – or is it? Prensky introduced the dichotomous *digital natives/digital immigrants* concept way back in 2001. Since then, several other ways of describing younger generations, youth and teenagers have been popularised, eg Tapscott's *net generation* in 'Growing Up Digital' (1998) and the follow-up study 'Grown Up Digital' (2009); *generations X, Y, Z and M* (Roberts et al, 2005; Wiedmer, 2015); the *app generation* (Gardner and Davis, 2013); and danah boyd's perspective (2014), *it's complicated*. But to return to the rather simplistic *digital natives* concept, it's certainly easy to locate endless YouTube video clips showing babies and infants demonstrating abilities to use digital technology, such as two-year-olds pressing, swiping and stretching the iPad screen with commanding dexterity as they select, open and engage with a range of age-appropriate apps. But even after a few moments thought, this is a far cry from being able to access and utilise many of the more sophisticated features that digital technology has to offer, quite apart from the need to develop criticality when using technology. It may be that babies in the digital age are born with a more enhanced innate scepticism regarding webpage content than their older brothers, sisters and parents… but many would be disinclined to believe that. The *able to work it out for themselves mentality* is fine to a point but it panders to superficial rather than to deep learning.

Brown and Czerniewicz (2010) provided a telling critique of the digital native concept in their research article entitled *Debunking the 'Digital Native': Beyond Digital Apartheid, Towards Digital Democracy*. The fact that their research was located within the South African context was particularly useful as it drew attention to negative cultural meanings associated with the terms *natives* and *immigrants*. From an educational point of view, they highlighted that the '*implications that people are born into something that determines them and which they cannot change*' are problematic (p 359). They drew attention to the inconclusive evidence from neuropsychology (McKenzie, 2007) and were also critical of Prensky's updated version of digital natives linked to *digital wisdom* (Prensky, 2011). They continued by presenting clear evidence that differences are better described in terms of *experience of* and *access to* digital technology rather than using generational concepts. In other words, they discovered that generational age wasn't a significant factor. They introduced the alternative category of *digital stranger* to describe those with limited experience due to lack of access to digital technology. Plowman et al's (2012) research similarly concluded that '*beliefs that there is a natural affinity between children and technology or that children of this age are more tech savvy than grown ups… seemed to be unfounded*' (p 2).

Critical question

» *Adopting the Brown and Czerniewicz (2010) model, based on experience of and access to technology, consider your own experiences. Further, critically reflect on the extent to which these experiences may have impacted on your pedagogical decisions to use technology in your setting to date. How might you modify your future pedagogical decisions in light of these insights?*

Childhood obesity and digital technology

Way back in 2000 the Alliance for Childhood published *Fool's Gold: A Critical Look at Computers in Childhood*, which included a focus in Chapter 2 on *Developmental Risks: The Hazards of Computers in Childhood*, covering physical, emotional, social, intellectual and moral hazards. The authors noted that:

> *Many health professionals believe childhood obesity has increased since 1994, in large part because children spend more time sitting in front of electronic media and less time actively playing, at home and school, and because they consume so many high-fat, high sugar foods.*

(Alliance for Childhood, 2000, p 25)

Other more recent studies help to develop a more evidence-based perspective on digital technology and obesity. Calvert et al (2013) referred to the *displacement effect* – the assumption that sedentary video game play and watching TV replaces more active physical activity. They noted that *'media use like television viewing seems to displace other indoor activities, such as board games, rather than vigorous outdoor activities'* (p 54). Burdette and Whitaker (2005) noted that pre-school children watched more TV in neighbourhoods perceived by mothers as unsafe, but the increased TV time was not correlated with obesity. On the other hand, numerous studies point to links between watching TV and obesity in young children and teenagers, such as when a TV is located in the child's bedroom (Strasburger 2011), which can also interfere with sleep patterns. Staiano and Calvert (2012) referred to *advergames*, which can include non-healthy food marketing on webpages and video games directed at children.

Of course, new digital technology is continuously being developed and the more recent *exergaming* can involve the whole body in physical activity using technology such as the Nintendo Wii game *Dance Dance Revolution* and Xbox Kinect. Sween et al (2014) identified a range of exergaming technology including dance simulation, motion capture games such as Sony Eye Toy and isometric resistance games such as Exerstation; there's also GameBike and the Gamercise Power Stepper – stop stepping on the pedals while working on your computer and the mouse stops working! But what are the health benefits of exergaming and can exergaming actually reduce childhood obesity? The literature reviewed by Sween et al (2014), based on 27 studies, concluded that *'exergaming is a new and exciting strategy to potentially improve physical activity levels and reduce obesity'* (p 1), particularly *'exergames of longer duration'* (p 3). However, a more recent systematic literature review by Zeng and Gao (2016), based on 12 studies drawn from 202 articles, suggested the evidence for the health-related effectiveness of exergaming was unclear but broadly positive for supporting weight loss/adiposity. The authors noted that *'evidence suggests that exergaming has the potential to attenuate weight gain for overweight or/and obese children and youth'* (p 282). Exergaming also helps to motivate children to be more active, develop physical skills, and has a positive psychological impact on sense of well-being (p 282).

Screen time: mobile technology, TV and violent video games

Attention problems and ADHD can be due to a range of factors, from genetic predisposition to environmental contaminants and even consumption of fast foods (Alderman, 2010). Several sources have noted the potential contribution of overstimulation from interacting with digital media. For example, psychologytoday.com (Dunkley, 2015) had an article entitled *Screen Time is Making Kids Moody, Crazy and Lazy* and recommends *'methodically eliminating all electronics use for several weeks – an "electronics fast" – to allow the nervous system to "reset"'*. Apps such as *Screen Limit*, *OurPact* (http://ourpact.com/support) and *Screentime* (https://screentimelabs.com) can be an effective way for parents to monitor and reduce screen time.

Evidence suggests that early and extensive use of computers, mobile technology and video games can lead to addiction so restricting use is a rational step. Sigman (2012) noted that *'screen "addiction", once a populist catch phrase, is increasingly being used by physicians to describe the growing number of children engaging in screen activities in a dependent manner'* (p 937). From 1999, the American Academy of Pediatrics (AAP) began issuing advice to parents: *'that children spend no more than one to two hours a day interacting with screen-based media, such as TV and video games. And ... for children under the age of two ... no TV at all'* (as cited by Guernsey, 2016). However, in 2016 the AAP abandoned *'its controversial recommendation to keep children under age 2 away from screen media'* (Guernsey, 2016). The 2016 AAP recommendations:

- *'allow for video chatting no matter what a child's age'*, citing new studies on how the use of FaceTime and Skype with distant relatives can benefit children;
- *advise parents of children 18 to 24 months old '"who want to introduce digital media" that they should choose high-quality programming and apps to watch and play with alongside their young children'*.

(AAP, 2016, as cited by Guernsey, 2016)

Screen time is clearly a serious issue: The governments in France, Australia and Canada have specific guidelines limiting screen time for children under three years old, and Taiwan, China and South Korea have legally enforced restrictions (Jary, 2016). The UK government recognised the issue of screen time in a guidance briefing paper entitled *How Healthy Behaviour Supports Children's Wellbeing* (PHE, 2013) but limited itself to *'rationing children's non-homework screen time'* (p 10) as part of a healthy lifestyle.

Gamification describes the process where terminology and rewards from game-playing scenarios are carried forward into everyday contexts; for example, using 'levels', 'merits' and 'bonus points' to motivate learners (Shapiro et al, 2016, p 8). *Games-based learning* refers to when games are used for educational purposes in the classroom (Shapiro et al, 2016, p 8).

But what about content? Evidence suggests that children younger than two and a half years old experience '*"video deficit": difficulty learning from 2-dimensional video representations*' (Chassiakos et al, 2016, p 4) but that '*building an emotional bond with an on-screen character improves learning potential*' (p 5) and that learning is more effective when there's interaction with the parents. The role of parenting approaches is reinforced by Wu et al (2014), who advocated a combination of '*restrictive, instructive and co-using approaches*' (p 7).

Shapiro et al (2016) reported on a study showing that '*playing fast-paced "action based" video games*' improved '*attentional processing*' and also '*induced long-lasting improvements in contrast sensitivity, a basic visual function*' (p 7). Research is continuing to emerge on how gaming can improve hand–eye co-ordination and reflex responses. In neuroscience terms, Shapiro et al (2016, p 8) reflected on research showing that playing games '*can contribute to neural plasticity*' due to the '*multitude of complex motor and cognitive demands*'.

Regarding violent content, Shapiro et al (2016, p 5) presented evidence showing that '*Preschoolers randomly assigned to change from inappropriate or violent content to high-quality prosocial programming were found to have significant improvements in their externalizing and internalizing behavior*'; the authors highlight such prosocial programmes as Sesame Street. On the other hand, Salonius-Pasternak and Gelfond (2005, p 18) noted that digital games can allow children '*to experiment with aggression in a safe setting without real world consequences, facilitating children's development of self-regulation of arousal*'.

Critical question

»   *In light of Chassiakos et al's (2016) proposition that technologies can play a prosocial role, can you identify examples (eg television programmes or games) from your own practice?*

Research by Granic et al (2014) '*identified four types of positive impact that video games have on the kids who play them: cognitive, motivational, emotional, and social*'.

- **Cognitive benefit:** *Games have been shown to improve attention, focus, and reaction time.*

- ***Motivational benefit:*** *Games encourage an incremental, rather than an entity theory of intelligence.*

- ***Emotional benefit:*** *Games induce positive mood states; and there is speculative evidence that games may help kids develop adaptive emotion regulation.*

- **Social benefit:** *Gamers are able to translate the prosocial skills that they learn from co-playing or multi-player gameplay to 'peer and family relations outside the gaming environment'.*

> (Granic et al, 2014, as cited by Shapiro et al, 2016, p 6)

Critical question

» *Shapiro et al (2016) posit that 'the real question is not whether or not technology belongs in early childhood education, but rather, how can we leverage the efficiency of digital tools to best serve young learners?' (p 12). What is your response to their question?*

Tablet devices

The 2016 CHILDWISE Monitor report states that:

> *This year, for the first time, tablet devices have overtaken laptops/PCs/netbooks as the main type of computer that children have in their homes. Four in five children (79%) now live in a house with a tablet device in it. This is a significant rise from just three in five (61%) last year.*

> (CHILDWISE, 2016)

The Technology and Play report (Marsh et al, 2015) presented a detailed analysis of 0–5 year olds' use of tablet technology, including details related to socio-economic status, ethnicity and gender. Most popular was the iPad, though 50 per cent of children had access to 4–10 devices and 32 per cent accessed 11–20 devices. These percentages related just to home use: other venues such as school, friends' or grandparents' houses extend the already substantial use of tablets. It was also noted that the main reason parents gave for the choice of apps to download for their children was *fun*, followed closely by *educational* and then *ease of use*. But the dominant form of educational app still has the *drill and practice* format (Kervin, 2016). Yet the potential of *digital play* for learning extends far beyond simply earning points for correctly matched number bonds, for example, or clicking on the missing word to complete the sentence.

Khoo et al (2013) focused on educational applications of iPads within the New Zealand Te Whāriki early years curriculum context and identified four key approaches. As a relational tool the iPad is able to support the development of positive relationships, which are key not only within the Te Whāriki curriculum but also within the EYFS curriculum. Evaluating the relationship between teacher, pupil, parents and the iPad, Khoo et al explained:

> *their interaction with the iPad led to Zach not only exploring his interests but also gaining the skills and confidence to navigate his way through the different apps on the iPad, to settle on a drawing activity and then to share his activity with his family. The iPad as a relational tool allowed for more seamless connections between home and Centre learning because Zach's parents were able to view and input into this learning episode.*

> (Khoo et al, 2013, p 10)

As a communicative tool, Khoo et al (2013) evaluated the use of the FaceTime app, connecting two iPads to provide a new communicating and exploring experience:

> *The children were fascinated with the fact they could communicate with one another virtually. Each child began to take turns carrying the mobile iPad and walking with it towards other areas of the Centre. The children based at the stationary iPad would ask the mobile iPad child questions about his location, the details of what he was seeing and so forth.*
>
> (Khoo et al, 2013, p 12)

Khoo et al also evaluated use of iPads as a tool for encouraging children to participate in documenting their learning using the iPad camera; and as an informational tool through accessing and exploring internet sources.

Several research-based studies provide a range of examples of educational uses of touchscreen tablets/iPads that extend beyond the typical drill and practice model (Kervin, 2016; Khoo et al, 2013; Spencer, 2013). Subject-specific research includes Spencer (2013), in relation to numeracy, which focused on '*personalisation; kinaesthetic, play based learning and motivation*' (pp 611–12); Outhwaite (2016), who reported on the positive educational value of four game-based *EuroTalk*© numeracy apps with foundation-stage children, regardless of background; and Faulder (2015), who focused on maths journals and use of the *My Story* app. In relation to literacy, results from the extensive annual survey on the use of touchscreen tablets to support emergent literacy in the home and school conducted by Pearson and the National Literacy Trust (Knowland and Formby, 2016) included the fact that younger parents are more likely to use touchscreens when reading with their children. On the other hand, almost all practitioners preferred printed versions of stories and regarded screen size as a barrier, while recognising the value of touchscreen tablets for boys and those with Special Educational Needs and Disabilities (SEND). The report noted that touchscreens don't aid vocabulary development and concluded with the observation that changes are occurring more quickly in the home than the school context, such as increased use of touchscreens at home for reading. Lynch and Redpath (2014), when reporting on the use of iPads in the Australian early years context noted '*tensions between print based traditions and new digital literacies, and those between standards-based classroom curricula and more emancipatory agendas*' (p 147). Kervin (2016) identified the educational value of five instances of digital play for literacy learning. In particular, Kervin evaluated using networks, the iPad camera and video, setting goals using the *Pocket Pond* app (https://itunes.apple.com/gb/app/pocket-pond-2/id498375421?mt=8), creating and negotiating scenarios using *Minecraft* (https://minecraft.net/en/) and storytelling using the *PuppetPals* app (https://itunes.apple.com/gb/app/puppet-pals-hd/id342076546?mt=8).

Digital play

The literature on play is extensive but it's immediately evident that the concept of play has been defined and categorised in a multiplicity of ways. More recently *digital play* has emerged as a qualitatively different type of play (Kulman, 2015; Salonius-Pasternak and Gelfond, 2005). Marsh et al (2016) reviewed a range of models of play in order to accommodate the concept of digital play and emphasised the value of Hughes' Taxonomy (2002), which identified 15 different types of play (see Table 3.2 below). For example, Hughes' definition of '*fantasy play as Play in which children can take on roles that would not occur in real life, e.g. be a Superhero*' is contrasted with Marsh et al's digital version of fantasy play as '*play in a digital context in which children can take on roles that would not occur in real life, e.g. be a superhero. This could be through the use of an avatar, but may also include taking on a character off-screen whilst they engage in on-screen activities in the fantasy scenario*' (no. 11 in Table 3.2). Similarly, Hughes' definition of '*mastery play as play in which children attempt to gain control of environments, e.g. building dens*' is contrasted with '*play in a digital context in which children attempt to gain control of environments, e.g. creating a virtual world*' (no. 13 in Table 3.2) (p 247).

Table 3.2 Summary of digital play types based on the work of Marsh et al (2016, p 6)

Digital play types based upon Marsh et al's (2016) adaptation of Hughes' (2002) framework	
1. Symbolic play	Occurs when children use a virtual object to stand for another object, eg an avatar's shoe becomes a wand
2. Rough and tumble play	Virtual rough and tumble play occurs when avatars that represent users in a digital environment touch each other playfully, eg bumping each other
3. Socio-dramatic play	The enactment of real-life scenarios in a digital environment that are based on personal experiences, eg playing house, going shopping
4. Social play	Play in a digital context during which rules for social interaction are constructed and employed
5. Creative play	Play that enables children to explore, develop ideas and make things in a digital context
6. Communication play	Play using words, songs, rhymes, poetry, etc in a digital context. Can include text messages, multimodal communication and so on
7. Dramatic play	Play in a digital context that dramatises events in which children have not directly participated, eg TV shows
8. Locomotor play	Virtual locomotor play involves movement in a digital context, eg child may play hide and seek with others in a virtual world
9. Deep play	Play in digital contexts in which children encounter risky experiences, or feel as though they have to fight for survival

Table 3.2 (cont.)

Digital play types based upon Marsh et al's (2016) adaptation of Hughes' (2002) framework	
10. Exploratory play	Play in a digital context in which children explore objects, spaces, etc through the senses in order to find out information, or explore possibilities
11. Fantasy play	Play in a digital context in which children can take on roles that would not occur in real life, eg be a superhero
12. Imaginative play	Play in a digital context in which children pretend that things are otherwise
13. Mastery play	Play in digital contexts in which children attempt to gain control of environments, eg creating a virtual world
14. Object play	Play in which children explore virtual objects through vision and touch through the screen or mouse. They may play with the virtual objects
15. Role play	Play in a digital context in which children might take on a role beyond the personal or domestic roles associated with socio-dramatic play
16. Recapitulative play	Play in a digital context in which children might explore history, rituals and myths and play in ways that resonate with the activities of our human ancestors (lighting fires, building shelters and so on)

Traditional educational skills versus digital capability

Mattoon et al (2015) found that the computational ability of pre-school children increased to the same extent when they used traditional physical manipulatives or digital manipulatives using touchscreen tablets and software. They concluded that:

> If children's experiences prior to school are changing to include digital technology so they are naturally seeking it out for learning or entertainment purposes, then early childhood educators can consider examining their curriculum and personal pedagogies in regard to the potential of the technology.
>
> (Mattoon et al, 2015)

Plowman et al (2012, p 4) similarly concluded that 'operational competence develops children's concepts of technological interactivity and makes visible their understanding that taking an action can produce a response'. There is a well-known tendency to look back at the past through rose-tinted glasses whereas progress and change typically encounter resistance. Heppell (2011) dwelt on this when noting opposition to the use of ballpoint pens in schools for fear that 'cursive script handwriting might be ruined'! But children are already using (digital) technology even before they start in pre-school, and it's not going away! So what are the pluses and minuses of digital capability versus traditional educational skills?

Critical questions

Guernsey (2014) posed a series of provocative questions for practitioners to reflect on, acknowledging that children are from birth immersed in a world of 'always on' media.

» What are some new ways to help turn children on to words, language and text, ideas?

» Could children feel even more agency and excitement about learning to read than the generations behind them?

» Could new technologies offer chances to children with reading difficulties that didn't exist before?

First of all, it's worth considering the meaning of traditional educational skills. Should traditional skills such as memorising facts, mental arithmetic and basic reading still be the major preoccupation of schools in today's world? More recently, child-centred progressive education introduced skills such as problem-solving, planning ability, decision-making and learning how to learn (Novak and Gowin, 1984; Wingra School, 2012). In the digital age where the pace of life is so much quicker, information retrieval, decision-making, communicating and critical thinking are now high on the agenda.

Evidence suggests that digital technology can have both a positive and negative impact on memory. For example, video games and social media such as Facebook may strengthen memory whereas text messaging, Twitter and YouTube may be argued to weaken working memory (Savage and Barnett, 2015). But it's a mixed picture: text messaging can actually help to improve spelling ability and literacy (Wood et al, 2011, 2014). And although concentration can be negatively impacted by frequent use of digital technology (Jeffries, 2013), research by Tapscott (2009) suggested that the Net Generation youth of today are far better at multitasking; and digital tools such as calculators and spreadsheets perform an emancipatory function, allowing users to use their energies for conjecture and reflection (Loveless, 1995). Of course, questions continue to be asked – for example, whether extended use of digital technology undermines critical thinking, and Greengard (2009) suggested that '*the verdict isn't in and a definitive answer about how technology affects critical thinking is not yet available*'.

Critical question

» *How can digital capability development and acquisition of traditional skills be complementary in your professional practice and the children's learning? Select an example from your future planning and consider how a dual approach could be adopted.*

Digital childhoods

Compared to the recent past children are born into a world saturated with digital media. From even a few months old babies are being soothed by a Fisher-Price (no date) *Cuddle Projection Soother*, a *Musical Teething Turtle* or a *4-in-1 Step 'n Play Piano*, which includes, among other features, an electronic keyboard, illuminating drums, microphone and head-phone – for the already plugged in and turned on baby from birth to five-year-old child! Touchscreen tablets in particular are pervasive among even very young children, and children are accessing the internet from an increasingly young age (Marsh et al, 2015). The Scottish Universities Insight Institute uses the term *digital childhoods* to describe being '*immersed in a world in which digital technologies are ubiquitous*' (SUII, no date) and highlights a range of ensuing issues – for example, whether children understand technology better than adults; whether digital play is replacing traditional forms of play; whether digital technology leads to social isolation; whether digital technology even has any place at all in pre-school and, on the other side, whether children have a right to develop their digital literacy. Carrington and Marsh (2005) refer to the need to '*move beyond the moral panics and hypes to raise important questions about curricula and pedagogy in the new media age*' (p 281); and that schools need to become more attuned to pupils' '*increasingly multimodal and multimedia out-of-school practices*' (p 284). Gibbons (2015) extends this theme through a more philosophical approach to the implications of technology and digital childhoods. For example, there is an assumption that although pervasive and taken for granted, technology is less natural as well as more problematic (eg a robotic doll contrasted with a rag doll).

But the practical issues continue to resurface: What knowledge and understanding of digital technology do children in the early years have? Ofcom reported that the average 6-year-old has an equivalent understanding of technology to that of an average 45-year-old, exceeded only by 14–15-year-olds who had the highest digital quotient score, ie this understanding involves '*awareness and self confidence around gadgets from tablets to smart watches, knowledge of superfast internet, 4G mobile phone networks and mobile apps*' (Garside, 2014). And as for implications, it would be unwise to conclude from this that young children don't need support to help them persevere with less intuitive technology (Jackson, 2016) or have nothing to learn, such as the need to develop digital literacy (Savage and Barnett, 2015).

Another of the questions raised by the concept of digital childhoods is whether digital technology leads to social isolation. But take a journey on a railway train before the mobile phone era and everyone would have had their heads buried in a newspaper, magazine or book (Huffington Post, 2016). In fact, digital technology can reduce social isolation. The Pew research report, a study of American social networking (Hampton et al, 2009), found '*larger and more diverse discussion networks*' although the social ties were weaker than non-digital locally based networks. This is a point emphasised by McGauran (2016), who suggests that digital technology leads to a decline in the quality of social relations through illusions of '*social connection and companionship*', development of negative self-images and reduced intimacy, a theme also explored by Gardner and Davis (2013) in *The*

App Generation. However, often individuals blend the two by reinforcing physical-world friendships with digital interactions when they are not in the same physical space.

Technology vs creativity

There can be the perception that use and/or overuse of technology is going to take time away from children using their imagination and engaging in creative activities. To begin to answer this question there are some underpinning assumptions to unravel. Firstly, you need to consider what is meant by the term *creativity* and whether this also extends beyond the traditional confines of *the arts* (Savage and Czismadia, 2017). Ott and Pozzi (2012) articulated that '*creative thinking is considered a key competence for the twenty-first century*' (p 1011). Creative thinking can be broken down into '*cognitive skills, affective attitudes*' and '*metacognition abilities*' (Ott and Pozzi, 2012, p 1013). Table 3.3 highlights the similarities between Robson's (2014) *Analysing Children's Creative Thinking Framework* (ACCT) for three to five year olds and Ott and Pozzi's (2012) descriptors of *creative thinking* used in their research on digital gaming. You will note the close relationship between Robson's (2014) ACCT framework and the three characteristics of effective learning embedded in the EYFS framework (Department for Education, 2014, p 11).

Critical question

» *Select a creative activity you carried out with a group of children recently. Identify the cognitive (mental processes), affective (emotional or attitudinal) and metacognitive (awareness of thought processes) capabilities these children demonstrated in completing the task. If you were to repeat the creative activity using technology, how might thc cognitive, affective and metacognitive dimensions change?*

Table 3.3 *Comparing Robson's (2014)* Analysing Children's Creative Thinking Framework *for 3–5-year-olds with Ott and Pozzi's (2012) descriptors of creative thinking*

Robson (2014): Category from ACCT framework for 3–5-year-olds (p 11) E. Exploration I. Involvement and enjoyment P. Persistence	Ott and Pozzi's (2012) descriptors of creative thinking (pp 1013–14) C. Cognitive A. Affective M. Metacognitive
E1. Exploring	A1. Receiving (*behaviours such as: be curious, be motivated, be frightened, etc*)
E2 Engaging in new activity	C1. Generating (*actions such as: combine, estimate, compare, state, etc*)
E3 Knowing what you want to do	C2. Planning (*actions such as: predict, infer, hypothesise, design, define, etc*)

Table 3.3 (cont.)

Robson (2014): Category from ACCT framework for 3–5-year-olds (p 11) E. Exploration I. Involvement and enjoyment P. Persistence	Ott and Pozzi's (2012) descriptors of creative thinking (pp 1013–14) C. Cognitive A. Affective M. Metacognitive
I1. Trying out ideas	A2. Responding (*behaviours such as: express joy, express disappointment, express fear, etc*)
I2. Analysing ideas	M3. Evaluating (*attitude towards judging/appraising the outcomes*)
I3. Speculating	M1. Monitoring (*attitude towards being aware of the global process enacted and of each single step made*)
I4. Involving others	
P1. Persisting	M1. Monitoring (*attitude towards being aware of the global process enacted and of each single step made*) A2. Responding (*behaviours such as: express joy, express disappointment, express fear, etc*)
P2. Risk taking	M2. Regulating (*attitude towards controlling/ adjusting the solution process*)
P3. Completing challenges	C3. Producing (*actions such as: build, enact, apply, test, verify, etc*)

Secondly, the technologies themselves vary enormously in terms of functionality, interactivity, and cognitive (C1, C2 and C3 in Table 3.3) and affective demand (A1 and A2 in Table 3.3). Sweeping statements about *technology* miss these important nuances. Plowman et al (2012) recognised that:

> concerns are sometimes raised about whether technology hinders the more play-ful, physical, and exploratory aspects of children's learning but this is more likely to happen when the items they use are limited to desktop computers with upright screens, a mouse and a keyboard.

> (Plowman et al, 2012, p 5)

Further, it is without argument that many children are experiencing digital media on a daily basis through viewing images or films, reading ebooks, listening to music and playing games. Therefore, do you want children to be only *consumers* of digital content or also *producers* (P3 and C3 in Table 3.3) of digital art, films, ebooks, music and games? Savage and Barnett (2015, p 9) argued that to be digitally literate children should be '*both a consumer and an author (producer) of digital content and having the skills, knowledge, understanding, values and attitudes embodied within both roles*'. Resnick (2013) underlined the fundamental importance of going beyond the consumer role and empowering children *to design, create and express themselves with new technologies*. Everyday opportunities to play and create, with some of the technologies listed in Chapter 2, begin to equip children with an appreciation of the processes and products of digital creation. Resnick (2013) recognised that through these experiences '*children begin to see themselves as creators and designers ... who can make things with digital media*' (M1, M2 and M3 in Table 3.3).

Arnott et al (2016) viewed creativity as '*inextricably linked to the development of representation and symbolism*'*;* ie visualisation (pp 162–3). Kim et al's (2016) research highlighted the potential of technology to support visualisation within the creative process. Ott and Pozzi's (2012) research concluded that '*digital mind games can be considered ... to foster creative thinking and, in particular, cognitive processes underpinning problem solution strategies and strategic decision making*' (p 1017).

Henriksen et al (2016) suggested that '*contemporary technologies often bring new possibilities for people to be creative*'; therefore, comparing the *traditional* and *digital* may be a false dichotomy (p 30). Further, Giovanni (2007) reminded practitioners that you '*must accept that only slight traces of the creative processes are uncovered in the product*' (pp 109–10). Arnott et al's (2016) research utilised iPad diaries with children in order to gain the child's perspective on creative play; multiple benefits were cited including:

> *The iPads afforded the benefit of, quite literally, offering the child's spatial perspective, if used during creative play. The portable nature of the resource means that children can record their creative play from their eyeline view and from the angle that they choose, rather than from an adult- focused bird's-eye view. Commentary about what the children were doing as they built a creation with the resources could supplement this recording.*
>
> (Arnott et al, 2016, p 164)

A resemblance can be drawn between the *Atelier* (workshop or studio), from the Reggio Emilia tradition, and conceptions of *Makerspaces* (Makerspaces.com). Within the *Maker Movement* (Cohen et al, 2016; Peppler et al, 2016), frequent references are made to playful learning as *tinkering*. Resnick and Rosenbaum (2013, p 2) described the tinkering approach as '*characterised by a playful, experimental, iterative style of engagement, in which makers are continually reassessing their goals, exploring new paths, and imagining new possibilities*'. Tinkering resonates with the view of the creative process articulated by, for example, Robinson with '*three distinct but related concepts*':

- *see – Imagination, seeing something in the mind's eye;*
- *think – Creativity, using imagination to solve problems;*
- *produce – Innovation, applying creative ideas and implementing solutions.*

(Robinson, 2006, cited by Wisconsin Task Force on
Arts and Creativity in Education, 2010, p 1)

Martin (2015) similarly recognised that although the popularity of the *Maker Movement* has come to the fore in digital technology-rich times, it is not philosophically '*a new phenomenon, but it is built from familiar pieces, and its relevance to education has deep roots*'. In the Montessori tradition, '*it has long been argued that children and youth can learn by playing and building with interesting tools and materials*'.

Giovanni's (2007) work posed the following question: Are creative processes different in the construction of real-world or virtual creations? For example, can you distinguish between the processes underpinning the creation of a painting from an image on a screen? Is it simply that technologies may offer new possibilities and forms for creative output; in Reggio terms, *new languages*?

> Technologies that continuously generate new materials and ways of gaining contact with the world offer novel expressive possibilities for children's art.
>
> (Giovanni, 2007, p 118)

Rather than be resistant to what may be unfamiliar, Giovanni (2007) prompted practitioners to learn this '*new language*' (p 119).

> Traditional languages are subject also to change and transformation when they are enriched by technology. The arrival of digital technology has generated new forms of language that enable children to structure knowledge and relationships in ways that frequently expose the imaginative limitations of adults. It offers opportunities to participate in images, to get inside them on a micro and macro scale, to shift points of view and see different images at the same time, to experience imaginary realities, immerse ourselves in light effects that cannot be found in nature, and transform sounds during their production.
>
> (Giovanni, 2007, p 119)

Conversely, Gill (2012) warned practitioners of the possible negative motivational impact of the *perfect* and *polished* digital product:

> One of the problems presented by new media is that they generate a visual language that is polished and packaged. This flood of perfectly rendered images can act as an emotional block for anyone who attempts to create an original drawing or painting of their own.
>
> (Gill, 2012, p 128)

However, is this any truer of digital media than traditional forms?

Savage and Czismadia (2017) compared models of creativity and technology-based computational thinking. Table 3.4 is a reproduction of an analysis of *descriptors for creative attitudes* (Winconsin Task Force on Arts and Creativity in Education, 2010) alongside *computational thinking learner attitude descriptors* (ISTE and CSTA, 2011); the synergy and alignment brings back to the fore the question of whether technology and creativity are really at odds.

Table 3.4 *Savage and Czismadia's (2017) analysis of the alignment between attitude descriptors for creativity and computational thinking*

Winconsin Task Force on Arts and Creativity in Education (2010) identified the following contributing attitudes for learners engaged in *creative* work:	ISTE and CSTA (2011) listed a number of attitudes needed when engaged in *computational thinking*:
• comfortable with ambiguity and there being more than one right answer	• tolerance for ambiguity
• curiosity	• ability to deal with open-ended problems
• willingness to take risks	• confidence in dealing with complexity
• being open and responsive to diverse perspectives	• ability to communicate and work with others to achieve a common goal or solution
• flexible and adaptable	• persistence in working with difficult problems

Conclusion

The discussions conducted in this chapter challenged you to probe behind the newspaper headlines and look at the evidence and reflect on pedagogical practices. Of course, complexities and conflicting opinions do not disappear but hopefully you have gained greater confidence in robustly critiquing what you may read or hear. To summarise, we know that *all* technologies, and the uses they are put to, are packaged together in the media and it is not usually fully taken into account whether they are passive or interactive, self-selected and initiated or adult-directed, together with the potential educational outcomes. The picture painted by the media is not always the same as the findings of research and as a practitioner you should pose the question: *What is the evidence*? For example, McPake (2011) noted that:

> There is a widespread view, particularly among media commentators, that young children now spend most of their time watching TV and playing computer games, and that this is at the expense of more valuable experiences, including listening to bedtime stories, playing traditional games, drawing and painting, and learning basic letter and number skills. Our research does not support this view.

> (McPake, 2011, p 4)

In this chapter a more detailed picture of *digital childhood* has been examined and notions of today's children as *digital natives* have been challenged. Plowman et al (2012) concluded that:

Because we looked at the big picture of children's everyday lives we found that technology did not dominate or hinder social interaction in the ways suggested by media coverage.

(Plowman et al, 2012, p 2)

Further, the distinction between digital and non-digital is very much an adult construct. As Plowman et al (2012, p 3) pointed out, '*children do not differentiate between technological and "traditional" activities to the same extent as adults and sometimes integrated their play seamlessly across different products*'. Similarly, it is not helpful to consider this an 'either/or' situation. Digital technologies are not used *instead* of traditional forms but *as well as* and are generally complementary. McPake (2011) found that:

the kinds of communicative and creative activities stimulated by digital technologies often complement those children are developing as a result of their early experiences with traditional texts.

(McPake, 2011, p 3)

Recommended further reading

- Plowman, L, Stephen, C and McPake, J (2010) *Growing Up With Technology: Young Children Learning in a Digital World*. London: Routledge.

- For practitioners wishing to engage in further dialogue you may wish to look at *EECERA Digital Childhood SIG* – Home: https://sites.google.com/site/eeceradigitalchildhoodssig/home.

- An extensive bibliography is provided by the *TapClickRead* organisation, listing peer-reviewed articles exploring many topics addressed in this chapter.

   Bibliography: Research Base for Tap, Click, Read (2015) TapClickRead.org at www.tapclickread.org/wp-content/uploads/2015/08/Research-Bibliography-for-TapClickRead-2015.pdf.

References

Alderman, L (2010) Does technology cause ADHD? [online] Available at: www.everydayhealth.com/adhd-awareness/does-technology-cause-adhd.aspx (accessed 1 March 2017).

Alliance for Childhood (2000) Developmental Risks: The Hazards of Computers in Childhood, in Cordes, C and Miller, E (eds) *Fool's Gold: A Critical Look at Computers in Childhood*. [online] Available at: http://drupal6.allianceforchildhood.org/sites/allianceforchildhood.org/files/file/pdf/projects/downloads/chapter2.pdf (accessed 1 March 2017).

Arnott, L, Grogan, D and Duncan, P (2016) Lessons from Using iPads to Understand Young Children's Creativity. *Contemporary Issues in Early Childhood*, 17(2): 157–73.

Boyd, D (2014) *It's Complicated: The Social Lives of Networked Teens*. New Haven, CT: Yale University Press.

British Broadcasting Corporation (BBC) (2015) Children spend six hours or more a day on screens. [online] Available at: www.bbc.co.uk/news/technology-32067158 (accessed 1 March 2017).

Brown, C and Czerniewicz, L (2010) Debunking the 'Digital Native': Beyond Digital Apartheid, Towards Digital Democracy. *Journal of Computer Assisted Learning*, 26: 357–69.

Burdette, H and Whitaker, R (2005) A National Study of Neighborhood Safety, Outdoor Play, Television Viewing, and Obesity in Preschool Children. *Pediatrics*, 116(3): 657–62. [online] Available at: www.imaginationplayground.com/images/content/2/9/2985/Neighborhood-Safety-Outdoor-Play-Television-www.imaginationplayground.com/images/content/2/9/2985/Neighborhood-Safety-Outdoor-Play-Television-Viewing-Obesity.pdf (accessed 1 March 2017).

Calvert, S, Staiano, A and Bond, B (2013) Electronic Gaming and the Obesity Crisis. *New Directions for Child and Adolescent Development*, 139: 51–7. [online] Available at: http://onlinelibrary.wiley.com/wol1/doi/10.1002/cad.20031/abstract (accessed 1 March 2017).

Canadian Broadcasting Corporation (CBC) (2015) Over-use of iPads, iPhones and smart screens hurting kids. [online] Available at: www.cbc.ca/news/canada/edmonton/over-use-of-ipads-iphones-and-smart-screens-hurting-kids-1.3221491 (accessed 1 March 2017).

Carrington, V and Marsh, V (2005) Digital Childhood and Youth: New Texts, New Literacies. *Discourse: Studies in the Cultural Politics of Education*, 26(3): 279–85.

Chassiakos, Y R, Radesky, J, Christakis, D, Moreno, M and Cross, C (2016) Children and Adolescents and Digital Media. *American Academy of Pediatrics*, 138(5): 1–18. [online] Available at: http://pediatrics.aappublications.org/content/pediatrics/early/2016/10/19/peds.2016–2593.full.pdf (accessed 1 March 2017).

CHILDWISE (2016) Childhood 2016 press release. [online] Available at: www.childwise.co.uk/uploads/3/1/6/5/31656353/childwise_press_release_-_monitor_2016.pdf (accessed 1 March 2017).

Cohen, J D, Jones, W M, Smith, S and Calandra, B (2016) Makification: Towards a Framework for Leveraging the Maker Movement in Formal Education. *Proceedings of Society for Information Technology & Teacher Education International Conference*, 2016(1): 129–35.

Department for Education (DfE) (2014) Statutory framework for the Early Years Foundation Stage: setting the standards for learning, development and care for children from birth to five. [online] Available at: www.gov.uk/government/uploads/system/uploads/attachment_data/file/335504/EYFS_framework_from_1_September_2014_with_clarification_note.pdf (accessed 1 March 2017).

Dunkley, V (2015) Screentime is making kids moody, crazy and lazy. [online] Available at: www.psychologytoday.com/blog/mental-wealth/201508/screentime-is-making-kids-moody-crazy-and-lazy (accessed 1 March 2017).

Faulder, M (2015) Enhancing practical maths with maths journals and MyStory app. [online] Available at: https://enabling environments.co.uk/2015/02/02/enhancing-practical-maths-with-math-journals-and-mystory-app/ (accessed 1 March 2017).

Fisher-Price (no date) 3 months old. [online] Available at: www.fisher-price.com/en_GB/playtime-guide/3-months/index.html (accessed 1 March 2017).

Gardner, H and Davis, K (2013) *The App Generation*. New Haven, CT: Yale University Press.

Garside, J (2014) Ofcom: six-year-olds understand digital technology better than adults. [online] Available at: www.theguardian.com/technology/2014/aug/07/ofcom-children-digital-technology-better-than-adults (accessed 1 March 2017).

Gibbons, A (2015) Debating Digital Childhoods: Questions Concerning Technologies, Economies and Determinisms. *Open Review of Educational Research*, 2(1): 118–27.

Gill, B (2012) Thinking Inside the Box Constrained Creativity and New Technology. *Gifted Education International*, 28(1): 127–9.

Giovanni, P (2007) On the Wave of Creativity: Children, Expressive Languages and Technology. *International Journal of Education through Art*, 3(2): 103–21.

Granic, I, Lobel, A and Engels, R (2014) The Benefits of Playing Video Games. *American Psychologist*, 69(1): 66–78.

Greengard, S (2009) Are We Losing Our Ability to Think Critically? *Communications of the ACM*, 52(7). [online] Available at: http://cacm.acm.org/magazines/2009/7/32082-are-we-losing-our-ability-to-think-critically/fulltext (accessed 1 March 2017).

The Guardian (2015) Tablets and smartphones may affect social and emotional development, scientists speculate. [online] Available at: www.theguardian.com/technology/2015/feb/01/toddler-brains-research-smartphones-damage-social-development (accessed 1 March 2017).

Guernsey, L (2014) Introducing seeding reading: Investing in children's literacy in a digital age. [online] Available at: www.joanganzcooneycenter.org/2014/06/23/introducing-seeding-reading-investing-in-childrens-literacy-in-a-digital-age/ (accessed 1 March 2017).

Guernsey, L (2016) The beginning of the end of the screen time wars. *Slate*. [online] Available at: www.slate.com/articles/technology/future_tense/2016/10/the_american_academy_of_pediatrics_new_screen_time_guidelines.html (accessed 1 March 2017).

Hampton, K, Goulet, L S, Her, E J and Rainie, L (2009) Social isolation and new technology. [online] Available at: www.pewinternet.org/2009/11/04/social-isolation-and-new-technology/ (accessed 1 March 2017).

Henriksen, D, Mishra, P and Fisser, P (2016). Infusing Creativity and Technology in 21st Century Education: A Systemic View for Change. *Educational Technology & Society*, 19(3), 27–37.

Heppell, S (2011) Mobile technologies and handheld devices for ubiquitous learning: Research and pedagogy. [online] Available at: http://workshop.heppell.mobi/ (accessed 1 March 2017).

Huffington Post (2016) Stop saying technology is causing social isolation. [online] Available at: www.huffingtonpost.com/hector-l-carral/stop-saying-technology-is-causing-social-isolation_b_8425688.html (accessed 1 March 2017).

Hughes, B (2002) *A Playworker's Taxonomy of Play Types*. London: Play Education.

International Society for Technology in Education (ISTE) and the Computer Science Teachers Association (CSTA) (2011) *Operational Definition of Computational Thinking for K-12. Education*. [online] Available at: www.iste.org/docs/ct-documents/computational-thinking-operational-definition-flyer.pdf?sfvrsn=2 (accessed 1 March 2017).

Jackson, R (2016) Digital childhoods: What technology means for the development of children. [online] Available at: https://theknowledgeexchangeblog.com/2016/01/06/digital-childhoods-what-technology-means-for-the-development-of-children/ (accessed 1 March 2017).

Jary, S (2016) How much screen time is healthy for children? Expert tips on screen safety, education, mental development and sleep. [online] Available at: www.pcadvisor.co.uk/feature/digital-home/how-much-screen-time-is-healthy-for-children-benefits-3520917/ (accessed 1 March 2017).

Jeffries, D (2013) Is technology and the internet reducing pupils' attention spans? [online] Available at: www.theguardian.com/teacher-network/teacher-blog/2013/mar/11/technology-internet-pupil-attention-teaching (accessed 1 March 2017).

Kervin, L (2016) Powerful and Playful Literacy Learning with Digital Technologies. *Australian Journal of Language and Literacy*, 39(1): 64–73.

Khoo, E, Merry, R, Nguyen, N H, Bennett, T and MacMillan, N (2013) Early Childhood Education Teachers' iPad-supported Practices in Young Children's Learning and Exploration. *Computers in New Zealand Schools: Learning, Teaching, Technology*, 25(1–3): 3–20. [online] Available at: www.otago.ac.nz/cdelt/otago065453.pdf (accessed 1 March 2017).

Kim, H, Park, J, Yoo, S and Kim, H (2016) Fostering Creativity in Tablet-Based Interactive Classrooms. *Educational Technology & Society*, 19(3): 207–20.

Knowland, V and Formby, S (2016) *The Use of Technology to Support Literacy in the Early Years in 2015*. National Literacy Trust. [online] Available at: www.literacytrust.org.uk/assets/0003/3324/The_Use_of_Technology_to_Support_Literacy_in_the_Early_Years_in_2015.pdf (accessed 1 March 2017).

Kulman, R (2015) What is Digital Play? Why is it Important? *LearningWorks for Kids*. [online] Available at: http://learningworksforkids.com/2015/07/what-is-digital-play-why-is-it-important/ (accessed 1 March 2017).

Loveless, A (1995) *The Role of IT: Practical Issues for the Primary Teacher*. London: RoutledgeFalmer.

Lynch, J and Redpath, T (2014) 'Smart' Technologies in Early Years Literacy Education: A Meta-narrative of Paradigmatic Tensions in iPad Use in an Australian Preparatory classroom. *Journal of Early Childhood Literacy*, 14(2): 147–74.

Makerspaces.com (2016) What is a makerspace? [online] Available at: www.makerspaces.com/what-is-a-makerspace/ (accessed 1 March 2017).

Marsh, J, Plowman, L, Yamada-Rice, D, Bishop, J C, Lahmar, J, Scott, F, Davenport, A, Davis, S, French, K and Piras, M (2015) Exploring play and creativity in pre-schoolers' use of apps: final project report. [online] Available at: http://techandplay.org/tap-media-pack.pdf (accessed 1 March 2017).

Marsh, J, Plowman, L, Yamada-Rice, D, Bishop, J and Scott, F (2016) Digital Play: A New Classification, *Early Years: An International Research Journal*, 36(3): 242–53. [online] Available at: http://eprints.whiterose.ac.uk/96760/22/5-24-2016_Digital%20pl.pdf (accessed 1 March 2017).

Martin, L (2015) The Promise of the Maker Movement for Education. *Journal of Pre-College Engineering Education Research (J-PEER)*, 5(1), Article 4.

Mattoon, C, Bates, A, Shifflelet, R, Latham, N and Ennis, S (2015) Examining Computational Skills in Prekindergartners: The Effects of Traditional and Digital Manipulatives in a Prekindergarten Classroom. *Early Childhood Research & Practice*, 17(1). [online] Available at: http://ecrp.uiuc.edu/v17n1/mattoon.html (accessed 1 March 2017).

McGauran, D (2016) 5 ways social media contributes to social isolation. [online] Available at: www.activebeat.com/your-health/women/5-ways-social-media-contributes-to-social-isolation/ (accessed 1 March 2017).

McKenzie, J (2007) Digital Nativism Digital Delusions and Digital Deprivation. *from now on*, 17(2). [online] Available at: http://fno.org/nov07/nativism.html (accessed 1 March 2017).

McPake, J (2011) *Rethinking Young Children Creating and Communicating. Research Briefing 3 for Digital Childhoods*. Glasgow: Scottish Universities Insight Institute.

National College for Teaching and Leadership (2013) Teachers' standards (early years). [online] Available at: www.gov.uk/government/uploads/system/uploads/attachment_data/file/211646/Early_Years_Teachers__Standards.pdf (accessed 1 March 2017).

Novak, J and Gowin, B (1984) *Learning How to Learn*. London: Cambridge University Press.

Peppler, K, Halverson, E and Kafai, Y B (eds) (2016) *Makeology: Makerspaces as Learning Environments* (Vol 1). London: Routledge.

Plowman, L, McPake, J, Stephen, C, Prout, A, Adey, C and Stevenson, O (2012) *Young Children Learning with Toys and Technology at Home*. Stirling: University of Stirling Research Briefing.

Prensky, M (2001) Digital Natives, Digital Immigrants. *On the Horizon*, 9(5): 1–6. [online] Available at: www.marcprensky.com/writing/Prensky%20-%20Digital%20Natives,%20Digital%20Immigrants%20-%20Part1.pdf (accessed 1 March 2017).

Prensky, M (2011) Introduction. *From Digital Natives to Digital Wisdom: Hopeful Essays for 21st Century Education*. Thousand Oaks, CA: Corwin/Sage. [online] Available at: http://marcprensky.com/writing/Prensky-Intro_to_From_DN_to_DW.pdf (accessed 1 March 2017).

Public Health England (PHE) (2013) *How Healthy Behaviour Supports Children's Wellbeing*. London: Public Health England. [online] Available at: www.gov.uk/government/uploads/system/uploads/attachment_data/file/232978/Smart_Restart_280813_web.pdf (accessed 1 March 2017).

Ott, M and Pozzi, F (2012) Digital Games as Creativity Enablers for Children. *Behaviour & Information Technology*, 31(10): 1011–19.

Outhwaite, L (2016) Effectiveness of an iPad intervention to support development of maths skills in foundation year children. [online] Available at: https://onebillion.org/downloads/dunkirk-primary-final-report.pdf (accessed 1 March 2017).

Resnick, M (2012) Reviving Papert's Dream. *Educational Technology*, 52(4): 42–6. [online] Available at: web.media.mit.edu/~mres/papers/educational-technology-2012.pdf (accessed 1 March 2017).

Resnick, M (2013) Teaching kids to code. [online] Available at: www.edsurge.com/n/2013-05-08-learn-to-code-code-to-learn (accessed 1 March 2017).

Resnick, M and Rosenbaum, E (2013). Designing for Tinkerability, in Honey, M and Kanter, D (eds) *Design, Make, Play: Growing the Next Generation of STEM Innovators*, pp 163–81. London: Routledge.

Roberts, D, Foehr, U and Rideout, V (2005) Generation M: media in the lives of 8-18 year olds. [online] Available at: https://kaiserfamilyfoundation.files.wordpress.com/2013/01/generation-m-media-in-the-lives-of-8-18-year-olds-report.pdf (accessed 1 March 2017).

Robson, S (2014) The Analysing Children's Creative Thinking Framework: Development of an Observation-led Approach to Identifying and Analysing Young Children's Creative Thinking. *British Educational Research Journal*, 40(1): 121–34.

Salonius-Pasternak, D E and Gelfond, H S (2005). The Next Level of Research on Electronic Play: Potential Benefits and Contextual Influences for Children and Adolescents. *Human Technology: An*

Interdisciplinary Journal on Humans in ICT Environments, 1(1), 5–22. [online] Available at: http:// humantechnology.jyu.fi/archive/vol-1/issue-1/salonius_pasternak-gelfond_harvard_medical_ school_center_for_mental_health_and_media_united_states_of_america1_5-22 (accessed 1 March 2017).

Savage, M and Barnett, A (2015) *Digital Literacy for Primary Teachers*. Northwich: Critical Publishing.

Savage, M and Czismadia, A (2018) Computational Thinking and Creativity in the Secondary Curriculum, in Younie, S (ed) & Bradshaw, P. *Debates in ICT and Computing* Education. Oxon: Routledge.

Scottish Universities Insight Institute (SUII) (no date) Digital childhoods. [online] Available at: www. scottishinsight.ac.uk/Portals/50/Digital%20Childhoods%20ResearchBriefin1.pdf (accessed 1 March 2017).

Shapiro, J, Tekinbaş, K, Schwartz, K and Darvasi, P (2016) Mindshift guide to digital games and learning. (Games and Learning Publishing Council). [online] Available at: www.kqed.org/assets/pdf/news/ MindShift-GuidetoDigitalGamesandLearning.pdf (accessed 1 March 2017).

Sigman, A (2012) Time for a View of Screen Time. *Archives of Disease in Childhood*, 97(11): 935–42.

Spencer, P (2013) iPads: Improving Numeracy Learning in the Early Years. In Steinle, V, Ball, L and Bardini, C (eds) *Mathematics Education: Yesterday, Today and Tomorrow* (Proceedings of the 36th Annual Conference of the Mathematics Education Research Group of Australasia), Melbourne: MERGA. [online] Available at: www.merga.net.au/documents/Spencer_MERGA36-2013.pdf (accessed 13 March 2017).

Staiano, A and Calvert, S (2012) Digital Gaming and Pediatric Obesity: At the Intersection of Science and Social Policy. *Social Issues and Policy Review*, 6(1): 54–81. [online] Available at: http://onlineli-brary.wiley.com/doi/10.1111/j.1751-2409.2011.01035.x/abstract;jsessionid=21FACEC78BDF7F 9C1C8C2A4623AB8132.f03t01 (accessed 1 March 2017).

Strasburger, V (2011) Policy Statement – Children. Adolescents, Obesity, and the Media. *Pediatrics*, 128(1): 201–08. [online] Available at: http://pediatrics.aappublications.org/content/pediatrics/ 128/1/201.full.pdf (accessed 1 March 2017).

Sween, J, Wallington, S, Sheppard, V, Taylor, T, Llanos, A and Adams-Campbell, L (2014) The Role of Exergaming in Improving Physical Activity: A Review. *Journal of Physical Activity and Health*, 11(4): 864–70. [online] Available at: www.ncbi.nlm.nih.gov/pmc/articles/PMC4180490/pdf/nihms486686.pdf (accessed 1 March 2017).

Tapscott, D (1998) *Growing Up Digital*. London: McGraw-Hill.

Tapscott, D (2009) *Grown Up Digital: How the Net Generation is Changing Your World*. New York: McGraw-Hill.

Wiedmer, T (2015) Generations Do Differ: Best Practices in Leading Traditionalists, Boomers, and Generations X, Y, and Z. *Delta Kappa Gamma Bulletin*, 82(1): 51–58.

Wingra School (2012) Differences between traditional and progressive education. [online] Available at: www.wingraschool.org/who/progressive.htm (accessed 1 March 2017).

Wisconsin Task Force on Arts and Creativity in Education (Updated on 19 February 2010) Towards a def-inition of creativity. [online] Available at: www.education.com/reference/article/towards-definition-creativity/ (accessed 1 March 2017).

Wood, C, Jackson, E, Hart, L, Plester, L and Wilde, L (2011) The Effect of Text Messaging on 9- and 10-year-old Children's Reading, Spelling and Phonological Processing Skills. *Journal of Computer Assisted Learning*, 27(1): 28–36. [online] Available at: http://onlinelibrary.wiley.com/doi/10.1111/ j.1365-2729.2010.00398.x/abstract (accessed 1 March 2017).

Wood, C, Kemp, N and Plester, B (2014) *Text Messaging and Literacy – The Evidence*. London: Routledge.

Wu, C, Fowler, C, Lam, W, Wong, H, Wong, C and Loke, A (2014) Parenting Approaches and Digital Technology Use of Preschool Age Children in a Chinese Community. *Italian Journal of Pediatrics*, 40(44): 1–8.

Zeng, N and Gao, Z (2016) Exergaming and Obesity in Youth: Current Perspectives. *International Journal of General Medicine*, 9: 275–84.

4 Understanding the world: technology

CHAPTER OUTLINE AND PROFESSIONAL LINKS

Understanding the world in one of the seven '*areas of learning and development*' specified in the EYFS Framework (DfE, 2014). Educational programmes must contain activities and experiences that include:

> *guiding children to make sense of their physical world and their community through opportunities to explore, observe and find out about people, places, **technology** and the environment.*
>
> (DfE, 2014, p 8)

The EYFS Framework breaks down *Understanding the world* into sub-areas including:

• *Technology: children recognise that a range of technology is used in places such as homes and schools. They select and use technology for particular purposes.*
> (DfE, 2014, p 12)

At the outset of the book, this sub-area was probably the EYFS strand you thought of first in relation to *technology-enhanced learning* (DfE, 2014). If children are working towards being able to *select* and *use* technologies *purposely* by age five, they must have broad and rich technology experiences up until then. Berry (2016) noted that '*it's not enough for children to use the tech they're given: they've got to have some say in what they use*'.

Critical questions

Reflect on how technologies are typically deployed in your setting. When and how are children given the opportunity to select technologies themselves? Berry (2016) posed the following questions that practitioners should consider.

» Are these things stored somewhere children can access them?

» Do children know the basics of how to keep themselves and the equipment safe?

» How will they be shared fairly?

(Berry, 2016)

The term places (*such as homes and schools*) was similarly underscored to emphasise that it is important to base experiences both directly within your setting, including real-world simulations, and where children encounter technologies when they are not in your care. You are aiming to help children understand the technology-rich world in which they live. In Chapter 3 the discussion on the *digital natives* concept suggested that children *do* need to be actively directed by practitioners in developing the skills, knowledge, concepts and attitudes related to living in a technology-rich world. As your learners move on to Key Stage 1, teachers continue to '*ensure that pupils become digitally literate*' working towards a '*level suitable for the future workplace and as active participants in a digital world*' (DfE, 2013, p 1).

In this chapter you will also be given technology-specific guidance on the assessment of children's progress, their needs, and developmental activities (eg Table 4.2) and support in this area of learning (DfE, 2014, p 13). The rationale for offering this lies in the principle that educators, irrespective of the age-phase, can only truly cater for children's developmental needs in a subject discipline if they have comprehensive professional knowledge and understanding of *what has come before* and *what will come next* for learners. Therefore, in addition to the overarching principle of the EYFS Framework to ensure children's '*school readiness*', including '*knowledge and skills* [as the] *foundation for ... progress through school and life*', it is pertinent to explore how the *technology* strand is developed after five years of age (DfE, 2014, p 5). While maintaining a broad and balanced approach in this chapter, you will be prompted to also think forward to the *Primary National Curriculum Programmes of Study for Computing* (DfE, 2013). Your work in this area lays the essential foundations for what comes next in primary computing. *Computer science*, *digital literacy* and *information technology* are the three components of primary computing (DfE, 2014) and provide a useful framework for exploring the early development of these complementary strands. Table 4.1 helps you to cross-reference these two sources.

Table 4.1 *Interpretation of* Development Matters: Development Statements *(The British Association for Early Childhood Education, 2012) categorised under the national curriculum for computing sub-themes of* computer science, digital literacy *and* information technology *(DfE, 2013)*

Development statements categorised by computing Programme of Study themes	Computer science theme:	Digital literacy theme:	Information technology theme:
Birth to 11 months	*The beginnings of understanding technology lie in babies exploring and making sense of objects and how they behave.*		
8–20 months			
16–26 months	*Anticipates repeated sounds, sights and actions, eg when an adult demonstrates an action toy several times.* *Shows interest in toys with buttons, flaps and simple mechanisms and beginning to learn to operate them.*	*Anticipates repeated sounds, sights and actions, eg when an adult demonstrates an action toy several times.*	
22–36 months	*Operates mechanical toys, eg turns the knob on a wind-up toy or pulls back on a friction car.*		*Seeks to acquire basic skills in turning on and operating some ICT equipment.*
30–50 months	*Knows how to operate simple equipment, eg uses remote control.* *Shows an interest in technological toys with knobs or pulleys.* *Shows skill in making toys work by pressing parts or lifting flaps to achieve effects such as sound, movements.*	*Shows an interest in technological toys … such as cameras or mobile phones.* *Knows that information can be retrieved from computers.*	*Knows how to operate simple equipment, eg turns on CD player.*

Table 4.1 (cont.)

Development statements categorised by computing Programme of Study themes	Computer science theme:	Digital literacy theme:	Information technology theme:
40–60+ months	*Completes a simple program on a computer.* *Children recognise that a range of technology is used in places such as homes and schools; eg traffic lights.*	*Children recognise that a range of technology is used in places such as homes and schools; eg ebooks.*	*Uses ICT hardware to interact with age-appropriate computer software.* *Children recognise that a range of technology is used in places such as homes and schools; eg tablets/iPads. They select and use technology for particular purposes.*

(The British Association for Early Childhood Education, 2012, and DfE, 2013)

Theoretical perspectives and pedagogical links

Berry (2016) explained that while *'computing may not be part of the EYFS Statutory Framework, ... there is much that goes on in the EYFS that provides a foundation for computational thinking'*. Table 4.1 demonstrates this by categorising the *development statements* for technology within the computing programme of study themes of computer science digital literacy and information technology (DfE, 2013). These themes are not mutually exclusive but are intertwined, complementary and overlapping. Occasionally, you do not even need to be using technology to be teaching aspects of computational thinking and you will note reference to *unplugged* activities in this chapter (http://csun-plugged.org).

Computer science and Early Years Foundation Stage technology

At first glance, the idea of *computer science* may sound very daunting, but once you look beyond the scary-sounding terminology (eg algorithms and debugging) you will see that there are concepts and approaches that very much resonate with early years practice.

→ Looking ahead, in Key stage 1 pupils will be taught to:

- *understand what algorithms are; how they are implemented as programs on digital devices; and that programs execute by following precise and unambiguous instructions*

- *create and debug simple programs*

- *use logical reasoning to predict the behaviour of simple programs.*

(DfE, 2013)

Figure 4.1 *Extract from KS1 Computing POS: Computer Science*

Defining computer science

Computational thinking is a core tenet of computer science. In the simplest terms, it requires thinking logically through a problem to generate and test solutions. No doubt you already create learning opportunities for your children to do this every day! An algorithm is simply a sequence of instructions or commands needed to perform a task; for example, making toast in the role-play kitchen (Figure 4.2).

> *In the early years, teachers naturally create opportunities for sequencing – a key element of algorithms. For example, sequencing lining up to leave the classroom, tidying up, or even how to play nicely with others by taking turns. Role play provides further opportunity for sequencing; for example the sequences of events that occur in the post office when going to post a letter.*

(Barefoot Computing, 2014)

Figure 4.2 *Barefoot Computing (2014) Algorithm for making toast (barefootcas.org.uk, 2014)*

Critical question

» *Identify any sequencing activities you have planned in the next few weeks. Consider how you can empower children to be the* programmers *and how they can scaffold each other's attempts at carrying out precise sequences to role-play or carry out tasks.*

Using Table 4.2, locate which (or similar) devices you already use in your setting. Working across Table 4.2, left to right, you can see the transition between using concrete apparatus and abstraction by representation on a screen. Similarly, children progress from instantaneous response programming, ie '*I press this button now and my car moves forwards until I take my finger off*', to programming increasingly more complex sequences of instructions that are delayed until the program is executed by pressing *Go*. Abstraction begins when the sequence of instructions (program or algorithm) begin to be transcribed or represented separately from the device in operation (eg *TacTile* or *Focus on Bee-Bot* software). Options towards the right also provide learners with the opportunity to debug; ie fix their programs if they do not perform as expected on execution.

Discussion of Table 4.2 introduced some new concepts (eg algorithm) and process terminology (eg debugging) and you will now have the opportunity to clarify meaning and delve a little deeper. Figure 4.3 from Barefoot Computing (2014) breaks down the *concepts* and *approaches* that form the basis of computational thinking.

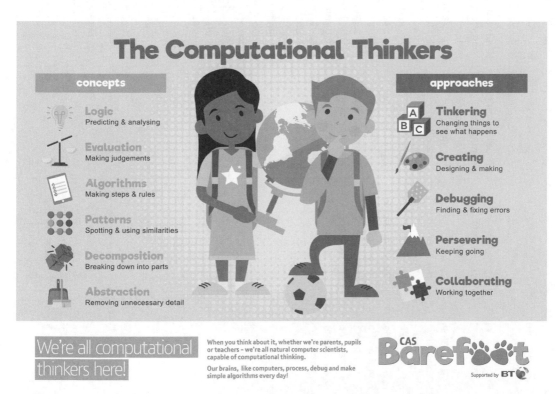

Figure 4.3 *The computational thinkers (reproduced by permission of Barefoot)*

Table 4.2 *Illustrative example of progressive early years programming language commands; moving from left to right the commands require greater cognitive demand*

Programming commands:	**Programming commands:**	**Programming commands:**	**Programming commands:**	**Programming commands:**	**Programming commands:**
On/off	On/off	On/off	On/off	On/off	Go/execute
Go by pressing and holding button and off/stop by releasing hold	Forwards	Forwards/accelerate	Go/execute	Go/execute	Pause
Reaction time: Instantaneous	Backwards	Reverse	Pause	Pause	Clear
Concrete or abstraction: Concrete	Left	Sound horn	Clear	Clear	Forwards (15cm steps)
	Right	Lights on/lights off	Forwards (15cm steps)	Forwards (15cm steps)	Backwards
	Reaction time: Instantaneous	**Reaction time:** Instantaneous	Backwards	Backwards	Left or right and 90 degree turns
	Concrete or abstraction: Concrete	**Concrete or abstraction:** Concrete	Left or right and 90-degree turns	Left or right and 90 degree turns	Aerial, angled or through the perspective of Bee-Bot's eyes
			Up to 40 steps can be programmed	Debug by swapping tiles.	Routes/programs can be planned and edited (debugged)
			Reaction time: Instantaneous or delayed until sequence executed by pressing Go	Up to 30 steps can be programmed by connecting three readers.	**Reaction time:** On execution of program
			Concrete or abstraction: Concrete moving towards Abstraction	**Reaction time:** Delayed until sequence executed by pressing go	**Concrete or abstraction:** Abstraction as no concrete apparatus used
				Concrete or abstraction: Concrete moving towards Abstraction with the use of written program via TacTile and Bluetooth connectivity	
Eg *One Stage Remote Control Spin and Go Triceratops* from TTS	Eg *Wonderbug Outdoor Waterproof Remote Control Bug* from TTS	Eg *Billy Big Wheels* from TTS	Eg *Bee-Bot and Constructa-Bot* from TTS	Eg *Blue-bot & TacTile Reader* from TTS	Eg *Focus on Bee-Bot* software or Bee-Bot app (https://itunes.apple.com/gb/app/bee-bot/id500131639?mt=8)

Berry (2016) suggested a list of questions, suitable for early years, that you could pose in your setting. These questions are related to exploring computing concepts (left-hand side of Figure 4.3):

- **Logical reasoning:** *What will happen if I do this? How do you know?*

- **Algorithms:** *What do I need to do to solve this? Is there a better way?*

- **Decomposition:** *Can we break this problem up? Could we each do different jobs to solve the problem?*

- **Patterns:** *Have you solved something like this before? What did you do then? What's changed?*

- **Abstraction:** *What's the most important thing here? Maybe we can draw a picture of this?*

- **Evaluation:** *What went well? Which way worked best? What would you do differently next time?*

(Berry, 2016)

The recommendation is *not* that you should introduce these vocabulary terms to children. Instead, consider how and when you pose similar questions to learners and scaffold their journey towards solutions and alternative approaches.

Referring to the *approaches* on the right-hand side of Figure 4.3, you will quickly recognise some similarities with the characteristics of effective teaching and learning from the EYFS Framework. Examples include the synergy between '*tinkering*', described below, and '*playing and exploring – children investigate and experience things, and "have a go"*' (DfE, 2014, p 9).

Tinkering

Barefoot Computing (2014) defined tinkering as '*trying things out*';

> *For young children, this is the vital play based, exploration and experimentation phase of learning about something.*
>
> (Barefoot Computing, 2014)

Further, it is argued that '*tinkering is closely associated with logical reasoning, as pupils try things out they start to build up experiences of cause and effect. "If I move this, then this happens"*' (Barefoot Computing, 2014). For three- to five-year-olds, you will no doubt already recognise the tinkering you witness daily; for example, in the role-play corner. Barefoot Computing (2014) recognised that typically '*early years environments abound with opportunities to try things out, how to explore and ask open questions such as 'why...?' and 'how...?'*'. Also, when children have access to '*digital devices, such as remote control toys, programmable floor turtles, cameras and computers*', tinkering will no doubt occur. Children in your setting may move beyond remote control toys to extend their programming experience by using Bee-Bots or Constructa-bots and toy-app combinations such as *Think & Learn Code-a-pillar* (Fisher-Price).

In summary, by including play-based tinkering activities regularly in the early years you are equipping children with an attitude that is essential for later computer programming:

by giving them time to direct their own exploration, asking pupils open ended questions, challenging pupils to find out more, encouraging confidence and play and giving pupils time to reflect on what they have discovered whilst tinkering.

(Barefoot Computing, 2014)

Creating

Similarly, the computational thinking approach of *creating*, defined by Barefoot Computing (2014) as '*about planning, making and evaluating things*', reminds you of the EYFS characteristic of *creating*, where children '*have and develop their own ideas*' (DfE, 2014, p 9). By *creating*, children are engaged in '*active learning*' (DfE, 2014). By '*designing and making pupils become active rather than passive learners as they use and applying computational thinking skills to create animations, games*' (Barefoot Computing, 2014).

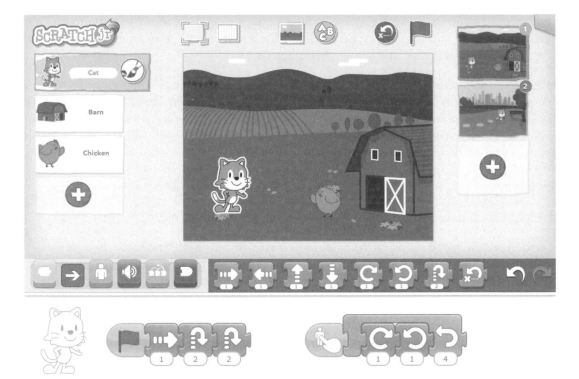

Figure 4.4 *A screenshot from ScratchJr (ScratchJr.org), a visual programming language (for children approximately five years old) where blocks are connected to create movement, sounds etc (reproduced by permission of Scratchjr)*

Debugging

Debugging is one of those terms that can sound more daunting than it actually is. When you have a plan to do something and it doesn't work, you go back to try and spot what the problem was and take remedial action; ie correct the mistake until it works in the way you intended. Barefoot Computing (2014) suggested a four-step model for *logical reasoning* that can easily be interpreted in an early years context:

1. *Predict what should happen.*

2. *Find out exactly what happens.*

3. *Work out where something has gone wrong.*

4. *Fix it.*
   (Barefoot Computing, 2014, http://barefootcas.org.uk/barefoot-primary-
   computing-resources/computational-thinking-approaches/debugging/)

You may be thinking about what debugging would look like as an activity. Barefoot Computing (2014) offers the following example:

> *In early years, pupils explore (tinker) in the role play corner to try things out and learn how things work, they are continually finding problems and fixing them and and in so doing are debugging. For example, they may organise the shoe shop and then serve a customer and can't find the matching pairs of shoes, so they reorganise their shoes in pairs to solve this 'bug' in their shop display. In doing this they are using logical reasoning to solve their problem.*
> (Barefoot Computing, 2014, http://barefootcas.org.uk/barefoot-primary-
> computing-resources/computational-thinking-approaches/debugging/)

Critical question

» *Above is an example of what debugging might look like in the early years. Can you think of other examples? Perhaps role-playing getting dressed in the morning or brushing your teeth, where actions need to happen in a precise sequence.*

Persevering

Working in the the EYFS you are seeking to foster perseverance by encouraging children to '*keep on trying if they encounter difficulties*', '*concentrate*' and '*think critically*' (DfE, 2014, p 9). You will already recognise the importance professionally, that young learners need to develop attitudes that will help them cope when things are hard and they want to give up. Being resilient and persevering is essential in being a successful learner. In Chapter 3 research on children playing computer games appeared to suggest that, alongside traditional activities, they can be constructive in developing both concentration and perseverance: '*Both coders and gamers report experiencing a state of "flow" in which they're utterly absorbed in and focussed on a single activity*' (Barefoot Computing, 2014).

Collaborating

Many of the activities you regularly build into practice encourage children to develop their capacity to work alongside, together or collaboratively with others. Gradually this builds into a wider sense of other perspectives and ideas. Again, this desirable attribute can be extrapolated into a programming context:

> When programming, many see 'pair programming' as a particularly effective way to write code, with two programmers sharing a screen and a keyboard, working together to create software. Typically one programmer acts as the driver, dealing with the detail of the programming, whilst the other takes on a navigator role, looking at the bigger picture.
>
> (Barefoot Computing, 2014, http://barefootcas.org.uk/barefoot-primary-computing-resources/computational-thinking-approaches/collaborating/)

Therefore, you can have confidence that when you are encouraging 'pupils to develop their emerging collaborative skills, such as how to take turns, how to wait in line, how to explain their ideas to another, listen to peers and work together on an activity with or without support', this will prepare them well when they later encounter opportunities to program with others (Barefoot Computing, 2014).

CASE STUDY

Programming my robot friend to navigate around the classroom

James and Amelia are playing a robot game. James is pretending to be a robot and moves his arms and legs in a robotic manner. He makes Amelia laugh by putting on a funny voice and repeatedly saying 'I am a robot' as he moves on the spot. Amelia joins in by pretending to turn James on and off by operating an imaginary switch on his back. They rehearse this several times, having a great deal of fun. James' key worker is nearby and encourages them to continue their game. After a few minutes she suggests that Amelia gives her robot vocal instructions: walk forwards, stop, turn around. James and Amelia continue in their roles, exploring this new dimension to their play for a further five minutes.

Commentary on case study

Dr Teckniko's website (https://drtechniko.com) contains descriptions of several simple how to train your robot activities suitable for use in the early years. It is easy to simplify or extend the ideas to match the learners you are working with. Similarly, vocal commands can be augmented by creating agreed pictorial symbols similar to those in Figure 4.5.

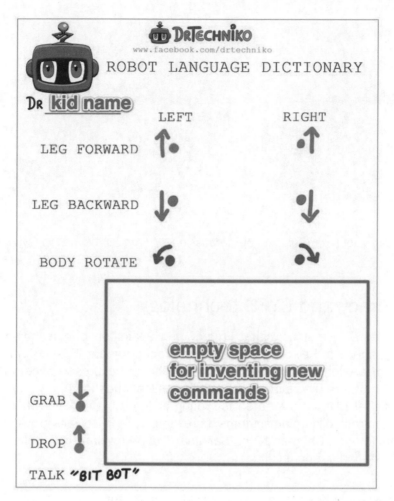

Figure 4.5 *Dr Techniko's pictorial robot commands (reproduced by permission of DrTechniko. com)*

Unsurprisingly, with the international growing emphasis on teaching children coding, from pre-school onwards, commercial toy retailers are responding by launching new products and apps to tap into this area. Earlier you were introduced to *Code-a-pillar* from Fisher-Price. Another example is the Dot and Dash robots illustrated in Figure 4.6. The robots connect wirelessly to your iPad/tablet and are operated by associated apps;

- *Path* app www.makewonder.com/apps/path
- *Go* app www.makewonder.com/apps/go
- *Xylo* app www.makewonder.com/apps/xylo

Figure 4.6 *Dash robot (reproduced by permission of Wonder Workshop) www.makewonder. com/dash*

Digital literacy and EYFS technology

Another key theme is that of digital literacy and again the origins begin in the early years. Looking ahead to Key Stage 1 curriculum requirements (Figure 4.7), we can identify key ideas of personal safety and privacy and how to express concerns and interact respectfully with others. There is also the philosophical question of ownership and ethics surrounding digital footprints created for young children by adults in their lives. Digital assessment and record-keeping systems, for example, Tapestry, are growing in popularity and have many merits. Chapter 12 on *Safeguarding and welfare* will delve much deeper into your professional responsibilities.

→ Looking ahead, in Key Stage 1 pupils will be taught to:

• *use technology safely and respectfully, keeping personal information private; identify where to go for help and support when they have concerns about content or contact on the internet or other online technologies.*

(DfE, 2013)

Figure 4.7 *Extract from KS1 Computing POS: Digital Literacy*

Defining digital literacy

Savage and Barnett (2015, pp 6–23) dedicated a chapter to discussing and defining literacy in a manner pertinent to children. Key conclusions with relevance to early years include:

• Instead of talking about digital literacy, it is important to recognise that really they are plural (litera**cies**) and they evolve over time in line with technology and cultural practices.

- For example, Grace (aged three) will role play taking *selfies* after witnessing older siblings and family members using this term.

- Jacob (aged two) interacts with granny using FaceTime.

• Digital literacies are a continuum rather than a threshold mastery construct. You will be at a certain point on that continuum, as will children in the early years based on their experiences of technology and digital media to date.

• Rather than being a list of technical competences, being *digitally literate* describes an informed sense of being and living in a digitally rich world. The key word here is *informed*, implying a sense of understanding.

- For example, children who have regular experiences of taking, manipulating and sharing digital photographs come to understand that the images they encounter (in print or on screen) have been *framed*, possibly altered (the Photoshop effect) and shared (published) by others.

• We have already discussed the topic of enabling children to be both *consumers* and *producers* of digital content; for example, creating their own artwork, films, music and audio recordings, however brief they may be.

• More than any other generation, today's children are growing up in an information-rich world. Slowly they are experiencing *information* in its many forms (graphics, animations, audio narration, sound effects, music, films, games etc). Gradually they are learning to distinguish between *forms*, *live* and *recorded*, *real*, *fictitious* or *layered* information (*layered* images are where a photograph and a graphic are blended together, as can be seen on a BBC website at www.bbc.co.uk/cbeebies/shows/andys-dinosaur-adventures).

Over time they will watch adults searching for information to answer questions or follow lines of interest. For example, Gabriel (aged two) asks what a *jellyfish* is after listening to *Commotion in the Ocean* (Andreae and Wojtowycz) being read; his key worker offers to look this up on the iPad to show him more images and tell him more information.

• Identities can be adopted online and in games; for example, choosing a *character* or an *avatar* to represent yourself. Materials such as *Hector's World* videos (available via CEOP at www.thinkuknow.co.uk/5_7/hectorsworld/) can be used to introduce e-safety issues to young children aged five.

• Technologies can be used to communicate; young children will see siblings and adults send SMS (short message service), MMS (multimedia messaging service), talk 'face-to-face' over FaceTime and Skype, send emails, chat, Tweet (Twitter), pin (Pinterest), 'friend' on social networks etc. You will notice these terms and practices may feature or be mimicked in role play.

• Individuals, families and groups are interconnected globally. Preston et al (2017) discuss the attitudes and values of digital citizenship and the responsibilities this may entail. Initiatives, partnerships and organisations in early childhood education may be connected digitally across states, countries and continents (eg. Global Village International Preschool, www.gvipreschools.org).

Critical question

» *Which values and dispositions do you believe are important in relation to digital literacies? What type of opportunities would you provide children with in order to enable them to develop positive values and dispositions?*

While some of the practices listed here may sound daunting and have e-safety implications, you need to acknowledge their existence and prevalence irrespective of personal preferences. Safeguarding practices and practitioner advice is addressed comprehensively in a later chapter. Simple protocols, such as not using personal devices (Savage and Barnett, 2015) are fundamental to safeguarding protocols. As children's e-safety education continues, the focus turns to empowering them to keep themselves safe by knowing and understanding what they are doing, including both benefits and potential risks.

Information technology and EYFS technology

At the beginning of this chapter we discussed Berry's (2016) reminder to practitioners that:

> the technology early learning goal states that children should '**select and use technology for particular purposes**'. There are a wide range of digital technologies that young children can use playfully and collaboratively, such as digital cameras, audio recorders, tablet computers, phones (smart or otherwise) and simple, programmable robots such as Bee-Bot. As they play with these devices, children will form their own mental model (schema) of how these work.

Defining information technology

This section focuses on what could be categorised as functional skills; the tools and capabilities needed to express knowledge, ideas, feelings etc in multiple digital formats alongside paint, crayons, glue, scissors etc. Throughout Chapters 4–11 you will be presented with ideas for developing these information technology capabilities in the early years. Practitioners and learners now have a varied and powerful toolkit to create, share and present with. Balanced with traditional tools, you have multiple digital tools at your disposal. As children gain experience (and reflect on those experiences) with a range of digital tools, they will gradually become confident and discerning users. Figure 4.8 illustrates how these early steps with you develop as children pass five years of age and commence Key Stage 1.

→ *Looking ahead, in Key Stage 1 pupils will be taught to:*

* *use technology purposefully to create, organise, store, manipulate and retrieve digital content*

* *recognise common uses of information technology beyond school.*

(DfE, 2013)

Figure 4.8 *Extract from KS1 Computing POS: Information Technology*

International perspective

You may have been surprised by the emphasis on *computer science* when reading this chapter. The primary computing curriculum certainly is very different compared to your prior educational experience. Was the new curriculum subject of computing, introduced in 2014, reflective of trends in the United Kingdom only or a wider international repositioning? You may well have heard of global STEM (science, technology, engineering and mathematics) initiatives and it frames the topics we have discussed in the book so far.

The *National Public Radio*'s (USA) 2015 headline drew attention to how things may be changing:

> *Coding Class, Then Naptime: Computer Science For The Kindergarten Set*
> (NPR.org, 2015, www.npr.org/sections/ed/2015/09/18/441122285/
> learning-to-code-in-preschool)

Globally educators have been prompted to rethink educational objectives in relation to technology and digital information. Children today are growing up in an information-rich world, where social, educational and commercial interactions are mediated by technology more often than not. The future jobs of these children will include roles and skill-sets we have yet to think of. Who ten years ago would have foreseen the career of the *social media strategy manager*?

Bloggers such as *Trendhunter.com* (2016) regularly report on storylines such as *Preschool coding – Parents rush to teach children about binary to get them ready for digital jobs*. We see commercial companies launching toys such as Fisher-Price's *Code-a-pillar*, referred to earlier, and the *Primo Play Set – Cubetto*, with physical shape blocks representing code.

- *Cubetto* is aimed at three year olds – where a '*a toddler can program a plywood robot*' (see video at https://youtu.be/yBJWKbv589Q) (Primotoys.com).

- And *KIBO Robot Kits* (http://kinderlabrobotics.com/kibo/) similarly aim to bring programming to four year olds (http://kinderlabrobotics.com/robotics-in-early-childhood/).

- Ozobots are another similar product (http://ozobot.com).

Figure 4.9 *Cubetto Playset by Primo Toys (photos reproduced by permission of Primo Toys, www.primotoys.com)*

Figure 4.10 *KIBO robot kit, by Kinderlab – children build their own robot and create a sequence of instructions using the wooden KIBO blocks (photo reproduced by permission of Kinderlab, www.kinderlabrobotics.com)*

Resnick's (2013) seminal phrase '*learn to code, code to learn*' reflects a growing mindset that reading and writing code is a desirable 21st-century literacy:

> *I see coding (computer programming) as an extension of writing. The ability to code allows you to 'write' new types of things – interactive stories, games, animations, and simulations.*

> (Resnick, 2013)

Resnick was not arguing that every child will grow up to be a programmer but that fundamental transferable capabilities are also developed in the process of developing computational thinking capability in young learners. Sometimes, a very direct correspondence is found; for example, Kazakoff and Ber's (2014) research concluded that activities '*programming robots*' had a positive impact on '*sequencing ability in early childhood*' (p 553). On other occasions these foster learning attitudes such as perseverance and managing difficulty.

Wolfram (2016) argued that:'*computational thinking is going to be a defining feature of the future, and it's an incredibly important thing to be teaching to kids today. But where does it fit into the standard educational curriculum? The answer, I think, is simple: everywhere!*' New York's mayor declared in 2016 that '*a computer science education is literacy for the 21st century*', backed up by $186 million being spent annually (as of 2016) to enable '*students from kindergarten through high school to learn the fundamentals of computer science, like coding, robotics and web design'* (www.wnyc.org/story/de-blasio-tackles-inequity-nyc-schools-computer-science/).

President Obama took part in the launch of the *Hour of Code* non-profit movement of 2016 (https://hourofcode.com/us):

> *The Hour of Code is a global movement reaching tens of millions of students in 180+ countries. Anyone, anywhere can organize an Hour of Code event. One-hour tutorials are available in over 45 languages. No experience needed. Ages 4 to 104.*

Reflecting back on the emphasis being placed on technology for learning in the United Kingdom, you can be confident that many of your international counterparts are doing likewise.

Conclusion

Children are naturally curious about the technology that surrounds them and how people interact with them: *'what happens when Mummy puts her card in the machine outside the bank? what is the machine called? why does she have to type a number in? why does she keep it secret?'* (Berry, 2016).

If you now return to Table 4.1 at the beginning of this chapter and re-read the statements listed, they now look very modest. The table began to categorise the development statements for technology under the computing curriculum sub-themes. This chapter has illustrated what this means and how it might look in practice.

Critical question

» *Table 4.1 also used age bands taken from* Development Matters *(with the proviso that development may not be linear) (The British Association for Early Childhood Education, 2012, pp 41–2). Returning to one of the questions posed in Chapter 3, how does experience of and access to technology impact upon these age bands both now and in the future as technology continues to evolve?*

Recommended further reading and product reviews

- Barefootcas.org.uk links to a number of relevant articles that would be useful to read including Bers et al's (2014) research in a kindergarten setting that found children *'were both interested in and able to learn many aspects of robotics, programming, and computational thinking with the TangibleK curriculum design'* (p 145).

  Bers, M, Flannery, L, Kazakoff, E and Sullivan, A (2014) Computational Thinking and Tinkering: Exploration of an Early Childhood Robotics Curriculum. *Computers & Education*, 72, 145–57. [online] Available at http://ase.tufts.edu/devtech/publications/computersandeducation.pdf.

- P Bagg has a number of appropriate Bee-Bot activities and resources for reception at http://code-it.co.uk/beebot.

Figure 4.11 App-based The Foos *from codeSpark Academy (reproduced by permission of codeSpark)*

- Using the *pre-reader* filter on the *Hour Of Code* website (https://hourofcode.com/us/learn), you can find a range of activities that can be used or adapted in your setting.

- BBC Computing Science and ICT for three- to six-year-olds can be accessed at www.bbc.co.uk/education/subjects/zst3d2p.

- The *DevTech Research Group* host an online community, the *Early Childhood Robotics Network*, at http://tkroboticsnetwork.ning.com and was involved in research around the *KIBO Robotic Kits* with Pre-Kindergarten children.

- *codeSpark Academy – The Foos* aims to teach play-based, word-free coding to four year olds (+) and offers free lesson plans and support materials at http://codespark.org/parents-teachers/.

Finally, you should read the Standards and Testing Agency (2014) EYFS profile exemplification for the level of learning and development expected at the end of the EYFS: *Understanding the world: ELG15 – Technology*.

References

Barefoot Computing (2014) [online] Available at: http://barefootcas.org.uk (accessed 1 March 2017).

Berry, M (2016) Laying the foundations for computing in the early years. Blog post. [online] Available at: http://milesberry.net/2016/01/laying-the-foundations-for-computing-in-the-early-years/ (accessed 1 March 2017).

The British Association for Early Childhood Education (2012) Development matters in the Early Years Foundation Stage (EYFS). [online] Available at: www.foundationyears.org.uk/files/2012/03/Development-Matters-FINAL-PRINT-AMENDED.pdf (accessed 1 March 2017).

codeSpark Academy (2016) [online] Available at: http://codespark.org/parents-teachers/ (accessed 1 March 2017).

Department for Education (DfE) (2013) Computing programmes of study: Key Stages 1 and 2, national curriculum in England. [online] Available at: www.gov.uk/government/uploads/system/uploads/attachment_data/file/239033/PRIMARY_national_curriculum_-_Computing.pdf (accessed 1 March 2017).

Department for Education (DfE) (2014) Statutory framework for the Early Years Foundation Stage: setting the standards for learning, development and care for children from birth to five. [online] Available at: www.gov.uk/government/uploads/system/uploads/attachment_data/file/335504/EYFS_framework_from_1_September_2014__with_clarification_note.pdf (accessed 1 March 2017).

Kazakoff, E and Bers, M (2014) Put Your Robot In, Put Your Robot Out: Sequencing through Programming Robots in Early Childhood. *Journal of Educational Computing Research*, 50(4): 553–73.

Preston, C, Savage, M, Payton, M and Barnett, A (2018) Towards Tomorrow's Successful Digital Citizens: Providing the Critical Opportunities to Change Mindsets, in Younie, S (ed) and Bradshaw, P. *Debates in ICT and Computing* Education. Abingdon: Routledge.

Primotoys.com (2016) Cubetto. [online] Available at: www.primotoys.com (accessed 1 March 2017).

Resnick, M (2013) Learn to code, code to learn. [online] Available at: www.edsurge.com/news/2013-05-08-learn-to-code-code-to-learn (accessed 1 March 2017).

Savage, M and Barnett, A (2015) *Digital Literacy for Primary Teachers*. St Albans: Critical Publishing.

Standards and Testing Agency (2014) *EYFS Profile Exemplification for the Level of Learning and Development Expected at the End of the EYFS. Understanding the World: ELG15 – Technology*. London.

Trendhunter.com (blog) Preschool coding. [online] Available at: www.trendhunter.com/protrends/preschool-coding (accessed 1 March 2017).

Wolfram, S (2016) Preparing students for the computational future. [online] Available at: www.edsurge.com/news/2016-09-11-preparing-students-for-the-computational-future (accessed 1 March 2017).

5 Communication and language

CHAPTER OUTLINE AND PROFESSIONAL LINKS

Communication and language is one of the prime areas for learning and development in the EYFS framework.

> Communication and language development involves giving children opportunities to experience a rich language environment; to develop their confidence and skills in expressing themselves; and to speak and listen in a range of situations.
>
> (DfE, 2014, p 8, author's emphasis)

This area is subdivided into three Early Learning Goals:

- **ELG 01 Listening and attention:** *children listen attentively in a* range of situations. *They listen to* stories, *accurately anticipating key events and* respond *to what they hear with relevant comments, questions or actions. They give their* attention *to what others say and respond appropriately, while engaged in another activity.*

- **ELG 02 Understanding:** *children* follow instructions *involving several ideas or actions. They* answer 'how' and 'why' questions *about their experiences and in response to stories or events.*

- **ELG 03 Speaking:** *children* express themselves effectively, showing awareness of listeners' needs. They use past, present and future forms accurately when talking about events that have happened or are to happen in the future. They develop their own narratives and explanations by connecting ideas or events.

(DfE, 2014, p 10, author's emphasis)

Both sets of Teachers' Standards also indicate the importance of communication and language development:

- **Teachers' Standards (Early Years)** (National College for Teaching and Leadership, 2013, author's emphasis)

    - **Standard 2.5** '*Communicate **effectively** with children from birth to age five, listening and responding sensitively*' (p 2);

    - **Standard 2.6** '*Develop children's confidence, social and **communication skills** through **group** learning*' (p 2);

    - **Standard 3.2** '*Demonstrate a clear understanding of how to **widen** children's* [communication and language] *experience*' (p 3);

    - **Standard 5.2** '*Demonstrate an awareness of the ... **communication needs** of babies and children, and know how to adapt education and care to support children at different stages of development*' (p 4).

- **Teachers' Standards (Qualified Teacher Status)** (DfE, 2011, author's emphasis)

    - **Standard 3** makes reference to teachers '*demonstrating an understanding of ... literacy, **articulacy** and the **correct use of standard English***' (p 11);

    - **Standard 5** makes reference to teachers having '*a clear understanding of the needs of all pupils, including those ... with **English as an additional language** ...* [and being] *able to use and evaluate distinctive teaching approaches to engage and support them*' (p 11).

Communication is conceptually quite sophisticated and nuanced; it involves:

- '*imparting or exchanging of information by speaking, writing, or using some other medium*';

- a '*message containing information or news*';

- a '*message*' that can be a mass broadcast or a bespoke interpersonal construction;

- choosing between multiple modes of transmission (a conversation, a letter, a text, a status update, video etc);

- an affective dimension;

- an active engagement or response from the recipient.

(Oxford Living Dictionary, 2016)

Communication technologies is the *CT* of *ICT*:

an umbrella term that includes any communication device or application, encompassing: radio, television, cellular phones, computer and network hardware and software, satellite systems and so on, as well as the various services and applications associated with them, such as videoconferencing and distance learning.

(Rouse, 2016)

Therefore, enabling experiences of a *'rich language environment'* across *'a range of situations'* suggests a wealth of possibilities (DfE, 2014, p10).

This chapter continues by exploring common assumptions in relation to *'communicative competencies'* (McPake et al, 2013, p 423). Now that a significant proportion of communication in our society is mediated by technology, do we need to revisit the traditional definition of communication? Young children are immersed in cultural practices of communication and language use from the outset. This chapter will consider examples from the spectrum of technology-mediated communication: from mass broadcast communications (eg a television programme) to interpersonal communications (eg FaceTime). Communication also involves *active listening*; not only *hearing* but being able to cognitively process and respond to that *message*.

Theoretical perspectives and pedagogical links

Language as a symbol system

Communication is the essence of social constructivist theory where *learning* is viewed as a *'social process'* (Kim, 2001). Cviko et al (2012) highlighted the importance of *'children learning to use language for authentic purposes'* in realistic scenarios (p 33). Kim (2001) explained that language is a culturally constructed *'symbol system'* and that:

> *without the social interaction with more knowledgeable others, it is impossible to acquire social meaning of important symbol systems and learn how to use them. Young children develop their thinking abilities by interacting with adults.*
>
> (Kim, 2001)

The notion of language as a system of symbols is very pertinent in an early years context as children, from birth onwards, are constructing their mental schema of that *symbol system* over and over again as they experience social interactions. Over time young children will learn to associate the situated practices and norms of expression, sometimes mediated by technology, and develop an awareness of the target audience. For example, they learn when a *lol* or an emoji are appropriate and when they are not! Savage and Barnett (2015) suggested that rather than dismissing everything that is not 'Standard English', irrespective of context, you should recognise the child's sophisticated reasoning in detecting *'characteristics of a sub-culture's'* language when immersed in a specific social-communicative context (eg. SMS) (p 12). Is that not part of the richness of language?

Early years professionals have been using symbols and pictures with children to aid communication for many years. For example, Figure 5.1 depicts *InPrint 3*, a tool to *'make books, flash cards, worksheets and accessible documents with Widgit Symbols'* and the *Widgit* app range (available from www.widgit.com/index.php).

Widgit Go for iPad...

Widgit Writer

Create symbol documents on your iPad with this new app that integrates with your Widgit Online account for free

Widgit Go

Symbol activities and grids for your iPad or Android tablet. Use it in the home, in the classroom or on the go.

App Bundles

Get the best deals on collections of Widgit Apps

Early Language Screening Tools

NEW: Assess early language and verbal comprehension - suitable for practitioners, teachers and parents.

Widgit Vocab

Widgit Vocab is a series of iPad apps designed to develop basic vocabulary. Widgit Vocab can help extend a user's vocabulary range with listening, speaking and reading activities

Symbols2Write

Apps for young learners and pupils who need support in learning about sentences and the elements that construct them.

Discover Series

Learning and communication support for children studying a new subject. The first three apps cover Tudors, Victorians and Egyptians.

Figure 5.1 *Products from Widgit.com including* InPrint 3, Widgit Go *for tablet devices and* Widgit app bundle *(reproduced by permission of Widgit: Widgit Symbols© Widgit Software 2002–2017; www.widgit.com)*

The use of symbols with young children resonates with the popularity of emojis or emoticons (see Figure 5.2). The BBC (2016) recently reported on a job listing for an '*emoji translator*' with the role of '*explaining cross-cultural misunderstandings in the use of the mini pictures*'!

Figure 5.2 *Emojis or emoticons*

Providing a rich language environment with technology

Both the prime area descriptor and ELG1 above make reference to children having the opportunity to be immersed in a '*rich language environment*' across a '*range of situations*' (DfE, 2014, pp 8–10). How can this be modelled in your setting? Is communication as a multisensory experience replicated digitally?

Non-verbal communication

Non-verbal cues such as gestures, facial expressions and body positioning are also key to understanding the 'message' being communicated. Paciga (2015) explained that when a digital text includes animation, '*the listener experiences an additional form of semiotic meaning – the gesture*' (p 479). Further, Paciga reflected on several studies (Ricci and Beal, 2002; Verhallen et al, 2006) showing '*positive correlations between animation containing gestures in digital storybooks and measures of story understanding*' (p 480).

Critical question

» *Consider how non-verbal communication cues are replicated or replaced in communications mediated by technology. How are they different or the same? Are they as effective? What can go wrong? Does this mean you need to model normative practices?*

What does communication entail?

Gooden and Kearns (2013) cited Bloom's (1998) description of '*communication development*' being guided by '*the need for* relevance *(i.e., communicating what is important),* discrepancy *(i.e., seeking to establish consistency of information), and* elaboration *(i.e., learning more complex language skills)* (p 1). McPake et al (2013) posed a thought-provoking question – in our digitally rich contemporary landscape, how do we decide what the '*communicative competencies*' are? (p 423). Traditionally there has been a focus on '*spoken language acquisition*' and it cannot be disputed as rightfully retaining a dominant position. However, we should consider the wider '*communicative means*' typically experienced by young children (McPake et al, 2013, p 423). This also echoes the description of the technological affordance of *communicability* used by the Primary National Strategy (2004): '*children can communicate their points of view using different* (digital) *platforms*' (p 76). The communication platforms experienced by young children range '*from traditional oral communication and written texts to screen-based media, including TV, computers, game consoles and touch screens*' (McPake et al, 2013, p 423). These communication exchanges can also be asynchronous; children can be sending or receiving the message when the recipient or sender is not located in the same geographical space or time frame. Craft (2012) articulated this as '*connectivity around the clock, with a parallel existence in virtual space ... seamlessly integrated with actual lives*' (p 1). Children of this generation may perceive '*self-actualisation through media use*' as the norm (Third et al, 2014, p 9).

Communicative competencies with technology

McPake et al (2013) offered a framework for breaking down the development of '*communicative competencies*' when '*young children learn to communicate with digital technologies*', including:

- acquisition of the operational skills *for communication (such as the prosody* of spoken language, symbol recognition and reproduction in written language, or keyboard or camera controls);*

- the purposes of communication; *cultural conventions (such as politeness, turn-taking, narrative structures);*

- and an understanding of audience.
                    (McPake et al, 2013, p 423; *prosody means 'patterns of stress and intonation in a language' (Google, 2016))

The following case study exemplifies how these competencies might look in practice.

CASE STUDY

Colin was three years old ... and already a proficient photographer. He was learning to store and retrieve photos electronically, with help from his mother. ... Colin and Emma, his five-year-old sister, were communicating with relatives in Australia, sending them photographs and messages containing emoticons (neither could write at this stage) and using a webcam for video calls.
                                        (McPake et al, 2013, p 427)

Commentary on case study

Colin's story shows several features of communicative competence in development: operational skills (such as taking, storing, retrieving and sending photographs), learning about the purposes of communication (building and maintaining social ties etc), about cultural conventions (choosing the most appropriate photographs to send) and about the need to understand the audience's point of view (learning, for example, that the Australian relatives needed explanations because his familiar world was strange to them).

In contrast to traditional means of communication, Colin and Emma had the opportunity to develop *'competences afforded by the combination of synchronous and asynchronous, multi-modal and multimedia communications'* (McPake et al, 2013, p 427).

Table 1: Comparing traditional and digital communicative and creative competences in the early years

	Traditional examples	Digital examples
Technical skills to support communicative practices	Shapes and sounds of letters, holding a pencil or a book, alphabet and spelling games	Main functions of different technologies (off, on, fast forward, alert sounds), keyboard symbols (recognition and location), using a mouse
Competence in communicating over time and distance	Letters, postcards, birthday cards	Text messages, email, sending and receiving digital photographs
Exploring, combining and transforming narrative expression	Listening to stories, telling stories	Watching TV/DVDs, engaging with interactive digital storybooks or websites: acting scenes from favourite programmes or films
Exploring, combining and transforming visual expression	Symbols, drawings, paintings	Emoticons, taking and editing photographs and videos
Exploring, combining and transforming musical expression	Listening to others sing and play instruments live, learning and performing familiar songs, making up own songs and music (with traditional instruments, including toy versions, where available)	Listening to music from a variety of digital sources (eg, radio, TV, MP3 players, YouTube), learning and performing familiar songs, making up own songs and music (with electronic instruments, including toy versions, where available)

Figure 5.3 *A reproduction of McPake et al's comparison of traditional and digital communicative competencies in the early years (McPake et al 2013 p 429)*

Critical question

» After studying the content of Figure 5.3, identify several forthcoming activities you have planned. Consider how you might utilise technology and complete Table 5.1 accordingly. After completion, reflect on whether the use of technology is likely to enhance the experience for children. The enhancement (or not) might relate to the outcome, levels of motivation and/or engagement.

Table 5.1 Planning for communicative competencies

Activity name and description	Is this activity a *narrative*, *visual* or *musical* expression?	Equipment needed	Operational skills required by child
1.	This example illustrates an activity using technology to enable the child to express a *narrative*.		
2.	This example illustrates an activity using technology to enable the child to express an idea *visually*.		
3.	This example illustrates an activity using technology to enable the child to express an idea *musically*.		

McPake et al (2013) concluded that, contrary to some popular opinion, '*digital technologies have ... greatly expanded the visibility and accessibility of graphic and written communication in children's lives*'. Further, the '*possibilities for young children to participate themselves are enhanced by the multi-modality of such communications, using visual symbols, photographs, video and sound as well as written texts*'. Importantly, '*these additional elements can make it easier for children to understand who is communicating and why, and to reply*'. The result being that young children have enriched opportunities to engage in authentic communication and to be '*part of social networks outside their immediate community at an earlier age and in more proactive ways than might have been possible even a decade ago*' (McPake et al, 2013, pp 426–7).

Augmentative and alternative communication

Chapter 11 explores technologies for inclusion in depth; however, some of the strategies that are used with children with communication-related SEND are also useful more generally. As the Communication Trust (2011) noted, '*Augmentative and Alternative Communication (AAC) describes a wide range of techniques children and young people can use to support spoken communication*':

Aided communication can be 'low- tech' or 'high-tech' and refers to methods which involve additional equipment, such as a picture or symbol chart or book, a talking computer or a Voice Output Communication Aid ... High-tech aids enable the child or young person to make choices and create messages using pictures, symbols, words or letters that can be linked to an electronic voice.

(Communication Trust, 2011, pp 13–14)

CASE STUDY

Callum is three years old, all areas of his development are delayed and he has low muscle tone which affects his ability to walk and talk. He was able to understand what he heard but had no way of communicating what he wanted or needed.

... At two and a half he was given a simple electronic communication aid (eg. Smart Speak), which brought voice to the symbols. By pressing the picture on his communication aid Callum can make choices and 'say' what he wants'.

(Communication Trust, 2011, p 31)

Figure 5.4 Smart Speak *from Inclusive Technology (reproduced by permission of Inclusive Technology)*

Commentary on case study

Very quickly Callum was able to communicate with the rest of the children in his nursery class and get them to sing the song he chose or listen to the story he wanted. Now he uses a range of ways to communicate including his communication aid ... these helped Callum take control.

(Communication Trust, 2011, p 31)

Products such as *Widget Online* '*allow you to create … symbol flashcards, timetables,* and *stories*' free of charge (Inclusive Technology). Similarly, the *Recordable Talking Wall Chart* (available from TTS at www.tts.org.uk) allows you to '*place cards, objects or drawings inside the 30 pockets and record a 10 second message for each one*'.

Active listening and learning

Listening is equally key to communication (ELG 01). Listening involves not only 'hearing' but also being able to cognitively process the information and add it to an evolving mental schema. Can technology contribute usefully to making messages and information more accessible?

Rushton et al (2003) recognised that *immersive,* '*real-life sensory and activity-based learning*' opportunities engender '*active engagement*' on the part of the learner. '*Neurons are triggered*' and '*complex connections*' are made as the child's '*brain maps out this experience in a unique manner*' (Rushton et al, 2003, p 17). Audio books, ebooks and book apps can make a valuable contribution to language development by enabling varied exposure to voices, expressive styles and vocabulary. Morgan (2013, p 477) defined ebooks as '*interactive electronic resources that combine text with sound, animation, and images and often include text that is read aloud and highlighted*'. Audio books, ebooks and book apps can create both autonomous or shared listening experiences. Paciga (2015, p 476) also drew attention to increased engagement when children are listening due to the '*motivational qualities of choice and control*'. Shuker and Terreni (2013, p 18) similarly made reference to the '*sense of agency*' and '*playfulness*' observed in young children interacting with digital texts. Hoffman and Paciga (2014, p 380) reminded practitioners that scaffolded and shared reading is just as important with digital texts; where '*the adult operates as a facilitator of children's meaning making from text*' as this is how young children '*develop oral language, vocabulary, and comprehension of written language (listening comprehension)*'.

Critical question

» *Consider how* active listening *may be observable when reading an electronic book or book app. Are* engagement *and* interactivity *suitable indicators of active listening?*

Sargeant (2015) argued '*that people read ebooks, whereas they use book apps, the latter being far more media-rich and interactive*' (p 454). Beautiful, tactile picture books with lift-up flaps, pop-out sections and buttons to press will always have a place in early years settings. However, book apps can potentially embody '*media-rich interactive features to further children's engagement with their literature*' (p 454). Can the humble picture book compete with '*hypermedia technology*', permitting the embedding of '*films, sound recordings, and video recordings*', arranged '*as non-linear systems*' and sometimes containing interactive features and gamification rewards? (Sargeant, 2015, p 456). Immersion in a digital book may indeed provide an accessible '*rich sensory experience*' for young children (p 457).

Critical question

» *It could be argued that* 'the convergence of animated film, game design and picture book conventions can lead to a destabilisation of narrative structures within children's digital books' *(Sargeant, 2015, p 457). Consider your response to this proposition.*

Technologies to support giving and following instructions

CASE STUDY

Gabriel is a lively three-year-old who enjoys having a go at everything. He responds enthusiastically to most activities and cannot wait to get started. He can become frustrated when things do not go as he intended and often has to return to ask, or get reassurance, about what to do next. His key worker wishes to set him a target of being able to listen and follow multiple-stage instructions without him needing continuous reassurance. His key worker decides to make him an outdoor activity challenge where he has to carry out in sequence a number of activities. He recognises numbers to ten so his key worker records mini tasks using the *'Big-Point Recordable Buttons'* they have (available from TTS). Number 1 says *'jump up and down'*, Number 2 says *'stand on one leg'...*

Commentary on case study

Simple technologies like the recordable buttons can provide a step towards independence and working through actions sequentially. While in this case study Gabriel's key worker was present throughout, the opportunity could be viewed as fostering an independent disposition in Gabriel by providing him with the scope of 'doing it by himself'. Tools like this can also be utilised for activities where the sequence of steps is crucial; for example, making a biscuit. A recordable wall panel could be populated with images of steps (eg weighing the butter) and ten-second recordings of what to do. If children are distracted, an instruction can be replayed. Devices vary in the number of steps and length of instructions that can be recorded. A recordable book would be suited to more complex instructions; effectively combining visual and aural prompts can foster independence and children working at their own pace. After these approaches and tools have been modelled, children will be eager to create and test their own sets of instructions with their peers. (Visit www.tts-group.co.uk for more information on all of these technology products.)

Speaking

Technologies may support children to express themselves in a number of ways. For example, they could use one of the recordable devices mentioned above to break down their message into manageable sequential chunks. They can rehearse, play back and refine sections of their message. For shy or reticent children, this intermediary step of communicating, mediated by technology, may provide a self-esteem or confidence boost. Technologies can give young children the opportunity to hear back their vocalisation of language. Audio recording and playback functionality can empower young children to give detailed verbal accounts of their unique perspective. In Chapter 2 some popular devices available from TTS were discussed, including the popular *Easi-Speak* recorders, the *Recordable Butterflies* and *Speak and Record Binoculars*. Other communication devices that could be deployed in play are *Rechargeable Mobile Phone Walkie Talkies*, *Recordable Talking Pest*, *Talking Point Recordable Buttons* and *Talk-Time Recordable Cards*.

English as an additional language

Regarding the use of English as an additional language, the Department for Education's (2014) expectations are that:

> providers must take reasonable steps to provide opportunities for children to develop and use their home language in play and learning, supporting their language development at home.
>
> (DfE, 2014, p 9)

Most of the technologies used to aid communication and language development highlighted in this chapter can also be put to good use in supporting children acquiring vocabulary and fluency when English is not their first language. Many online texts may be available in multiple languages. Recording and playback tools may be used to scaffold learning of key vocabulary. Immersive and authentic role-play opportunities will be key in supporting bilingual or multilingual children. You may have the opportunity to work with relatives to create digital books with audio embedded in the children's first language. Paciga (2015) reported on Verhallen and Bus's (2010) study demonstrating '*improved second-language preschoolers' receptive vocabulary learning through experiences with animated digital storybooks*' (p 480).

International perspective

In the United States of America over one million children are undertaking the equivalent of EAL programmes (Leacox and Wood-Jackson, 2014, p 176). '*Children from migrant families represent an emerging bilingual population with biliteracy needs.*' Leacox and Wood-Jackson's (2014) study of '*preschool and kindergarten English language learners*' (aged four to six) explored the children's vocabulary acquisition using both traditional and '*technology-enhanced methods*' (p 175). One group of children experienced an adult-mediated, '*technology-enhanced English shared reading with Spanish-bridging vocabulary instruction*' with an electronic book (ebook). Audio prompts and definitions were available via hypertext in the e-books (p 175). '*Target vocabulary words were pictured on the right side of the screen. When the picture was clicked, a prerecorded audio file provided the Spanish-bridging (ie a short definition in Spanish)*' (p 184). Leacox and Wood-Jackson concluded that the children working with the digital texts showed the greatest '*word learning gains'*. The technology also '*allowed for adaptations to different linguistic groups'* (p 193).

Conclusion

A social constructivist perspective highlights the importance of social experiences in the development of mental schemas and the synthesis of situated practices. '*Children's experiences in the early years play an important part in the development of communicative and creative competences ... young children are learning about the roles digital technologies can play in supporting communicative and creative activities'* both within and beyond their setting (McPake et al, 2013, pp 428–9). Over time, young children gain a broader *repertoire of possibilities* for communication. Not all digital media is well made or has educational merit, which is also the case with traditional forms.

Recommended further reading and product reviews

Guidance on choosing quality ebooks can be found in the following two articles:

- Morgan, H (2013) Multimodal Children's E-books Help Young Learners in Reading. *Early Childhood Education Journal*, 41: 477–83. On p 480 there is a useful '*checklist for selecting multimodal e-Books for children'*.

- Hoffman, J and Paciga, K (2014) Click, Swipe, and Read: Sharing E-books with Toddlers and Preschoolers. *Early Childhood Education Journal*, 42(6). On p 383 see '*Table 2: Additional considerations for selecting high-quality e-books'*.

References

British Broadcasting Corporation (BBC) (2016) Emoji translator wanted – London firm seeks specialist. [online] Available at: www.bbc.co.uk/news/world-38287908 (accessed 1 March 2017).

Communication Trust (2011) Other ways of speaking: supporting children and young people who have no speech or whose speech is difficult to understand. [online] Available at: www.talkingpoint.org.uk/sites/talkingpoint.org.uk/files/Other%20Ways%20of%20Speaking%20FINAL.pdf (accessed 1 March 2017).

Craft, A (2012). Childhood in a Digital Age: Creative Challenges for Educational Futures. *London Review of Education*, 10(2): 173–90.

Cviko, A, Mckenney, S and Voogt, J (2012) Teachers Enacting a Technology-rich Curriculum for Emergent Literacy. *Educational Technology Research & Development*, 60: 31–54.

Department for Education (DfE) (2011) Teachers' standards: guidance for school leaders, school staff and governing bodies. [online] Available at: www.gov.uk/government/uploads/system/uploads/attachment_data/file/301107/Teachers__Standards.pdf (accessed 1 March 2017).

Department for Education (DfE) (2014) Statutory framework for the Early Years Foundation Stage: setting the standards for learning, development and care for children from birth to five. [online] Available at: www.gov.uk/government/uploads/system/uploads/attachment_data/file/335504/EYFS_framework_from_1_September_2014__with_clarification_note.pdf (accessed 1 March 2017).

Gooden, C and Kearns, C (2013) The Importance of Communication Skills in Young Children. *Human Development Institute Research Brief.* [online] Available at: www.hdi.uky.edu/wp-content/uploads/2015/03/ResearchBrief_Summer2013.pdf (accessed 1 March 2017).

Hoffman, J and Paciga, K (2014) Click, Swipe, and Read: Sharing E-books with Toddlers and Preschoolers. *Early Childhood Education Journal*, 42(6): 379–388.

Kim, B (2001). Social Constructivism, in Orey, M (ed) *Emerging Perspectives on Learning, Teaching, and Technology*. [online] Available at: http://cmapsconverted.ihmc.us/rid=1N5QXBJZF-2OSG67F-32D4/Kim%20Social%20constructivism.pdf (accessed 1 March 2017).

Leacox, L and Wood-Jackson, C (2014) Spanish Vocabulary-bridging Technology-enhanced Instruction for Young English Language Learners' Word Learning. *Journal of Early Childhood Literacy*, 14(2): 175–97.

McPake, J, Plowman, L and Stephen, C (2013) Pre-school Children Creating and Communicating with Digital Technologies in the Home. *British Journal of Educational Technology*, 44(3): 421–31.

Morgan, H (2013) Multimodal Children's E-books Help Young Learners in Reading. *Early Childhood Education Journal*, 41: 477–83.

National College for Teaching and Leadership (2013) Teachers' standards (early years). [online] Available at: www.gov.uk/government/uploads/system/uploads/attachment_data/file/211646/Early_Years_Teachers__Standards.pdf (accessed 1 March 2017).

Oxford Living Dictionary (2016) Communication. [online] Available at: https://en.oxforddictionaries.com/definition/communication (accessed 1 March 2017).

Paciga, K (2015) Their Teacher Can't Be An App: Preschoolers' Listening Comprehension of Digital Storybooks. *Journal of Early Childhood Literacy*, 15(4): 473–509.

Primary National Strategy (2004) *Key Features of ICT in Excellence and Enjoyment: Learning and Teaching in the Primary Years*. Department for Education and Skills: London.

Rouse, M (2016) ICT (information and communications technology – or technologies) [online] Available at: http://searchcio.techtarget.com/definition/ICT-information-and-communications-technology-or-technologies (accessed 1 March 2017).

Rushton, S, Eitelgeorge, J and Zickafoose, R (2003) Connecting Brian Cambourne's Conditions of Learning Theory to Brain/Mind Principles: Implications for Early Childhood Educators. *Early Childhood Education Journal*, 31(1): 11–21.

Sargeant, B (2015) What is an Ebook? What is a Book App? And Why Should We Care? An Analysis of Contemporary Digital Picture Books. *Children's Literature in Education,* 46(4):454–66.

Savage, M and Barnett, A (2015) *Digital Literacy for Primary Teachers*. St Albans: Critical Publishing.

Shuker, M and Terreni, L (2013) Self-authored E-books: Expanding Young Children's Literacy Experiences and Skills. *Australasian Journal of Early Childhood*, 38(3): 17–24.

Third, A, Bellerose, D, Dawkins, U, Keltie, E and Pihl, K (2014) *Children's Rights in the Digital Age: A Download from Children Around the World*. Melbourne: Young and Well Cooperative Research Centre.

Widgit (no date) [online] Available at: www.widgit.com/sectors/education/early-years.htm (accessed 1 March 2017).

6   Physical development

CHAPTER OUTLINE AND PROFESSIONAL LINKS

This chapter will prompt you to consider the potential role of technology in relation to the area of learning – *physical development* (DfE, 2014, p 7), encompassing both fine and gross motor skills and physical exercise. The Department for Education (2014) defines *physical development* as follows:

> *Physical development involves providing opportunities for young children to be active and interactive; and to develop their co-ordination, control, and movement. Children must also be helped to understand the importance of physical activity, and to make healthy choices in relation to food.*
>
> (DfE, 2014, p 8, author's emphasis)

The relevant Early Learning Goals are articulated as:

- **Moving and handling:** *children show good* control *and* coordination *in* large *and* small movements. *They move confidently in a range of ways, safely negotiating space. They* handle equipment *and* tools *effectively...*

- **Health and self-care:** *children know the importance for good health of* physical exercise, *and a healthy diet, and talk about ways to keep healthy and safe.*
  (DfE, 2014, pp 10–11, author's emphasis)

The EYFS framework states that children must have the opportunity to learn how to '*handle equipment and tools effectively*' and this chapter will ask you to consider what this means within the wider notion of object affordances (DfE, 2014, p 10). Some of the questions raised in Chapter 3, regarding the impact of computer-game playing on exercise, health and well-being, will be revisited.

Theoretical perspectives and pedagogy

When thinking about technology-enhanced learning related to physical development, it is important that you draw from the range of digital devices that include cameras, video cameras, microphones, audio recording devices, tablets such as iPads and technology which supports *exergaming* (see Chapter 3) such as the Nintendo Wii and the *Dance Dance Revolution* app. You should never replace exercise with *exergaming* but instead recognise its enjoyment and motivational potential to extend opportunities (Hatch, 2011, pp 12–13).

Models of physical development in childhood

The *moving and handling* Early Learning Goal requires that '*children show good control and coordination in large and small movements*' (DfE, 2014, p 10). Established theory on physical development can be overlaid with an analysis of *control* and *co-ordination* when interacting with technologies. Oswalt (2007) outlined physical development during infancy. Piaget's stages of development locate the very young infant at the *sensorimotor* stage where knowledge of the world comes through the senses. Gradually, reflexes such as grasping, head turning and stepping are replaced by voluntary actions as motor skills develop. By six months babies will be able to hold objects and transfer an object from one hand to another. By about nine months babies will have more control over the objects they hold, such as being able to place them rather than just throw them down; they'll also be crawling, sitting independently and playing with toys. By about 18 months babies can use tools, such as holding a cup and making marks with a crayon; they can also turn pages in a book and build with blocks.

Critical question

»   *The section above identified some of the key physical development milestones referred to by Oswalt (2007) from birth to three years old. What are the typical milestones for gross and fine motor development for three- to five-year-olds? What might these milestones look like in relation to interacting with technologies?*

Controlling and operating technology tools

Many of you will have witnessed first hand, or seen video footage of, very young children demonstrating high levels of dexterity – '*small movements*' (DfE, 2014, p 10) when interacting with tablet or smartphone devices (for example, iPads and iPhones). Sometimes children appear to acquire these technology *gestures* quite easily. Further, they seem to make the connection between a *gesture* (*tap*, *swipe*, *pinch* and *drag*) and an action happening on screen relatively quickly. The nature of the tablet interface design and usability by young children is an interesting area for you to explore. Is being able to interact with digital interfaces from an early age a 21st-century equivalent of the *pencil grip*? Of course, that is a provocative question but that is precisely what new technologies prompt educators to do – reflect and question. Barnardo's (2006) reported that technologies can make positive contributions to developing both children's fine motor skills and their hand–eye co-ordination:

> ICT equipment like digital cameras, recorders, and computers all require some dexterity to use them effectively. Learning to use small and large equipment builds children's confidence and gives children a sense of control, autonomy and achievement. Using the keyboard, mouse or the buttons, levers and knobs on a piece of equipment such as a digital camera is an excellent way of developing finer motor skills. Workers involved in Barnardos' projects observed improved eye/hand coordination in children using ICT.
>
> (Canavan Corr, 2006, p 8)

Similarly, Ernest et al (2014) reported that the research literature concluded that '*playing games had been shown to be an important component of promoting visual and kinesthetic response-related skills*' (p 184). They referred to the notion of '*visual-reasoning skills*' – a sequence of *seeing*, *processing* and *reacting* with a physical response (Ernest et al, 2014, p 184; Hatch, 2011, pp 12–13).

Plowman and McPake's (2013) research highlighted the importance of '*operational learning – learning how to control and use technologies, getting them to do the things you want them to do, and having opportunities to make your own inputs and get a personalised response*' (p 30). Plowman and McPake go on on to explain the correspondence between *interactivity* and physical movement:

> Typically, 'interactive' refers to the operational aspects involved in creating a response from an action, such as clicking, pressing, or scrolling. Creating this interactivity can be an impediment to learning if children do not understand what they need to do or lack the fine motor skills to achieve it … Tablet computers can solve some of these operational problems … the touch screen and gestural interface, the portability, and the ease of sharing offer new dimensions of interactivity…
>
> (Plowman and McPake, 2013, p 30)

Object affordances

The EYFS framework states that children must have the opportunity to learn how to '*handle equipment and tools effectively*' (DfE, 2014, p 10). How does the notion of *object affordance* interrelate with the design of technologies for young children? Technologies with buttons, levers, switches and knobs appeal to children's curiosity and kinesthetic approach. VTech's *Kidizoom Action Cam* (see Figure 6.1) offers a 'through the eyes of' action-experience to filming as it can be mounted on a helmet or floor robot. But do the design ergonomics and appeal of *made for children* devices justify the additional expense or should we use the standard grown-up version?

082421

Figure 6.1 *VTech's* Kidizoom Action Cam, Kidizoom Duo (reproduced by permission of VTech)

Critical question

» *Surveying the technology devices in your setting, which are purpose-designed for children and which are real or close replicas of standard equipment? What are the advantages and disadvantages of using child versions of technologies?*

Activity, movement and technology

Chapter 3 challenged the idea that technology means children being stationary, passive and indoors. This section looks at how using technologies can embrace the characteristics of effective learning and promote interactivity, motivation, levels of physical activity and being outdoors! The implications of *characteristics of effective learning* are wide-ranging. For example, they might be taken to suggest that *non-interactive screen time* is not a desirable substitute for engaging *inter*-actively with digital media. They could also highlight the value of children playing with a metal detector, where they are developing their critical thinking by testing their ideas; operating the tool with precision and spatial awareness (BrightMinds, 2016; Watts, 2013). You may agree that '*passive use of technology and any type of screen media is an inappropriate replacement for active play, engagement with other children, and interactions with adults*' (NAEYC, 2012, p 4).

CASE STUDY

Funky Footsteps *from the Early Learning Centre*

Eliza and Ethan are intrigued by the new toy that has appeared in the toddler department. They are attracted by the bright colours and visual stimuli. Ethan crawls over to touch the new mat while Eliza sits and watches. He touches the footsteps, running his fingers across the textured footprints. His exploration is accompanied by excited babbling. Eliza walks over to see more. A practitioner touches the footprint and repeats the word *'feet'*. Eliza looks at her feet and where the practitioner is pointing. By *'accident'* she triggers a sound and reacts with surprise. After reassurance from the practitioner, Ethan starts to pat the footprint near him.

Commentary on case study

The Funky Footsteps toy appeals to Eliza and Ethan in respect of its object affordances; the scale and bright colours are visually stimulating; the textured footprints are a recognisable symbol and instinctively invite the children to place their own feet on top of them. The children quickly discover that the action of applying pressure results in sounds being generated. This sequence happens reliably and encourages the children to become more confident and deliberate in their actions.

Critical question

» *What physical development observations do you think you might make of Eliza and Ethan interacting with this toy? How would you scaffold any interventions to extend the physical development learning opportunities?*

Exploring movement with digital cameras

You might, for example, help a small group record a dance performance as well as reflect with the children on ways to improve this. Being able to *capture, play back, pause, restart* offers children an immensely powerful *performance refinement* opportunity. The child can augment their sensory experience of moving their body by seeing an asynchronous 'reflection' of how it looked. For example, digital video recording and playback may provide a vehicle for young children to 'see' review and modify how they move; for example, in holding a position. Barnardo's detailed how digital photography could be used to scaffold learning by breaking down movements into discrete steps:

> *Digital cameras are a great way to record their achievements and celebrate them with the children and their families. Balancing on a plank, skipping, hopping and other gross movements can be recorded in single frames or, if your camera has the feature, recorded as a sequence over short intervals. This fascinates children as they see all the movements they need to make in order just to jump, for example.*
>
> (Canavan Corr, 2006, p 8)

Selecting developmentally appropriate technology

The *Development Matters* document (Moylett and Stewart, 2012) is useful for identifying interconnections between moving, handling, health and self-care and the EYFS key themes (unique child, positive relationships, enabling environments, areas of learning). This will enable you to consider the developmentally appropriate use of digital technology.

Table 6.1 focuses attention on *moving and handling* and ways in which this guidance can be linked to digital technology.

Table 6.1 *Key themes from* Development Matters *and digital technology connections*

Key themes in EYFS and guidance within *Development Matters*	Digital technology connections
Unique child: 22–36 months • *Beginning to use three fingers (tripod grip) to hold writing tools* • *Imitates drawing simple shapes such as circles and lines* 40–60 months • *Shows increasing control over an object in pushing, patting, throwing, catching or kicking it* • *Handles tools, objects, construction and malleable materials safely and with increasing control*	iPad apps such as the free *Know Number 123*, which includes tracing numbers, and a *reflect* game that requires the player to tilt the iPad in order to move the numbers until they overlay the target number Shaking the iPad is used to clear the screen in the free *Fingerpaint* app Bee-Bots and Blue-Bots as well as remote control toys, computer mice/roller-ball type mice, touchscreen devices, digital devices operated by pressing buttons including cameras (for both indoor and outdoor use)
Positive relationships – 8–20 months • *Show babies different ways to make marks in dough or paint by swirling, poking or patting it* 30–50 months • *Use music of different styles and cultures to create moods and talk about how people move when they are sad, happy or cross*	Finger painting using the '*iPad may promote more and a wider variety of touch-based interaction*' (Crescenzi et al, 2014, p 92) YouTube music videos: teachers can also encourage moving to the music and creating mood music using electronic keyboards and computer apps
Enabling environments – 8–20 months • *Provide novelty in the environment that encourages babies to use all of their senses and move indoors and outdoors* • *Provide resources that stimulate babies to handle and manipulate things, eg toys with buttons to press or books with flaps to open* 22–36 months • *Provide CD and tape players, scarves, streamers and musical instruments so that children can respond spontaneously to music*	The Reggio Emilia-inspired light box, light room, use of lighting effects The Fisher-Price *4-in-1 Step 'n Play Piano* provides an immersive environment for '*developing coordination and gross motor skills*' Nintendo Wii's *Dance Dance Revolution* and other *exergaming* forms of digital technology (see Chapter 3 for more on this.)

Critical question

» *What developmentally appropriate apps can you find to support fine and gross motor skill development?*

CASE STUDY

Using iPads for finger painting

Eli (aged 26 months) is introduced to the *Fingerpaint Magic* app on the iPad. He instinctively touches the blank screen. He repeats this several times, staring intently at the screen. After a few moments he moves his finger away from the screen and turns his hands over. He looks at the finger he has been using. He returns to touching the screen and as his confidence grows he uses bolder and longer movements. He remains silent throughout. Over the next few minutes he repeats looking at his fingertips. The practitioner thinks he may be checking to see if he has paint on his fingers. He is observed trying short movements, dragging his finger, patting and hitting the screen to see what happens to the digital paint. As his confidence grows some of the movements are accompanied by sound effects.

Commentary on case study

Very young children explore their worlds most naturally and intuitively through touch. Touchscreen technology such as iPads is therefore already well designed to respond to poking, pressing, swiping and stretching by the small fingers of even the youngest infants. But does interacting with the iPad through touch enhance or hinder a child's learning in any way?

Crescenzi et al (2014) used a wider range of types, qualities and sequences of touching to evaluate the potential of the iPad for '*"digit" skill development*' (p 93). In particular, they compared finger painting using paper and paints with finger painting using apps on an iPad, including the free apps *DoodleBuddy* (by Dinopilot), *Fingerpaint Magic* and *Fingerpaint with Sounds* (by Inclusive Technology). They found that tapping, straight strokes, circular strokes, repeated touches and sequences of continuous touching including longer sequences occurred more with the iPad compared to when using paper and paints for finger painting. On the other hand, they found that when the children used paper and paints, pressing was more common; more fingers were used; different amounts of pressure were used when pressing; textural experiences were richer; and opportunities for reflection were greater as the child moved from paper to palette and looked at and experienced the feeling of paint on the fingers. Interestingly, they found that children had different repertoires of touch – for example, a child might show more restricted circular movements but more frequent tapping on the iPad, more pressing on the paper and equal amounts of repetition and continuous touching. They concluded that:

> *digital technology shapes young children's touch-based interaction: in particular, it engenders broader use of a wider range of types of touch, which include more complex and longer sequences of continuous touch interactions, fostering more elaborate touch repertoires.*

(Crescenzi et al, 2014, p 94)

Critical question

» *It's reasonable to consider that the different ways of touching when finger painting with paper and the iPad are influenced by the different affordances of these media. What other affordances do iPads have and how might these affordances provide support for young children's physical development?*

Physical development towards Key Stage 1

When using the STEP model for teaching PE you focus on Space, Task, Equipment and People (Black and Stevenson, 2011). Judicious use of digital technology can add to enjoyment and attainment. Videoing performance can also be an affordable and easy way for children to start analysing their own performance. And, of course, music is freely available on the internet so children could be encouraged to select their own music and then interpret this through dance.

Critical question

» *What health, welfare and safeguarding aspects do you need to take into consideration when planning a PE lesson that incorporates digital technology?*

Barnardo's advocated that technology can contribute to staying healthy:

> *The Internet has a vast range of health-related websites aimed specifically at children. These can support children's learning about themselves and their bodies. They can find out about diet, exercises and sport. Tape recorders, CD players and websites can play music that encourages children to move and dance. Children can hold a tape recorder and listen to recorded instructions guiding them through a series of obstacles outside (put a sticker on the pause button so that they can put the recorder down between listening to each of the instructions and carrying them out). ICT equipment can support children's physical development, enabling them to see that what they do has a positive effect on their well-being.*

(Canavan Corr, 2006, p 8)

Maliszewski (2011) reported on research showing the value of '*Wii games for physical development purposes*' with children with Special Educational Needs and Disabilities (as cited by Ernest et al, 2014, p 184).

International perspective

Saúde et al (2005) reported on a 2003 survey of European early childhood practitioners in Bulgaria, England, Portugal, Spain and Sweden, which aimed to explore their perceptions of the importance of technology in areas of the curriculum. Across all participating countries, technology was perceived as having the least importance in relation to *physical development and movement*; the percentage importance for each country was as follows: Bulgaria (6%), England (18.4%), Portugal (7.9%), Spain (7.6%) and Sweden (12.4%). In many ways this is not surprising as traditional notions of sitting at a computer do not appear to be very physical. Has the growth in mobile devices over the last decade changed perceptions?

Conclusion

Both *gaming* and *gamification* strategies can be channelled for positive motivational outcomes in relation to physical movement. A recent example is the *Pokémon Go* craze that swept the UK in the summer of 2016 and saw families, siblings and children walking distances that many government-funded health promotion strategies would be very envious of. 'Playing' makes it more fun for adults and children alike. The Office of Disease Prevention and Health Promotion in the USA (2016) acknowledged that real-world computer games like '*Pokémon Go – whatever its future or potential implications on kids' physical activity – provides some interesting food for thought*'.

Before concluding this chapter let us look ahead into the future. Will the careers of the future require people to interact with technology in a plethora of physical ways: voice commands, eye tracking, gesturing on a tablet screen, gesturing with large movements read by sensing cameras (eg Kinect) and immersive virtual reality headsets (eg Occulus Rift)? This might sound far-fetched at first but actually the seeds are already evident – people will be using physical and sensory interaction to a greater degree. There is already very convincing evidence that in relation to surgery, '*video game skill correlates with laparoscopic surgical skills*' in terms of speed, accuracy and mistake reduction due to enhancement of psychomotor skills (Rosser et al, 2007, p 181).

> *Psychomotor learning is the relationship between cognitive functions and physical movement. Psychomotor learning is demonstrated by physical skills such as movement, coordination, manipulation, dexterity, grace, strength, speed; actions which demonstrate the fine motor skills such as use of precision instruments or tools.*
>
> (Wikipedia, 2016, https://en.wikipedia.org/wiki/Psychomotor_learning)

Motion sensing input devices may already be in your home and those of children you work with; for example, the *Kinect* system used with Xboxes. In ten years' time, will physical development, including the development of psychomotor capabilities, look very different as a result of technological innovation? No doubt a great deal of research is to be done to unravel the developmental impacts of, for example, processing and connecting moving your arm in virtual reality with cognitive functions!

Recommended further reading and product reviews

- *Doodle Buddy* (https://itunes.apple.com/gb/app/doodle-buddy-for-ipad-paint/id364201083?mt=8). Free, easy and intuitive to use though it costs 79p to hide adverts. The app includes a range of backgrounds or you can select a photo or other image. Tools include brush, chalk, glitter, smudge, eraser and stamp. Shaking the iPad clears the screen.

- *LeapBand* is an activity watch for 4–7-year-olds (www.leapfrog.com/en-gb/products/leapband). This is a lively activity watch which includes 50 challenges and an activity tracker.

- *Fingerpaint Magic* (https://itunes.apple.com/gb/app/fingerpaint-magic/id586165483?mt=8). It's really quite enthralling the way the paint spreads and there's also a neat mirror effect. As usual the app comes with a range of backgrounds or you can select one of your photos or another image.

- Corr, A (2006) *Children and Technology: A Tool For Child Development*. Dublin: The National Children's Resource Centre. [onlne] Available at: www.barnardos.ie/assets/files/publications/free/chidlren%20and%20technology(1).pdf.

- Plowman, L (2012) Press for play: using technology to enhance learning in the early years. [online] Available at: www.academia.edu/1842491/2012._Press_for_Play_Using_technology_to_enhance_learning_in_the_early_years.

References

Black, K and Stevenson, P (2011) The inclusion spectrum incorporating STEP. [online] Available at: www.sportdevelopment.info/index.php/browse-all-documents/748-the-inclusion-spectrum (accessed 1 March 2017).

BrightMinds (2016) [online] Available at: www.brightminds.co.uk/metal-detectors/c13 (accessed 1 March 2017).

Canavan Corr, A (2006) *Children and Technology: A Tool for Child Development*. Barnardo's National Children's Resource Centre. [online] Available at: www.barnardos.ie/assets/files/publications/free/chidlren%20and%20technology(1).pdf (accessed 1 March 2017).

Crescenzi, L, Jewitt, C and Price, S (2014) The Role of Touch in Preschool Children's Learning Using iPad versus Paper Interaction. *Australian Journal of Language and Literacy*, 37(2): 86–95.

Department for Education (DfE) (2014) Statutory framework for the Early Years Foundation Stage: setting the standards for learning, development and care for children from birth to five. [online] Available at: www.gov.uk/government/uploads/system/uploads/attachment_data/file/335504/EYFS_framework_from_1_September_2014__with_clarification_note.pdf (accessed 1 March 2017).

Ernest, J, Causey, C, Newton, A, Sharkins, K, Summerlin, J and Albaiz, N (2014) Extending the Global Dialogue about Media, Technology, Screen Time, and Young Children. *Childhood Education*, 90(3): 182–91.

Extreme Tech (2016) Can we finally admit that Kinect is dead? [online] Available at: www.extremetech.com/gaming/230252-can-we-finally-admit-that-kinect-is-dead (accessed 1 March 2017).

Hatch, K (2011) Determining the Effects of Technology on Children. Senior Honors Projects, Paper 260. [online] Available at: http://digitalcommons.uri.edu/cgi/viewcontent.cgi?article=1212&context=srhonorsprog (accessed 1 March 2017).

Hodson, E and Basford, J (2008) *Teaching Early Years Foundation Stage*. Exeter: Learning Matters Limited.

Moylett, H and Stewart, N (2012) *Development Matters in the Early Years Foundation Stage (EYFS)*. London: Early Education. [online] Available at: www.gov.gg/CHttpHandler.ashx?id=104249&p=0 (accessed 1 March 2017).

Office of Disease Prevention and Health Promotion (2016) Pokémon Go: A game changer for kids' physical activity? [online] Available at: https://health.gov/news/blog/2016/09/pokemon-go/ (accessed 1 March 2017).

Oswalt, A (2007) Infancy physical development. [online] Available at: www.mentalhelp.net/articles/infancy-physical-development/ (accessed 1 March 2017).

Plowman, L and McPake, J (2013) Seven Myths about Young Children and Technology. *Childhood Education*, 89(1): 27–33.

Pokémon Go (2016) [online] Available at: www.pokemongo.com/en-uk/ (accessed 1 March 2017).

Rosser, J, Lynch, P, Cuddihy, L, Gentile, D, Klonsky, J and Merrell R (2007) The Impact of Video Games on Training Surgeons in the 21st Century. *Archives of Surgery*, 142(2): 181–6.

Saúde, S, Carioca, V, Siraj-Blatchford, J, Sheridan, S, Genov, K and Nuez, R (2005) KINDERET: Developing Training for Early Childhood Educators in Information and Communications Technology (ICT) in Bulgaria, England, Portugal, Spain and Sweden. *International Journal of Early Years Education,* 13(3): 265–87.

TTS Group (nd) TTS Group. [online] Available at: www.tts-group.co.uk (accessed 5 April 2017).

Watts, A (2013) *Outdoor Learning through the Seasons.* Abingdon: Routledge.

Wikipedia (2016) Pokémon Go. [online] Available at: https://en.wikipedia.org/wiki/Pokémon_Go (accessed 1 March 2017).

Wikipedia (2016) Psychomotor learning. [online] Available at: https://en.wikipedia.org/wiki/Psychomotor_learning (accessed 12 March 2017).

7 Personal, social and emotional development

CHAPTER OUTLINE AND PROFESSIONAL LINKS

This chapter examines technology-enhanced learning in relation to the '*prime area of personal, social and emotional development*' as defined by the statutory framework for the EYFS (DfE, 2014, p 7). Throughout, consideration is given to how the use of technologies may support the guiding principle of building '*positive relationships*' and the '*characteristics of effective teaching and learning*' (DfE, 2014, pp 6 and 9). Both the Teachers' Standards for QTS primary teachers (DfE, 2011) and early years teachers (NCTL, 2013) make direct reference, in Standard 5, to the requirement for professionals to:

- '*demonstrate an awareness of the physical, social and intellectual development of children, and know how to adapt teaching to support pupils' education at different stages of development*' (DfE, 2011).

- '*demonstrate an awareness of the physical,* emotional, *social and intellectual development* and communication needs of babies and children, *and know how to adapt education* and care *to support children at different stages of development*' (NCTL, 2013, p 4, author's emphasis).

The chapter continues by reviewing some of the research to date on this topic and prompts you to reflect on your professional responsibilities in light of these findings. A case study of a toddler and practitioner is shared to facilitate your analysis of elements of learning and development related to technology. Prompted by the popular Mosaic Approach, you are encouraged to consider how simple technologies can be used to empower children to articulate and express their unique voices. Finally, the chapter explores beyond the United Kingdom to consider what can be learnt from practice in New Zealand.

Debates

This book argues for a broad conceptualisation of technology and for you to think beyond the scope of the *Understanding the World: Technology* component of the EYFS (DfE, 2014, p 12). This is critically important in relation to personal, social and emotional development, as this is typically one of the components where technologies receive their greatest criticisms, including claims of *contributing to children's lack of social skills* and the *rise of anti-social behaviour*. You may question whether technologies can really be powerful enough to change innate behaviours. You might want to query the source, validity and scope of frequently made claims in the popular press. This chapter presents a neutral stance for you to consider and make up your own mind on these emotive issues that concern both parents and practitioners.

In recent years there has been a high-profile public debate about young children and *screen time* following paediatric advice from the US that there should be an outright ban for children under two years of age. Subsequently, this was revised to recommend families to take a *balanced approach*. It is important to note that the initial recommendation itself only discouraged passive screen time. The distinction of passive and interactive is often key in these debates. For example, it would be difficult to argue that using Skype or FaceTime with a family member or loved one, when not physically present, inhibits social interaction and connectedness. McPake (2011, p 2) argued that the functionality of these technologies in fact enables children to become '*part of social networks outside their immediate community at an earlier age and in a more proactive way than would have been possible even a decade ago*'.

Critical question

» *To what extent do you agree with Plowman's (2011) question: 'Does it make sense to talk about digital childhoods?'*

Plowman (2011) directly commented on the often-cited perspective that children need '*protection*' from the harmful side-effects of technology and that '*childhood should be a time of innocence and play … because children are still developing cognitively and socially*', concluding that a causal link, either way, was impossible due to the variables involved (p 3). Plowman (2011) also tackled the question of whether technology really dominates children's lives, concluding that '*although technology is ever-present … it does not necessarily influence day-to-day life for children of this age as much as its ubiquity might suggest*' (p 3). Subsequently, Plowman et al (2012) found, in their analysis of family practices, that technologies '*directly supported the process of children developing an awareness of cultural practices that had value and significance to the family*' (p 5). They recommended that as a practitioner you should acknowledge '*the ways in which parents, siblings and carers induct children into culturally significant technological practices*' (Plowman et al, 2012, p 5).

Theoretical perspectives and pedagogy

The strong interconnections between personal, social and emotional development (PSED) leads them to be considered together (DSCF, 2008). For the purposes of this chapter they have been redefined as follows to make reference to technology:

- *Personal development (being me)*: how technologies can contribute to a child's sense of who they are and what they can do; for example, recording and playing back a series of actions or looking at images of themselves.

- *Social development (being social):* how technologies can contribute to a child's understanding of him or herself in relation to others; foster and reinforce friendships; and support understanding of behaviours in social settings; for example, conversation protocols re-enacted with a mobile phone.

- *Emotional development (having feelings)*: how technologies can support children in understanding their own and others' feelings and the development of empathy and understanding someone else's point of view; for example, offering insight to another person's perspective by watching a recording they have made.

CASE STUDY, PART 1

Read and consider this example involving a toddler, Lucy.

Stephanie works in a private nursery. She is supervisor for the toddler room, which facilitates activities and learning opportunities for three- to four-year-olds. Various members of staff have been supporting children to use a range of objects to form their own constructions. Stephanie is using a digital camera and takes pictures periodically, capturing the evolving constructions. One female child, Lucy, has watched Stephanie take photos but has not asked to see them. She moves to the home corner and removes a play mobile phone from its charger. Lucy then proceeds to take her own photographs, changing her stance and moving around the construction to take photographs at different angles of her work. She stands and presses a few buttons and taps parts of the screen talking through her processes of sending the pictures to various people. Lucy is animated and happy to share her experiences with another. Lucy returns to her construction and changes some elements of it; taking the play mobile phone from her pocket, she continues to take photographs, talking to herself. Lucy identifies the changes to her construction and praises herself for doing 'a good job'. Another child moves to look at Lucy's construction; she quickly takes a photo and says 'I'll send it to you ... you can have a photo too. You're smiling in this one. That's good. Yes that's a good one,' Lucy states quickly, scanning the last photograph taken. She presses buttons and touches the screen, 'All done'. Lucy looks at Stephanie and says 'Mummy's got mine now'. Turning to the other child, Lucy asks 'Shall I send yours as well to your mummy?' Pressing buttons and touching the screen, she talks herself through this process and smiles, placing the phone back into her pocket.

Commentary on case study, part 1

In this scenario the practitioner, Stephanie, was able to observe and capture this role play involving technology. Even though Lucy was unable to send the photographs to her mother, the implications for using technology in context were without doubt supporting Lucy's emotional and social development. Lucy had no hesitation about the functionality digital tools can offer and the potential real-world connections. Through Lucy's own experiences of observing how technology is used, she was able to reflect on which technologies she needed to be able to do what she wanted, which was to share her experiences in the nursery with her mother. Lucy recognised the affordances and understood how she could transfer her learning skills and disposition to be a creative communicator (Smidt, 2013). Lucy's ability to apply these skills in context was evident as she manipulated the toy version of the mobile phone to capture, store, retrieve and send images to a virtual space. These affordances support the virtual bonds of attachment that Roberts-Holmes (2014) articulated and how such innovations are strongly motivational and provide opportunities for sustained shared thinking. McPake (2011, p 2) recalled how during his studies:

> children's play activities incorporated technologies in ways which demonstrated that they saw technological tools as part of their everyday environment and understood their purposes.

Critical question

Hughes' (2002) taxonomy of play types includes socio dramatic, imaginative, fantasy and role-play – for example, children can act out scenarios with a microwave oven and swipe a card cash register in the role-play area set up as a cafe.

» *How can the provision of technologies in role-play areas underpin the characteristic of 'active learning' (DfE, 2011)?*

Parton (2003) suggested that everyday technology tools should be embedded in role-play areas and offered illustrations for some of the common areas seen in early years settings; for example:

- an office including (real or replica) telephones (landline and mobile), fax machine, printers, computer keyboards, laptop, tablets etc;
- a doctor's surgery including (real or replica) digital thermometers, weighing scales, computers, oxygen finger-monitors, printers, touchscreens to log in on arrival, television screen appointment alerts etc.

Critical question

» *Consider an office-themed role-play area. How might the technologies incorporated contribute, positively and negatively, to the three elements of personal, social and emotional development?*

Which technologies do you use regularly to feel connected to your family members, friends and loved ones? Your answer probably includes at least one of the following: capturing, sharing and accessing digital images, video and audio, VoIP services, SMS, phone calls, and online social networks. As a professional you would only utilise age-appropriate tools and services for safeguarding reasons, but many children will want to rehearse what they experience adults in their environment using. Technologies embedded within educational activities may support children to '*develop a positive sense of themselves, their abilities and their relationship to others by capturing, viewing, manipulating and sharing digital images and recordings*' (DfE, 2014, p 8).

CASE STUDY, PART 2

This second part of the case study returns to how Lucy is making links between technologies and the continual opportunities to develop relationships and enhance her social and emotional well-being.

> *Lucy has been talking to other children about how she sent her mummy photographs of her building and continued to tell others in the sharing time circle that her grandma had said they were very good. Stephanie asked Lucy if this was the grandma who lived in Germany. Lucy nodded, 'but I see her all the time at tea time'. Stephanie was able to discuss with Lucy how grandma had seen the photos. Lucy pointed towards the ceiling, 'Up there in the sky … all photos go up there and then fly to grandma's and Jenny so she can see them and talk to me'. Stephanie was able to talk to Lucy's mother who identified that her family communicate via social media and FaceTime, as their wider family are distributed throughout four different countries. It was a way in which Lucy could understand that she had other family which she did not live with, but who were still part of her life, and not just seen at holidays. Lucy has regular contact with all of her family. At home Lucy's mother would often take photos of Lucy and post them to social media accounts as a way of allowing others to see and know what Lucy was doing in her life.*

Commentary on case study, part 2

McPake (2011, p 3) noted the common practice within early years of using digital cameras for assessment and how children like to see themselves on screen. They often showed animated engagement in dialogue, which recognises their thoughts, feelings and emotions related to their experiences and achievements at that given time. Gibbons (2015), however, suggested that the arguments surrounding identities, especially those of young children, are yet to be fully challenged or understood. Lindahl and Folkesson (2012) prompt you to recognise the additional needs of children in a digital environment and how these digital representations can contribute to their understanding of who they are. This aligns with the Third Space Theory based on Moje et al (2004), which identifies the spaces of nursery, home and the third space, which bridges both environments. For Lucy, this third space allows her the unique opportunity of capturing what she believes to be important and significant enough to share. What is more impressive is Lucy's ability to believe that once she has pressed the buttons and manipulated the screen her images have gone where she has sent them. This obviously increased her self-awareness and her ability to act autonomously within such situations.

Mosaic Approach

The Mosaic Approach is a popular child-centred, participatory research approach that includes '*one-to-one interactions, observations, digital photography, bookmaking, guided tours and map-making to co-construct the child's perspective*' (Harcourt et al, 2011, p 33). Clark (2005), in reference to the Mosaic Approach, asks '*what does it mean to be you in this place now – in this present moment?*'. This resonates with the notion of personal development articulated as '*being me*' (p 17). Audio and visual capture and playback technologies, in the hands of children, can '*allow them to communicate how they perceive the world in a meaningful way*' (Coleyshaw et al, 2010, p 6; Harcourt et al, 2011). Mukherji and Albon (2010) explain that the use of a camera '*aims to encourage children to document the people, places and events that have particular meaning for them*' (p 178). Importantly, the child has control of the camera and the images are of what the child is choosing to reveal about their sense and interpretation of the world, filtered or focused by a lens.

Critical questions

» *How might the narrative of images captured by the child contrast with observational photos captured by key workers?*

» *Which might reveal more in relation to PSED?*

With the growing use of iPads and tablet devices there are a plethora of early-years appropriate books, map making, video and animation applications you could adopt to empower children to be '*the documenters, photographers, filmmakers and audio curators of their world*' (Clark, 2005, p 25).

> *Taking photographs, leading a tour or watching slides provide different mirrors for reflecting on the central question: 'What does it mean to be in this place?'. Some young children would be barred from answering this question if they were only offered one traditional research tool, such as interviewing*
>
> (Clark, 2005, pp 17–18)

Critical question

Children today probably encounter digital images and audio themselves repeatedly at a level that is much more pervasive than your own experience.

» *What does this mean for children and what might be the positive and negative associations in relation to PSED?*

International perspective

As a professional you will be familiar with national priorities and policies within the United Kingdom. This section encourages you to briefly explore practice in another country and consider how this may complement or contrast with your understanding of PSED. The strong emphasis on social identity and active learning within New Zealand's Te Whāriki make it an ideal choice for this chapter.

A focus on Te Whāriki

The framework for ICT in early years in New Zealand is based on the socio-cultural foundations of the Te Whāriki curriculum, which emphasises children as active learners and recognises that ICT should be used in conjunction with other learning and teaching tools. The Te Whāriki curriculum (Ministry of Education, New Zealand, 1996) has four interwoven principles:

1   Relationships;
2   Holistic development;
3   Family;
4   Community and empowerment;

with five strands:

1   Well-being;
2   Belonging;
3   Contribution;
4   Communication;
5   Exploration;

and a series of learning goals and outcomes.

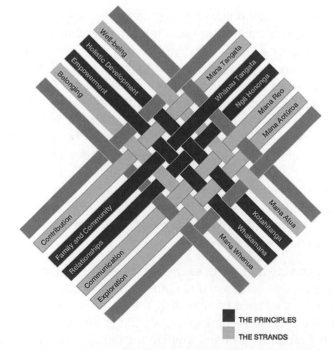

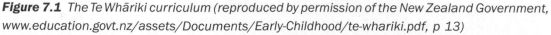

Figure 7.1 *The Te Whāriki curriculum (reproduced by permission of the New Zealand Government, www.education.govt.nz/assets/Documents/Early-Childhood/te-whariki.pdf, p 13)*

The weaving together of the curriculum principles, strands, indicative goals and outcomes is a central feature of Te Whāriki (which means 'woven floor mat' in the Maori language). Consequently, when focusing on technology-enhanced learning within the Te Whāriki context, it's important to consider impact in relation to each of the principles and strands as these are woven together. For example, Lee et al (2013) explain that the relationships principle '*is elaborated as "children learn through responsive and reciprocal relationships with people, places, and things"*' (p 44). So, if you think about relationships with people, you can include a focus on the family and community (*principle*) as well as on children's relationships with each other and with teaching staff.

Implications of Te Whāriki for practice

You might recognise that a virtual learning environment (VLE) would enhance communication (*strand*) between the early years setting and the family. Practitioners and children themselves (empowerment strand) can take photos of significant moments and make these available for parents and community. You may already have recognised the value of this as many UK early years settings use online learning journals when communicating with parents. It's also worth thinking about printing and displaying within the setting large-scale colour photos of children and their accomplishments together with comments and reflections, including those of the children – which is part of the responsive approach to planning and assessment within Te Whāriki. If you want to involve parents and children in the planning and assessment process (belonging and empowerment strands) then you can consider Te Whāriki, where documentation is publicly displayed as part of a living record (Lee et al, 2013).

You can easily approach considering technology-enhanced learning (TEL) within Te Whāriki systematically by taking each principle and strand in turn and identifying TEL in relation to the different combinations. The indicative learning outcomes can also be used as a guide. For example, when reflecting on digital technology in the context of responsive and reciprocal relationships, *well-being*, which includes being able to '*enjoy a moderate degree of change, surprise, uncertainty and puzzling events*' (Lee et al, 2013, p 54), can involve children playing with a range of early-years appropriate computer software; *belonging* can be developed through '*interest and pleasure in discovering an unfamiliar wider world*' (p 54) when watching and talking about video clips and the internet; *exploration* can involve taking photos of discoveries in the natural environment such as minibeasts; *communication* can be developed through children using sound recorders to record their ideas; *contribution* includes '*respect for children who are different from themselves and ease of interaction with them*' (p 55) and can be approached using the internet to find out about and respond to different cultures.

Carr and Lee (2009) provide numerous exemplars of early childhood settings using ICT to enhance learning based on the Te Whāriki curriculum. The report includes some particularly interesting accounts of children exploring the behaviour of mice using digital video cameras, documenting their learning experience using still cameras, publishing stories, sending and receiving emails, eg when investigating skeletal remains that one of the children found on the beach, and creating an interactive story.

Critical question

Te Whāriki doesn't include a specific personal, social and emotional area of learning and development.

» *What similarities and differences do you notice between Te Whāriki and the EYFS personal, social and emotional area of learning and development?*

Home and nursery links

The importance of communication and partnership working, between you as a professional and parents, is well recognised as good practice for PSED. You are asked to review the case study a final time and consider how technologies can support this process.

CASE STUDY, PART 3

During the planning meeting Stephanie shared her findings with others and recognised that the use of digital communications for some children and parents may be useful in providing a link between the home and the nursery. The advantages of this were discussed openly within the group and the following ideas were recorded:

- *the possibility of using technologies in the setting to support transitions from home into settings;*

- *a consideration of using iPads for children to capture their learning journeys and the implications of this for emotional development and enhancements of being able to see through the eyes of the child.*

Stephanie recognised the issues and opportunities within the staff team for development and using technologies in context. Stephanie realised that this was something that needed to be considered in consultation with the team in order to promote the safe and effective use of technologies. The staff team considered the achievements of Lucy and how this engagement benefitted her emotional and social development significantly.

Digital footprints and ethics

Trevarthen and Reddy (2007) recognised the importance of engagement with parents and guardians in supporting children's development in terms of emotional and social well-being. Online learning journals are growing in popularity as a mechanism for fostering this ongoing communication and dialogue about learning and development. However, one area of growing significance relates to the ethicacy of children's digital footprints, whereby even at a relatively young age they may already have an extensive digital footprint created by adults. Nurseries and parents/carers store many photographs of children on laptops and desktop computers, saving them for sharing with parents in online or paper-based learning journals and in some cases for marketing purposes. This is an important dimension for the entire early years sector to reflect on.

Conclusion

Despite the occasional alarmist newspaper headlines, your experiences as educators will probably echo Plowman et al's (2012) research in that '*technology did not dominate or hinder social interaction in the ways suggested by media coverage*' (p 2). Many technologies provide opportunities for young learners to gain a sense of themselves by playing with and exploring their unique *image, motion* and *sound* via photos, video and audio. These opportunities can contribute developmentally to their sense of self from both internal and external (*how I appear to others*) perspectives. When this is extended to include digital artefacts of friends and family, positive relationships can be actively reinforced. Similarly, the very act of selecting, sharing and taking turns with the technology can also have an impact on social development. A positive aptitude to creating by trying out ideas and new things resonates with the provisionality component of technology.

Recommended further reading and product reviews

Online learning journals

These have been suggested as a way of supporting children's learning and development. Although this relates to all aspects of learning, the shared and supportive dialogue that can be enabled between parents and practitioners can potentially have a significant impact on PSED. Two popular systems being used in UK settings you may wish to explore are as follows:

- *Tapestry: an online journal recording all the learning and fun of children's early years education* (https://tapestry.info).

- *2Build a Profile: capturing observations on the move* (www.2simple.com/2buildaprofile).

Images, video and audio

To obtain early-years appropriate image, video and audio recording devices, a recommended UK supplier is:

- TTS (www.tts-group.co.uk/primary/computing-ict/).

Inspired by the Mosaic methodology you might want to explore devices to:

- *capture and play back images and video*, for example: the talking mirror;

- *capture and play back audio*, for example: the See and Speak binoculars or magnifiers, Easispeak recorders, recordable pegs, cubes etc;

- *enhance walking tours*, for example: the Magic Garden includes talking trees, flowers and rocks, see www.tts-group.co.uk/magic-garden/1006036.html;

- *book making*, for example: Talk-Time Postcards, talking books, talking postcards, sequencer (www.tts-group.co.uk/story-sequencer/1001420.html) or the sound bar (www.tts-group.co.uk/sound-bar/1001536.html) for an audio book.

References

2Simple (2016) 2BuildaProfile [online] Available at: www.2simple.com/2buildaprofile (accessed 1 March 2017).

Carr, M and Lee, W (2009) *Information and Communication Technology (ICT) Te Hangarau Pàrongo me te Whakawhitiwhiti.* New Zealand: Ministry of Education, Wellington. [online] Available at: www.education.govt.nz/assets/Documents/Early-Childhood/Kei-Tua-o-te-Pae/ECEBk20Full.pdf (accessed 1 March 2017).

Clark, A (2005) Ways of Seeing: Using the Mosaic Approach to Listen to Young Children's Perspectives, in Clark, A, Kjørholt, A T and Moss, P (eds) *Beyond Listening: Children's Perspectives on Early Childhood Services.* Bristol: Policy Press.

Coleyshaw, L, Whitmarsh, J, Jopling, M and Hadfield, M (2010) *Listening to Children's Perspectives: Improving the Quality of Provision in Early Years Settings.* Part of the Longitudinal Study of Early Years Professional Status CeDARE. University of Wolverhampton & Department for Education. [online] Available at: www.gov.uk/government/publications/listening-to-childrens-perspectives-improving-the-quality-of-provision-in-early-years-settings (accessed 12 March 2017).

Department for Children, Schools and Families (DCSF) (2008) Social and emotional aspects of development. The national strategies early years. [online] Available at: www.foundationyears.org.uk/wp-content/uploads/2011/10/SEAD_Guidance_For_Practioners.pdf (accessed 1 March 2017).

Department for Education (DfE) (2011) Teachers' standards. [online] Available at: www.gov.uk/government/publications/teachers-standards (accessed 1 March 2017).

Department for Education (DfE) (2014) Statutory framework for the Early Years Foundation Stage: setting the standards for learning, development and care for children from birth to five. [online] Available at: www.gov.uk/government/uploads/system/uploads/attachment_data/file/335504/EYFS_framework_from_1_September_2014__with_clarification_note.pdf (accessed 1 March 2017).

Gibbons, A (2015) Debating Digital Childhoods: Questions Concerning Technologies, Economies and Determinisms. *Open Review of Educational Research,* 2(1): 118–27.

Harcourt, D, Perry, B and Waller, T (2011) *Researching Young Children's Perspectives.* New York: Routledge.

Hughes, B (2002) *A Playworker's Taxonomy of Play Types.* London: Play Education.

Lee, W, Carr, M, Soutar, B and Mitchell, L (2013) *Understanding the Te Whāriki Approach.* London: David Fulton.

Lindahl, M and Folkesson, A (2012) ICT in Preschool: Friend or Foe? The Significance of Norms in a Changing Practice. *International Journal of Early Years Education,* 20(4): 422–36.

McPake, J (2011) *Rethinking Young Children Creating and Communicating.* Research Briefing Three for Digital Childhoods, Stirling: Scottish Universities Insight Institute.

Ministry of Education, New Zealand (1996) Te Whāriki curriculum. [online] Available at: www.education.govt.nz/assets/Documents/Early-Childhood/te-whariki.pdf (accessed 1 March 2017).

Ministry of Education, New Zealand (2016) 0–6 early learning. [online] Available at: www.education.govt.nz/early-childhood/teaching-and-learning/kei-tua-o-te-pae-2/sociocultural-assessment-he-aromatawai-ahurea-papori/ (accessed 1 March 2017).

Moje, E B, Ciechanowski, K M, Kramer, K, Ellis, L, Carrillo, R and Collazo, T (2004) Working toward Third Space in Content Area Literacy: An Examination of Everyday Funds of Knowledge and Discourse. *Reading Research Quarterly,* 39(1): 40–70.

Morgan, A and Siraj-Blatchford, J (2013) *Using ICT in the Early Years.* London: Practical Pre-School Books.

Mukherji, P and Albon, D (2010) *Research Methods in Early Childhood.* London: Sage.

National College for Teaching and Leadership (NCTL) (2013) Teachers' standards (early years). [online] Available at: www.gov.uk/government/uploads/system/uploads/attachment_data/file/211646/Early_Years_Teachers__Standards.pdf (accessed 1 March 2017).

Parton, G (2003) *Early Years Activities to Promote the Use of Information and Communication Technology.* Dunstable: Belair Publications.

Plowman, L (2011) *Rethinking Young Children and Technology.* Research Briefing One for Digital Childhoods, Stirling: Scottish Universities Insight Institute.

Plowman, L, McPake, J, Stephen, C, Prout, A, Adey, C and Stephenson, O (2012) *Young Children Learning with Toys and Technology at Home.* Stirling: Economic and Social Research Council.

Roberts-Holmes, G (2014) *Doing Your Early Years Research Project: A Step by Step Guide.* London: Sage.

Smidt, S (2013) *The Developing Child in the 21st Century.* Abingdon, Oxfordshire: Routledge.

Tapestry Online Learning Journal (2016) [online] Available at: https://tapestry.info (accessed 1 March 2017).

Trevarthen, C and Reddy, V (2007) Consciousness in Infants, in Velmans, M and Schneider, S (eds) *The Blackwell Companion to Consciousness.* Malden, MA: Blackwell Publishing.

8 Literacy

CHAPTER OUTLINE AND PROFESSIONAL LINKS

This chapter begins by identifying the Early Learning Goals for literacy within the EYFS and the sections within the national curriculum for English in Key Stage 1. The chapter continues by helping you to consider some of the key themes within literacy and technology-enhanced learning, such as the meaning of the concept of literacy and whether there is a place for teaching typing skills in the curriculum. You'll also be directed to guidance and resources for using digital technology to enhance literacy learning in the context of models relating to literacy curriculum development. There's also a particular focus on the use of iPads to support development of writing and reading in the early years.

Literacy in the Early Years Foundation Stage

Literacy development involves encouraging children to link sounds and letters and to begin to read and write. Children must be given access to a wide range of reading materials (books, poems, and other written materials) to ignite their interest.

(DfE, 2014, p 8)

The Early Learning Goals (ELGs) for reading and writing are stated in the guidance document *Development Matters* (Moylett and Stewart, 2012), which also includes age-related teaching strategies linked to the key themes (unique child, positive relationships and enabling environments).

This area is subdivided into two Early Learning Goals (bold text: author's emphasis):

- **ELG 09 – Reading:** *Children read and understand simple sentences. They use **phonic** knowledge to **decode regular words** and read them aloud accurately. They also read some common irregular words. They demonstrate **understanding** when talking with others about what they have read* (DfE, 2014, p 29).

- **ELG 10 – Writing:** *Children use their **phonic knowledge to write words** in ways which match their spoken sounds. They also write some irregular common words. They **write simple sentences** which can be read by themselves and others. Some words are spelt correctly and others are phonetically plausible* (DfE, 2014, p 31).

Both sets of Teachers' Standards also indicate the importance of literacy:

- **Teachers' Standards (Early Years)** (National College for Teaching and Leadership, 2013)

    - **Standard 3.4** *'Demonstrate a clear understanding of **systematic synthetic phonics** in the teaching of early reading.'*

                                (National College for Teaching and Leadership, 2013, p 3)

- **Teachers' Standards (Qualified Teacher Status)** (DfE, 2011)

    - **Standard 3:** *'Demonstrate good subject and curriculum knowledge'* (p 11), particularly:

        o   *'demonstrate an understanding of and take responsibility for promoting high standards of **literacy**, **articulacy** and the correct use of **standard English**, whatever the teacher's specialist subject'*;

        o   *'if teaching early reading, demonstrate a clear understanding of **systematic synthetic phonics**'.*

Theoretical perspectives and pedagogy

Literacy or literacies?

You'll find it useful to take a broader perspective and develop a wider understanding of the concept of literacy as children progress through the EYFS into Key Stage 1 and beyond. What does it mean to be literate in the early years of the 21st century? The national curriculum (DfE, 2013) emphasises that *'Fluency in the English language is an essential foundation for success in all subjects'* (p 10) and focuses on aspects of fluency in spoken language, reading, writing and vocabulary development and *'love of literature through widespread reading for enjoyment'*(p 10).

> *All the skills of language are essential to participating fully as a member of society; pupils, therefore, who do not learn to speak, read and write fluently and confidently are effectively disenfranchised.*
>
>   (DfE, 2014, p 10)

In order to participate fully in society, fluency in reading and writing using a wide range of multimodal texts is required. Merchant (2006, p 3) suggests that *'Digital media in general, and digital writing in particular, have begun to reinforce this sense of a new social order'*. And the National Council of Teachers of English (NCTE, 2013) begins its position statement with an affirmation of the need to develop *'proficiency and fluency with the tools of technology'* and reinforces the view that we should be considering literacies rather than literacy, noting that '*the 21st century demands that a literate person possesses a wide range of abilities and competencies, many literacies*'. The national curriculum is intended to be regarded as part of the encompassing *school curriculum*, which is where these constituents of a more authentic reading and writing experience are likely to be located.

Critical question

»   *The National Council of Teachers of English asserts that* 'As society and technology change, so does literacy' *(NCTE, 2013). How is literacy changing and what might it mean to be literate 25 years from now?*

Using digital technology with the Early Learning Goals for reading and writing

Development Matters (Moylett and Stewart, 2012) provides useful starting points though it's essential to use your most up-to-date awareness of what digital technology is available and possibilities for use. So, for example, with regard to reading and specifically for 16–26-month-old babies, *Development Matters* indicates that the enabling environment should include '*CDs of rhymes, stories, sounds and spoken words*' as well as '*books with accompanying CDs*' (p 28). But a moment's thought suggests that YouTube videos, online interactive websites and iPad apps will increase the range and are likely to be more accessible. Nonetheless, you'll find some good ideas for ways of using digital technology from looking at *Development Matters* – using '*different voices to tell stories*'; and for 40–60+ months, matching letters to sounds and modelling segmentation and blending of words and sounds (you could use the drag and drop feature of the interactive whiteboard as one of many applications of a range of software, hardware and mobile apps). Similarly, for writing, role-play opportunities for 30–60+ months can include using a computer keyboard for writing and printing useful shopping lists, signs, labels and captions. Early years keyboards with lower-case letters are available from www.inclusive.co.uk.

CASE STUDY

A group of three five-year-old children are playing in the role-play area which has been set up as a travel agent and passport office. Holiday brochures and photos of destinations are on display. Two of the children are looking through one of the brochures and decide they want to visit Paris. They show the child acting as travel agent the brochure with their chosen destination. The children help each other to type their names and destination onto a simple ticket design template set up by the teacher using a word processing tool, for example, 2Publish Plus (available via www.purplemash.com) and then click print. The two children then take their tickets and go to another part of the Reception classroom to board the aeroplane for Paris.

Commentary on case study

Using the keyboard helps the children to communicate through writing using *'clearly identifiable letters'* (Moylett and Stewart, 2012, p 31). If this role play is organised as a teacher-directed activity to start with, then the teacher could help take photos for the passports and support children's writing when they fill in passport details before printing. Depending on the physical space available, the role play could be extended to include a cafe for children to visit when they arrive at their destination. This would of course provide further opportunities for developing reading, writing and also numeracy, such as printing menus and till receipts.

Critical question

» *What other role-play themes can you think of that will provide a natural way for children to develop their reading and writing skills enhanced through use of digital technology?*

Using digital technology with systematic synthetic phonics schemes

Although Levy (2009, p 361) expressed concerns that reading schemes can actually *'discourage some children from attempting to read any book'*, phonics schemes such as *Jolly Phonics* and *Letters and Sounds* have a central place in schools and early years in particular. The Rose Report (2006) drew attention to the value of interactive technology for the teaching of reading in the early years, such as helping teachers *'to plan and teach sequences of work that captured children's interest, intensified their concentration and sustained their attention'* (p 25). It's therefore not surprising that reading schemes and phonics schemes are supported by specifically designed digital resources.

Jolly Phonics

The good news is that there are demo versions available on the Jolly Phonics website (www.jollylearning.co.uk), though the range of games and features that you can try out is quite limited. The Jolly Phonics Games CD introduced by Inky Mouse (easy, medium and hard) includes *Vowel Forest*, which involves listening to the word and matching the sound; *Letter Sounds*, which supports recognition and pronunciation of letter sounds; *Writing Letters*, which models how to write individual letters; and *Frogagrams*, which is quite an entertaining way of writing words by clicking on frogs. There's also *Jolly Phonics for the Whiteboard*, which is based on five key skills: letter sounds, letter formation, blending, identifying sounds and tricky words. This interactive resource provides structured whole-class lessons organised into 12-week units. The Jolly Phonics website includes an informative short video introducing *Jolly Phonics for the Whiteboard* (http://jollylearning. co.uk/jolly-shop/jolly-phonics-for-the-whiteboard/). Jolly Phonics also has apps for the iPad, iPhone and Android that can be purchased for a couple of pounds.

There are a large number of touchscreen apps for learning phonics but you might want to encourage parents to download apps complementary to the phonics scheme in use in your school.

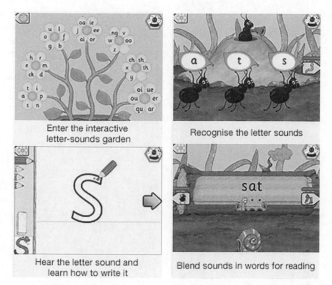

Enter the interactive letter-sounds garden

Recognise the letter sounds

Hear the letter sound and learn how to write it

Blend sounds in words for reading

Figure 8.1 *Screenshots from* Jolly Phonics Letter Sounds *app including letter formation and matching sounds to letters activities (reproduced by permission of Jolly Learning, 2016, https:// itunes.apple.com/gb/app/jolly-phonics-letter-sounds/id897894552?mt=8)*

S *(Tune: The Farmer in the Dell)*

The snake is in the grass.
The snake is in the grass.
/sss/! /sss/!
The snake is in the grass.

Action: Weave your hand in an 's' shape, like a snake, and say, sssssss.

Figure 8.2 *A screenshot from the* Jolly Phonics Songs *app from Jolly Learning (Jolly Learning, 2016, https://itunes.apple.com/gb/app/jolly-phonics-songs/id1096113645?mt=8)*

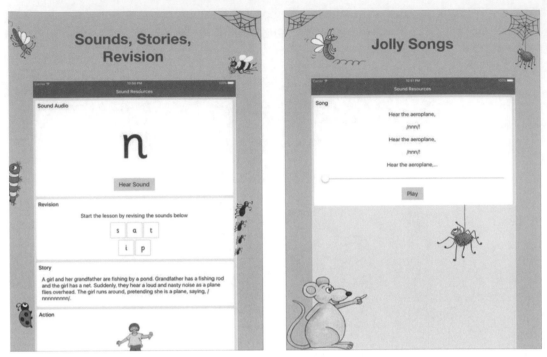

Figure 8.3 *The Jolly Phonics Lesson app designed for early years practitioners and teachers (Jolly Learning, 2016, https://itunes.apple.com/gb/app/jolly-phonics-lessons/id1149029299?mt=8)*

Letters and Sounds

The document *Letters and Sounds: Principles and Practice of High Quality Phonics*, produced by the Department for Children, Schools & Families as part of the Primary National Strategy (DCSF, 2008) provides a detailed view of the Letters and Sounds approach, including lesson plans for each of the six phases and suggestions for using the interactive whiteboard within some of the lessons. As with the Jolly Phonics scheme, digital resources are readily available:

- The **letters-and-sounds.com** website includes resources and interactive games for each of the six phases of Letters and Sounds (www.letters-and-sounds.com/). The introduction to each phase usefully identifies the letter sets. The resources section includes a range of free downloadable resources such as letter fans, letters in rainbow colours and words on trucks. There are several interactive games which you can customise for the phase the children are at by combining letters from the different sets.

- The Topmarks website (www.topmarks.co.uk/Interactive.aspx?cat=38) includes a range of interactive games for foundation stage and Key Stage 1 though you'll need to be selective and ensure the activities and letters match the phase.

- It's also worth exploring other resource websites even though they may involve paying a small yearly subscription; for example, Early Learning HQ (www.earlylearninghq.org.uk/literacy/) has a range of phase-related resources supporting Letters and Sounds.

Oxford Reading Tree

The Oxford Reading Tree (ORT) *'is currently used in over 80% of primary schools'* (Oxford Owl, 2016) – and who isn't familiar with stories about Biff, Chip, Kipper and Floppy? As a resource the Oxford Reading Tree is extensive with more than 800 books and videos, including phonics teaching matched to Letters and Sounds, fiction, non-fiction, poetry and ebooks. The ORT case studies (ORT, 2016) are a series of short video-clip testimonials and examples showing how schools have used the ORT. Particularly useful for parents, the Oxford Owl website provides free access to 135 ORT books, and also include activities such as rearranging the pictures into the correct order. All that's required is to register as a parent or teacher with www.oxfordowl.co.uk. YouTube is a useful source of animated versions of The Magic Key and other ORT stories, for example: www.youtube.com/watch?v=4XzkdHGuW24.

Critical question

» *Considering your experience of phonics and reading schemes, how might you use some of the available interactive digital resources to enhance the children's learning experience?*

Literacy curriculum development

Returning to the broader encompassing context of digital reading and writing, one way of justifying the lack of explicit reference to digital technology in the Key Stage 1 national curriculum for English is to take a sequential approach to curriculum development. Merchant (2006) explains that in this model digital writing and reading would be introduced gradually once traditional reading and writing skills have been mastered. This prioritises paper and pencil and physical books and regards digital technology as a dispensable tool from the point of view of literacy. Incidentally, this also panders to the misgivings of those who are opposed to the early introduction of digital technology. But this is surely not what's being advocated, given that both the EYFS and national curriculum clearly value digital technology and computing across all the age ranges, and given the scope and quality of currently available digital technology. What's more, Kennedy et al (2012) in *Literacy in Early Childhood and Primary Education (3–8 Years)*, a research report commissioned by the National Council for Curriculum and Assessment, affirm *'the importance of ensuring continuity between home and school'* and emphasise that:

> *Children are active users of technology in their everyday lives across a range of media, and this can be described as both creative and active.*
>
> (Kennedy et al, 2012, p 109)

An alternative approach is to introduce the technology in parallel to the literacy focus, ie when children are learning to use full stops and capital letters they would also be shown how to produce these using a computer keyboard; when learning a new letter they would also see this on the keyboard and respond interactively when playing with an appropriate app or when using word-processing software. On the other hand, this approach is quite inflexible and doesn't accommodate differences in children's experiences and the ways they develop; children may already be well advanced in their knowledge of computer keyboards, for example. A potentially more productive model involves the infusion of technology into the literacy curriculum.

> *When technology becomes a natural part of the classroom literacy environment, the highest level of infusion has been achieved.*
>
> (Shettel and Bower, 2013, p 7)

This approach is more child-centred and encourages children to be autonomous learners who are able to make effective use of the particular affordances of digital technology. Shettel and Bower (2013, p 8) describe several examples including podcasting, newscasts, digital storytelling, '*book trailers to promote books in the classroom library*' and '*simulated talk shows with the author and characters of the book*'.

CASE STUDY

Digital story writing

The Reception class teacher is conscious of the need for a thematic approach in order to enhance meaning and purpose in the children's learning. The classroom environment has therefore been arranged to reflect a seaside theme. The role-play area has been equipped with Punch and Judy puppets. In another part of the room, a seaside display has been created behind the sand area. The teacher has also brought a deckchair and airbed into the classroom. There's a writing area where children are encouraged to write souvenir postcards. The children have just finished listening and singing along to a YouTube version of 'There's a hole in the bottom of the sea' (www.youtube.com/watch?v=R1Qn2bcZRTo) and are now deciding on how to use their free choosing time. The teacher selects several children to support sentence writing using www.purplemash.com – 2Create a Story, related to the seaside theme.

Commentary on case study

Using a thematic approach encourages interconnections between learning experiences. An interesting way to develop the seaside theme would be for the children to take photos of themselves, such as when sitting on a deckchair, or to video-record their own Punch and Judy show. The photos can then be imported into the www.purplemash.com 2Publish

Plus using the Diary template. Children can then be supported when writing simple sentences about their day at the seaside.

Critical question

» *By now you might be thinking that the* infusion *model is an ideal to be aimed for because it helps to provide a more authentic learning experience. How might you develop this infusion model as part of your own creative approach to teaching and learning?*

A role for iPads in pre-school literacy development

A large percentage of pre-school children have access to tablet technology outside of the pre-school setting, and this more often than not includes the iPad (Marsh et al, 2015). This may help to account for research findings which suggest that when iPads are made available for use in pre-school settings, children don't suddenly choose to stop using pencils and paper (Knight and Dooley, 2015). Having said this, of course, iPads are extremely popular among children and so questions arise about their educational value and potential contribution to literacy development.

Particularly with regard to writing, a key affordance is provisionality, ie the ability to edit, which can help to enhance engagement and persistence as children try to improve and explore alternatives. But a downside is that assessment can be more challenging as children may delete what they produce before it's seen by the teacher. Another commonly held opinion is that children are taking longer to learn how to hold and use pencils because they are spending so much time on iPads which use the finger as pointer, presser and for swiping. But then children find iPad apps highly engaging and research by Knight and Dooley (2015, p 57) noted that '*children demonstrated highly developed fine and gross motor skills as they manipulated their hands and fingers to perform writing and drawing tasks in the apps*'. iPads can also be used to help create a more inclusive learning environment by providing additional opportunities for children with greater tactile sensitivity, ie who have less preference for contact with paints and the waxy feel of crayons and other 'messy' media.

Critical question

» *Do paper-based mark-making/writing and drawing have more value than their digital counterparts? What's your view on this?*

As for reading, digital books accessed via the iPad can motivate children who show limited interest in books during free choosing time. Also, the multimodal nature of digital books can effectively distribute the cognitive load through use of images, animations and sound, which can enhance memory and comprehension (Moreno and Mayer, 2000; Savage and Barnett, 2015). But some ebooks are going to be better than others, and just as with physical books, as a teacher, you'll need to ensure that children are able to access good-quality ebooks. So, what makes a good-quality ebook for early years children? Cahill and McGill-Franzen (2013) reviewed ebook design and provided a taxonomy of desirable features. They focused attention on the more recent ebooks, which are '*"film-like" productions with user activated "hotspots" and additional levels of information and interaction*' (p 31), eg *Pat the Bunny* (www.youtube.com/watch?v=sHryMwL-lRk). Another useful feature to look for is the facility to customise the ebook by adding the child's name and photo, eg *Starring You Storybooks* (http://mamaknowsitall.com/2013/03/storybooks-starring-you.html) and the ability to record the child/teacher narrating the story, eg the *Best Apps for Kids* website includes an extensive list of reviews (www.bestappsforkids.com/category/book-apps-2/ebooks-with-record-your-voice/).

The list of key features you need to consider includes the following.

- The quality of the text: You'll need to focus on word choice, the '*rhythm of the language*' (p 34) and the evocativeness of the text as a '*springboard for discussion and reflection*' (p 34).

- The quality of the images and illustrations used in the book: Assess whether these are clear, well positioned and likely to appeal to the children.

- Is the story narrated? Being able to choose the voice for narration can be a particular strength of ebooks as is also the ability to set narration and text to different languages. Cahill and McGill-Franzen (2013) refer to *Pete's Robot* from the iTunes Store; *Best Apps for Kids* (referred to above) includes apps where the reader can record their own narration of the text.

- The interactivity of the ebook: Typically you'll find ebooks for early years have multiple *hot spots* and different activities but you'll need to evaluate accessibility, ease of navigation and whether the interactivity is enhancing or distracting.

A practical framework for using iPads in the classroom

It's not the technology in itself but how you use it that enhances learning. Although iPad apps are typically highly engaging, fun and easy to use, younger children in particular '*may be able to correctly work the app and click through the appropriate buttons, but actually have limited understanding of the specific literacy concept*' (Northrop and Killeen, 2013, p 536). It's important to acknowledge that the technology doesn't actually replace the teacher but is one of the tools that you'll use to help enhance children's learning. An effective strategy for using iPads explained by Northrop and Killeen (2013, pp 533–5) is to begin by teaching the literacy concept without the iPad, then '*explain and model the app*', provide opportunity for '*guided practice with the app*' and then progress to '*independent practice with the app*'. This helps children to use the app in a more focused way and during the guided practice step you can assess and respond to any misconceptions. As with your teaching approach more generally, it's useful to identify key questions and scaffold learning within each child's zone of proximal development (McLeod, 2012).

International perspective: typing vs handwriting

Woollaston (2015) drew attention to the international context when noting that schools in Finland now have the option to teach typing instead of handwriting, following '*changes made to the Common Core Standards Initiative in the US, in September 2013, in which the US similarly removed cursive handwriting as a compulsory skill*'. Similarly, teaching cursive handwriting is not a mandatory part of the UK national curriculum. The core of the argument seems to be that what matters is legibility rather than style and being able to express yourself without needing to concentrate on letter formation. And by the age of eight, with practice children can type faster than they can write (Woollaston, 2015). Also, Merchant (2006) referred to research studies reporting that children write more extended texts, do more editing and produce writing of a higher quality when word processing. Certainly, it's more efficient to edit writing using the provisionality affordance of word processing software, though it's worth noting inconsistencies – for example Hopman (2014, p 2) suggests that handwriting '*helps build more complicated sentences than with typing, and leads to a better composition of a written text*'. Woollaston drew attention to research findings which suggest the practice of cursive handwriting helps to improve '*students' motor and visual skills, eye-to-hand co-ordination, spatial awareness, hand and finger dexterity, cognitive function and brain development*'. And Hopman (2014, p 2) also notes that handwriting leads to '*better reading performance*' and that '*bad handwriting can have disastrous consequences in professional fields*'.

Critical question

» *In light of the evidence and reflecting on your own experience, how much time should be given to learning to type in the EYFS/national curriculum?*

Conclusion

This chapter has covered several topics relating to literacy and digital technology in the early years. By now you'll be aware that there are not always simple answers to apparently simple questions, such as should children in the early years start to learn how to type and what's the best way to make the most effective use of iPads for teaching literacy? New apps become available all the time but there's no one *super app* to replace the teacher. You need to be thinking about how to integrate digital technology into your teaching approach in order to enhance the children's learning. This means making the most of the affordances of the technology, using what it has to offer to best effect. Hopefully you'll be developing confidence to experiment and try out your ideas as part of your own creative approach to teaching.

Recommended further reading and product reviews

- *Best Apps for Kids* (www.bestappsforkids.com/)
- Cahill, M and McGill-Franzen, A (2013) Selecting 'App'ealing and 'App'ropriate Book Apps for Beginning Readers. *The Reading Teacher*, 67(1): 30–9.

- Morgan, H (2013) Multimodal Children's E-books Help Young Learners in Reading. *Early Childhood Education Journal*, 41: 477–83.

- Reutschlin Schugar, H, Smith, C A and Schugar, J T (2013) Teaching with Interactive Picture E-books in Grades K-6. *The Reading -Teacher*, 66(8): 615–24.

- Thoermer, A and Williams, L (2012) Using Digital Texts to Promote Fluent Reading. *The Reading Teacher*, 65(7): 441–5.

- www.purplemash.com. Useful collection of *2Simple* software, available through paid subscription.

- NALDIC: Supporting bilingual children in the early years –www.naldic.org.uk/eal-initial-teacher-education/resources/early-years.

References

Department for Children, Schools & Families (DCSF) Letters and sounds: principles and practice of high quality phonics. (DCSF Publications.) [online]. Available at: www.gov.uk/government/uploads/system/uploads/attachment_data/file/190537/Letters_and_Sounds_-_Phase_One.pdf (accessed 13 April 2017).

Department for Education (DfE) (2011) Teachers' standards. [online] Available at: www.gov.uk/government/uploads/system/uploads/attachment_data/file/301107/Teachers__Standards.pdf (accessed 1 March 2017).

Department for Education (DfE) (2013) The national curriculum in England framework document [online] Available at: www.gov.uk/government/uploads/system/uploads/attachment_data/file/425601/PRIMARY_national_curriculum.pdf (accessed 1 March 2017).

Department for Education (DfE) (2014) Statutory framework for the Early Years Foundation Stage: setting the standards for learning, development and care for children from birth to five. [online] Available at: www.gov.uk/government/uploads/system/uploads/attachment_data/file/335504/EYFS_framework_from_1_September_2014__with_clarification_note.pdf (accessed 1 March 2017).

Hopman, L (2014) Cursive over typeface: the importance of teaching handwriting instead of typing. MA thesis. [online] Available at: https://openaccess.leidenuniv.nl/bitstream/handle/1887/28826/MA_Thesis_Hopman.pdf?sequence=3 (accessed 12 March 2017).

Kennedy, E, Dunphy, E, Dwyer, B, Hayes, G, McPhillips, T, Marsh, J, O'Connor, M and Shiel, G (2012) Literacy in early childhood and primary education (3–8 years). [online] Available at: www.ncca.ie/en/Publications/Reports/Literacy_in_Early_Childhood_and_Primary_Education_3-8_years.pdf (accessed 1 March 2017).

Knight, L and Dooley, K (2015) Drawing and Writing on the Screen, in Dezuanni, M, Dooley, K, Gattenhof, S and Knight, L (eds) *iPads in the Early Years: Developing Literacy and Creativity*. London: Routledge.

Levy, R (2009) Children's Perceptions of Reading and the Use of Reading Scheme Texts. *Cambridge Review of Education*, 39(3): 361–77.

Marsh, J, Plowman, L, Yamada-Rice, D, Bishop, J C, Lahmar, J, Scott, F, Davenport, A, Davis, S, French, K, Piras, M, Thornhill, S, Robinson, P and Winter, P (2015) Exploring play and creativity in pre-schoolers' use of apps: final project report. [online] Available at: www.techandplay.org/reports/TAP_Final_Report.pdf (accessed 1 March 2017).

McLeod, S A (2012). Zone of proximal development. [online] Available at: www.simplypsychology.org/Zone-of-Proximal-Development.html (accessed 1 March 2017).

Merchant, G (2006) Digital writing in the early years. [online] Available at: www.google.co.uk/url?sa=t&rct=j&q=&esrc=s&source=web&cd=5&cad=rja&uact=8&ved=0ahUKEwjmu7WjtIzRAhWVMlAKHYB9D9cQFgg2MAQ&url=http%3A%2F%2Fextra.shu.ac.uk%2Fbvw%2FMerchantfinalSept06.doc&usg=AFQjCNHjAwdQODATi1zXe1iEDFR6tWPjUA&sig2=vYsAWLt4-b81Cqe9Jg3_gQ&bvm=bv.142059868,d.ZWM (accessed 12 March 2017).

Moreno, R and Mayer, R (2000) A Learner Centred Approach to Multimedia Explanations: Deriving Instructional Design Principles from Cognitive Theory. *Interactive Multimedia Electronic Journal of Computer-Enhanced Learning*, 2(2). [online] Available at: http://imej.wfu.edu/articles/2000/2/05/index.asp (accessed 1 March 2017).

Moylett, H and Stewart, N (2012) Development matters in the Early Years Foundation Stage (EYFS). London: Early Education. [online] Available at: www.gov.gg/CHttpHandler.ashx?id=104249&p=0 (accessed 1 March 2017).

National College for Teaching and Leadership (2013) Teachers' standards (early years). [online] Available at: www.gov.uk/government/uploads/system/uploads/attachment_data/file/211646/Early_Years_Teachers__Standards.pdf (accessed 1 March 2017).

National Council of Teachers of English (NCTE) (2013) The NCTE definition of 21st century literacies. [online] Available at: www.ncte.org/positions/statements/21stcentdefinition (accessed 1 March 2017).

Northrop, L and Killeen, E (2013) A Framework for Using iPads to Build Early Literacy Skills. *The Reading Teacher*, 66(7): 531–7.

Oxford Owl (2016) Oxford reading tree. [online] Available at: www.oxfordowl.co.uk/for-home/starting-school/oxford-reading-tree-explained/ (accessed 1 March 2017).

Oxford Reading Tree (ORT) (2016) ORT case studies and testimonials. [online] Available at: https://global.oup.com/education/content/primary/case-studies/pages/ort?region=uk# (accessed 1 March 2017).

Rose, J (2006) *Independent Review of the Teaching of Early Reading*. London: Department for Education and Skills. [online] Available at: http://dera.ioe.ac.uk/5551/2/report.pdf (accessed 1 March 2017).

Savage, M and Barnett, A (2015) *Digital Literacy for Primary Teachers*. Northwich: Critical Publishing.

Shettel, J and Bower, K (2013) Infusing Technology into the Balanced Literacy Classroom. *e-journal of Balanced Reading Instruction*, 1(2): 3–11. [online] Available at: www.balancedreadinginstruction.com/uploads/1/8/9/6/18963113/ejbri_v1i2_shettel__bower_infusing_technology_into_balanced.pdf (accessed 1 March 2017).

Woollaston, V (2015) The death of handwriting? Schools are ditching pens and papers for computers – but could it harm your child's development? *Mail Online*. [online] Available at: www.dailymail.co.uk/sciencetech/article-2936600/The-death-handwriting-Schools-ditching-pens-papers-computers-harm-child-s-development.html (accessed 1 March 2017).

9 Mathematics

CHAPTER OUTLINE AND PROFESSIONAL LINKS

This chapter begins by considering challenges related to mathematics teaching and the use of digital technology. The early years context is then highlighted, with a focus on the EYFS Early Learning Goals and Teachers' Standards. This is followed by discussing child development and mathematical knowledge related to the Early Learning Goals. A model for key characteristics of teaching and learning with digital technology is then used as a framework for technology-enhanced learning of mathematics in the early years.

The challenge

Heather Lowe (2009, p 37) emphasised that children need to '*explore and experiment so that they will grow up without some of the hang-ups about ICT that many of us experience*'. Put this together with the common performance motivation mindset (Dweck, 2012) that many people have about mathematics, eg '*I'm no good at maths therefore I'm not even going to try*' and TEL and mathematics looks like it could be a challenging topic. It doesn't have to be! You can learn a lot from the EYFS *Characteristics of Effective Learning* such as the value of curiosity; of having a 'can do' attitude, of persisting and bouncing back in the face of difficulties; developing problem-solving strategies and realising that making an extra effort can make all the difference.

If you're still not convinced, then pause for a moment and think back to what you know about learning theory and the nature of intelligence, such as the developmental perspective of Piaget, and your experiences when learning mathematics. Howard Gardner (1993), well known for his theory of multiple intelligences, expressed the view that intelligences '*are subject to being considerably modified by changes in available resources and ... in one's perceptions of one's own abilities and potentials*' (p xxvii). Carol Dweck's (2012) concept of the growth mindset reinforces this view of the potential of the human mind, as do more recent studies on brain plasticity (Banks, 2016) – cognitive abilities are not fixed!

The EYFS Early Learning Goals for number, shape, space and measures

The Early Learning Goals provide a clear statement of the mathematical knowledge and ability that children need to develop. Detailed guidance relating to the four key themes (unique child, personal relationships, enabling environments and areas of learning) is available in *Development Matters* (Moylett and Stewart, 2012).

- **ELG 11 – Numbers:** *'Children count reliably with numbers from one to 20, place them in order and say which number is one more or one less than a given number. Using quantities and objects, they add and subtract two single-digit numbers and count on or back to find the answer. They solve problems, including doubling, halving and sharing'* (EYFS, 2014a).

- **ELG 12 – Shape, space and measure:** *'Children use everyday language to talk about size, weight, capacity, position, distance, time and money to compare quantities and objects and to solve problems. They recognise, create and describe patterns. They explore characteristics of everyday objects and shapes and use mathematical language to describe them'* (EYFS, 2014b).

Teachers' Standards and Teachers' Standards (early years)

The Teachers' Standards and Teachers' Standards (early years) reinforce the need for teachers to have a good understanding of early years pedagogy and also of children's cognitive development in mathematics in the early years.

Teachers' Standard 3: *'Demonstrate good subject and curriculum knowledge'*.

- *'If teaching early mathematics, demonstrate a clear understanding of appropriate teaching strategies'* (NCTL, 2013, p 11).

The Teachers' Standards (early years):

Teachers' Standard 3.5: *'Demonstrate a clear understanding of appropriate strategies in the teaching of early mathematics'* (NCTL, 2013).

Gifford (2008) points out that simply providing three- to five-year-olds with opportunities for child-initiated learning is not in itself sufficient to ensure progress in mathematical development; the teacher needs to take a more active role. You'll find that Bruner's stages of cognitive representation are particularly important when teaching mathematics: *enactive*, which involves manipulation of objects and concrete experience; *iconic*, which involves pictorial representation; and *symbolic*, which involves use of words and symbols (McLeod, 2008). This is central to the University of Worcester's prime five approach to teaching mathematics (the other four constituents are a focus on questioning, language and talk, and problem-solving and reasoning).

Teachers' Standard 5: *'Adapt teaching to respond to the strengths and needs of all pupils'*.

- *'demonstrate an awareness of the physical, social and intellectual development of children, and know how to adapt teaching to support pupils' education at different stages of development'* (NCTL, 2013, p 11).

Gifford (2008) considered the pedagogical implications of cognitive, affective, physical and socio-cultural aspects of learning. Within the cognitive dimension she emphasises the value of cumulative learning and instant feedback, looking for patterns, modelling skills, problem-solving and provoking discussion. Digital technology is well designed to support daily routines with rhymes, games and repetitive structures. It can also be used to help address the Williams Review (2008) finding that children were underachieving in more creative and problem-solving type mathematical activities. In particular, within the physical dimension and re-emphasising the importance of Bruner's enactive stage, Gifford (2008) referred to the value of manipulatives, which suggests a range of mathematical activities using Bee-Bots, Blue-Bots, Roamer Too and other programmable robotic toys. You can also explore tangibles such as Makey Makey for their potential to support number activities (www.youtube.com/watch?v=rfQqh7iCcOU). Gifford notes that *'socio-economic status is a major predictor of mathematical achievement, particularly in the UK'* (p 217) and emphasises the value of home learning as part of a socio-cultural dimension. Bronfenbrenner's (2005) systems approach also draws attention to the influence of the environment beyond the early years setting.

NB. The equivalent early years Teachers' Standards are 3.5 and 5.2 (NCTL, 2013).

Critical question

» *Teachers' Standards 3 and 5 require that you choose appropriate teaching strategies matched to the particular learning needs of the children. Identify the mathematical misconceptions held by one or more children In your class. How might you use digital technology to progress this child's learning?*

Theoretical perspectives and pedagogical links

Child development and mathematical knowledge

The views of Piaget and Gardner provide a useful foundation for understanding the Early Learning Goals for numbers, shape, space and measures. Piaget's theory of a child's cognitive development is useful when focusing on the EYFS learning goals for mathematics. Although criticised because the age-related findings weren't replicated by research carried out in naturalistic settings (Donaldson, 1978), in general terms the stage theory is still influential. And more recently, Gardner (1993) related Piaget's stage theory to logical-mathematical and spatial intelligences.

With regard to logical-mathematical intelligence, during the sensorimotor stage the very young child comes to realise the permanence of objects; that objects continue to exist even when they are not in sight. It then becomes possible for the child to compare one object with another and grouping becomes possible. As the child enters the concrete operational stage, the ability to conserve number develops. Physical manipulation of objects is an important characteristic of learning during this stage. To start with, the child may compare a shorter and longer line of the same number of counters by saying that the longer line has more counters. Younger pre-school children may be able to count by rote but may not yet have learnt one-to-one correspondence and it's not until after the concepts of one more and one less have developed that understanding addition and subtraction becomes possible. Computer and iPad apps such as *123 Genius – First Numbers and Counting Games for Kids* can help develop one-to-one correspondence, ordering numbers and simple addition and subtraction.

With regard to spatial intelligence, during the sensorimotor stage the child becomes capable of moving around in space while not yet being able to represent this. By the end of this stage the child is capable of mental imagery in the absence of the object or event. As the child moves from the pre-school to the primary school, the concrete operational stage, objects and images of objects and events can be more effectively manipulated. For example, the child becomes capable of reversible spatial operations such as being able to imagine what the object looks like from the other side. The abstract reversible spatial operations of geometry become possible as the child enters the formal operational stage.

Schema theory is particularly influential within early years practice. Common early schemas include the *container* schema where the pre-school child will frequently put one thing into another and may enjoy putting themselves into a container such as a large cardboard box. Nutbrown (2015) refers to a range of simple schemas which include vertical, horizontal and circular movement such as jumping, drawing vertical or circular marks, spinning round or spinning the wheels on a toy car. As an early years teacher, you'll need to develop an awareness of the mathematical connections to these basic schema and to create learning experiences to build on and extend the child's budding interest. For example, if you notice that a child starts collecting things and puts them into a bag, you might aim to extend this schema by introducing a sorting game on the computer or iPad, eg the iPad app *Tiny Hands* includes sorting/collecting washing from the clothes line of the same colour into matching colour baskets.

Critical question

» *Which mathematical concepts and schemas are able to be supported effectively by the software and apps at your school and where are the gaps, if any, in your school's provision for supporting mathematical development?*

Characteristics of good-quality teaching and learning with digital technology

The BECTA publication, *Key Characteristics of Good Quality Teaching and Learning with ICT* (Bacon et al, 2001), focuses on autonomy, capability, creativity, quality and scope. These characteristics resonate well with principles of good practice in early years, such as the *Characteristics of Effective Learning*, as well as with approaches to supporting effective learning in mathematics (Bennett and Weidner, 2012; Price, 2009; Sangster, 2016).

Mathematics, independent learning and digital technology

Learning to be independent and independent learning in the cognitive sense are valued goals within the early years and digital technology context.

> *Pupils develop their own ways of thinking about the task and develop their own strategies for overcoming problems. They seem confident, prepared to take risks and learn from their mistakes.*
>
> (Bacon et al, 2001, p 2)

Programmable toys are particularly useful for encouraging more open-ended learning, exploration and problem-solving, encompassing a range of learning outcomes related to number, shape, space and measures. However, research by Janka (2008) and Stephen and Plowman (2008, 2013) emphasised the importance of the learning context and effective intervention by teachers to promote motivation and move learning forward.

CASE STUDY

Janka (2008) evaluated ways of teaching with Bee-Bots and recommended organising the class into small groups with one group programming the Bee-Bots with support from the class teacher while the other groups were *'designing, drawing, painting or building parts for Bee-Bot scenery'* (p 120). A familiar scenario using a thematic or topic approach to teaching would begin with you, as the teacher, reading a story to the children and then asking the class how they could act out the story using the Bee-Bots.

Commentary on case study

Choosing a suitable and familiar story that involves movement will help focus the children's attention. For example, the picture book by Maurice Sendak, *Where the Wild Things Are*, includes Max going to his room, a forest scene, Max sailing in a boat, Max pausing while talking to the wild things, a dance-like rumpus and Max sailing back to his room (www.youtube.com/watch?v=6cOEFnppm_A). As a topic in Key Stage 1, the children could find out about the wild animals in the rainforest; they could also investigate floating, sinking and forces in science related to Max sailing in a boat. Topics can be a creative cross-curricular approach to teaching that supports independent learning.

Critical question

» *Exploration, problem-solving and open-ended activities are constituents of independent learning. Think back to* Where the Wild Things Are. *How can a problem-solving approach be introduced when programming the Bee-Bots?*

Resources

Blue-Bots are the latest version of the popular *Bee-Bot* floor robot (see www.tts-group.co.uk/blue-bot-bluetooth-programmable-floor-robot/1007812.html). Its transparent body allows children to see inside the robot. The directional arrows have been improved to suggest rotation rather than the misleading left/right arrows on the Bee-Bots. Another improvement is the addition of a 45-degree rotation option. Blue-Bots can be programmed via Bluetooth from a tablet or PC/Mac. The Blue-Bot app enables pupils to *'use sequence, selection, and repetition in programs; work with variables and various forms of input and output'*(DFE, 2013, p 179). The app has both an explore and challenge mode and allows children to voice-record commands when programming.

The *Roamer Too* is the latest version of Roamer from Valiant Technology (see www.valiant-technology.com/us/pages/roamertoohome.php). This is an altogether more power-ful floor robot but one which can also be customised for even the youngest children. There are different keyboard overlays for different ages and abilities. As with the Classic Roamer, rotation can be one degree at a time rather than only 90 degrees or 45 degrees. Sequences using repeat as well as procedures based on the Logo programming language continue to be supported. Roamer Too can be programmed to travel at different speeds and with different amounts of push or pull force – useful for science activities. A pen module can be added which allows Roamer Too to draw graphic designs as it executes programs designed by the children. Roamer Too is also able to speak, eg ask and answer questions and respond to pupils' programming decisions.

Mathematics, capability and digital technology

Even the youngest nursery school children have demonstrated the ability to locate and open apps on an iPad and to press, swipe and stretch effectively. There are also a wide range of apps available for learning mathematics in the early years. Key features to look out for are ease of use, clear links to the Early Learning Goals, appropriate level of challenge, fun activities, interactivity, instant feedback and support for embodied learning. Spencer (2013) undertook a crossover study with groups of foundation-stage children using the app *Know Number Free* for the iPad and iPhone, downloadable from the iTunes store. The results of the research suggested that *'a week of daily exposure to iPads improved numeracy and this type of digital play advanced children's development in recognising, writing and quantifying num-bers'* (p 615). Spencer emphasised that effective modelling by the teacher can help improve progress, that the needs of higher-achieving children need to be considered and that some teachers still need to develop confidence in using digital technology. The seven activities that comprise this app appear well designed for nursery/kindergarten children. The activi-ties use a range of different motivating approaches; for example, the *Reflect* game requires the player to tilt the iPad in order to move the numbers until they overlay the target number. The other activities include sorting, counting, connecting, memorising and matching.

Mathematics, creativity and digital technology

McDonald and Howell (2012) focused on the use of *'creative digital technologies for the development of literacy, numeracy and science'* (p 642) in the early years.

'Creative' technology ... refers to computer-based programs and equipment that are not pre-prepared or constructed. They allow students to design, build and program with as little or as much support as is needed; thereby, requiring some conceptual and procedural understandings rather than simply engaging with the manufacturer's thinking.

(McDonald and Howell, 2012, p 642)

Just as natural resources can easily be assigned multiple meanings, open-ended digital technology resources also provide support for creative learning opportunities. For example, a small block of wood could act as a mobile phone with an imagined keypad for dialling phone numbers to support imaginative role play. Children might phone orders to the role play takeaway restaurant. Staff at the takeaway might use a computer to record orders and produce till receipts as part of the role play.

Mathematics, quality and digital technology

The BECTA (2007) publication, *Quality Principles for Digital Learning Resources*, focuses specifically on '*the design and use of digital learning resources to support effective learning and teaching*' (p 1). It separates pedagogic principles from design principles. The guidance suggests that when choosing digital technology resources you need to ensure that they're matched to the curriculum, easy to use and engaging for the children. You also need to consider inclusion (the focus of a separate chapter) and assessment to support learning. Of course, it's not just the end result that counts; children need to value the process through which they achieve their goals. But when thinking about quality it's important to look for the potential of digital technologies to enable children to produce and present high-quality work.

CASE STUDY

The children in a Year 1 class were working on the topic of patterns in mathematics. The teacher wanted to create a more authentic learning experience by using a cross-curricular approach so started this lesson by showing the children a range of wrapping papers for presents. The class was asked to look closely and say what they could see. They noticed that the wrapping papers had repeating patterns using stamped images or lines and shapes. The teacher then challenged the children to use graphics (eg Dazzle03) software to produce symmetrical designs using different coloured squares, triangles and circles. The printing facilities at the school were limited to A4-size paper but within their Design & Technology lesson the children had designed and made fridge magnets as presents and they were able to use their A4 wrapping paper to wrap these.

Commentary on case study

Most art programs can be customised to match the abilities of children throughout the primary school. The software includes a range of art and drawing tools that can be used for producing patterns. The split-screen feature allows accurate positioning of straight lines, shapes and stamped images in order to produce high-quality repeating patterns. As the teacher had selected a simplified interface, the children found using the software easy and they immediately felt confident enough to try out their ideas.

Mathematics, scope and digital technology

The concept of *scope* includes using digital technology to extend the range of learning, technology resources and context for use. This is extensive and includes mobile apps and games; interactive teaching programs; generic resources such as word processors, spreadsheets and presentation software; computers and old laptops; programmable toys; sound recorders; listening area; microphones; video and still-image cameras.

Bennett and Weidner (2012) suggest several mathematics activities and topics incorporating digital technology. Examples include: digital and analogue clocks, where pre-school children can make their own digital numbers using lollipop sticks; phones with keypads (and the older dial version), where pre-school children can make their own phonebooks to use within role play. Other mathematics-related ideas for role play include programming a toy microwave and using a toy swipe card cash register.

Websites

There are a seemingly endless flow of websites related to all aspects of early years mathematics. You simply need a basic search strategy – for example, you could use the following search terms in Google (changing the Key Stage and last word to match your specific interest):

- interactive maths games – Key Stage 1 *shape*;
- interactive maths games – Key Stage 1 *number bonds*;
- interactive maths games – Key Stage 1 *subtraction*;

or a more general search such as

- early years mathematics websites.

You'll find that Google also suggests similar searches related to your search terms that will be worth exploring. Good websites are related to your curriculum focus, easy to navigate, pitched at the right level, appealing to the age group, interactive and safe. You'll need to evaluate each website before use to check for suitability and then save it in the Bookmarks or Favourites folder of your web browser.

Some examples to get you started:

www.bbc.co.uk/bitesize/ks1/maths/shapes/play/

www.mathplayground.com/number_bonds_10.html

www.topmarks.co.uk/Flash.aspx?f=TakeAway

International perspective

The Singapore approach to teaching mathematics is a developmental approach moving from concrete, through pictorial to abstract modes of learning, and features opportunities for children to explain their mathematical reasoning and ideas. Sharpe (2009) reported on several studies that led specifically to the development of the Singapore numeracy curriculum for early years (MoE, 2012). Although the curriculum doesn't include a particular focus on the applications of digital technology, the support for multimodal learning that characterises digital technology relates well to this developmental approach. Sharpe emphasises that in Singapore there's more autonomy and that currently the British audit culture makes it difficult 'to sustain a developmental approach when targets have to be met and administrators appeased' (p 410). Yet, from reading *Development Matters* you'll have noticed that the EYFS does already include references to the use of digital technology to help children achieve the Early Learning Goals.

Conclusion

Now that you've reached the end of this chapter you should feel more confident about teaching mathematics in the early years and about using the potential of digital technology as part of your teaching approach. You should also have developed your understanding and awareness of children's mathematical development and have started to think about the theoretical underpinnings of effective mathematics teaching. You should also be more aware of the range of digital technology resources.

Recommended further reading and product reviews

- Williams, P (2008) *Independent Review of Mathematics Teaching in Early Years Settings and Primary Schools*. Nottingham: DCFS. [online] Available at: http://dera.ioe.ac.uk/8365/7/Williams%20Mathematics_Redacted.pdf.

- Blue-Bots. www.bettshow.com/library_10/2531429_assocPDF.pdf.

References

Bacon, S, Sanderson, R, Warner, H and Walker, H (2001) *Key Characteristics of Good Quality Teaching and Learning with ICT: A Discussion Document*. BECTA. [online] Available at: http://archive.naace.co.uk/implementingict/resources/Good%20Teaching%20and%20Learning.doc (accessed 1 March 2017).

Banks, D (2016) What is brain plasticity and why is it so important? [online] Available at: www.open.ac.uk/research/main/news/brain-plasticity (accessed 1 March 2017).

BECTA (2007) Quality principles for digital learning resources. [online] Available at: http://mirandanet.ac.uk/wp-content/uploads/2015/05/quality_principles.pdf (accessed 1 March 2017).

Bennett, E and Weidner, J (2012) *Everyday Maths through Everyday Provision: Developing Opportunities for Mathematics in the Early Years*. London: Routledge.

Bronfenbrenner, U (2005) (ed) *Making Human Beings Human: Bioecological Perspectives on Human Development*. London: Sage.

Department for Education (DfE) (2013) The national curriculum in England framework document. [online] Available at: www.gov.uk/government/uploads/system/uploads/attachment_data/file/425601/PRIMARY_national_curriculum.pdf (accessed 1 March 2017).

Donaldson, M (1978) *Children's Minds*. London: Fontana.

Dweck, C (2012) *Mindset*. London: Robinson.

EYFS (2014a) EYFS profile exemplification for the level of learning and development expected at the end of the EYFS mathematics ELG11. [online] Available at: www.gov.uk/government/uploads/system/uploads/attachment_data/file/360535/ELG11___Numbers.pdf (accessed 1 March 2017).

EYFS (2014b) EYFS profile exemplification for the level of learning and development expected at the end of the EYFS mathematics ELG12. [online] Available at: www.gov.uk/government/uploads/system/uploads/attachment_data/file/360537/ELG12___Shape__space_and_measures.pdf (accessed 1 March 2017).

Gardner, H (1993) *Frames of Mind: The Theory of Multiple Intelligences*. London: Fontana.

Gifford, S (2008) How Do You Teach Nursery Children Mathematics? In Search of a Mathematics Pedagogy for the Early Years, in Thompson, I (ed) *Teaching and Learning Early Number* (2nd ed). Maidenhead: Open University Press, pp 217–27.

Indigo Learning (no date). Dazzle03. [online] Available at: http://teemeducation.org.uk/primary/art/dazzle-03 (accessed 1 March 2017).

Janka, P (2008) Using a Programmable Toy at Preschool Age: Why and How. *Workshop Proceedings of the International Conference on Simulation, Modelling and Programming for Autonomous Robots*, Venice (Italy), November 3–4, pp 112–21. [online] Available at: www.terecop.eu/downloads/simbar2008/pekarova.pdf (accessed 1 March 2017).

Lowe, H (2009) Children's Independence, in Price, H *The Really Useful Book of ICT in the Early Years*. London: Routledge, pp 25–37.

McDonald, S and Howell, J (2012) Watching, Creating and Achieving: Creative Technologies as a Conduit for Learning in the Early Years. *British Journal of Educational Technology*, 43(4): 641–51.

McLeod, S A (2008) Bruner. [online] Available at: www.simplypsychology.org/bruner.html (accessed 1 March 2017).

Ministry of Education (MoE) (2012) Nurturing early learning: a curriculum framework for kindergartens in Singapore – a guide for parents. [online] Available at: www.moe.gov.sg/docs/default-source/document/education/preschool/files/kindergarten-curriculum-framework-guide-for-parents.pdf (accessed 1 March 2017).

Moylett, H and Stewart, N (2012) *Development Matters in the Early Years Foundation Stage (EYFS)*. London: Early Education. [online] Available at: www.gov.gg/CHttpHandler.ashx?id=104249&p=0 (accessed 1 March 2017).

National College for Teaching & Leadership (NCTL) (2013) Teachers' standards (early years). [online] Available at: www.gov.uk/government/uploads/system/uploads/attachment_data/file/211646/Early_Years_Teachers__Standards.pdf (accessed 1 March 2017).

Nutbrown, C (2015) Schemas and young children's learning. [online] Available at: www.sheffield.ac.uk/polopoly_fs/1.441757!/file/Schemas.pdf (accessed 13 April 2017).

Price, H (2009) *The Really Useful Book of ICT in the Early Years*. London: Routledge.

Roamer Too (no date) [online] Available at: www.valiant-technology.com/us/pages/standard_roamers.php (accessed 1 March 2017).

Sangster, M (2016) *Engaging Primary Children in Mathematics*. London: Bloomsbury.

Sharpe, P (2009) Numeracy Matters in Singapore Kindergartens, in Yoong, W K, Yee, L P, Kaur, B, Yee, F P and Fong, N S (eds) (2012) *Mathematics Education: The Singapore Journey* (vol 2). London: World Scientific, pp 387–412.

Spencer, P (2013) iPads: Improving Numeracy in the Early Years, in Steinle, V, Ball, L and Bardini, C (eds) Mathematics education: yesterday, today and tomorrow (Proceedings of the 36th Annual Conference of the Mathematics Education Research Group of Australasia). Melbourne: MERGA. [online] Available at: www.merga.net.au/documents/Spencer_MERGA36-2013.pdf (accessed 1 March 2017).

Stephen, C and Plowman, L (2008) Enhancing Learning with Information and Communication Technologies in Pre-school. *Early Childhood Development and Care*, 178(6): 637–54. [online] Available at: www.tandfonline.com/toc/gecd20/178/6?nav=tocList (accessed 1 March 2017).

Stephen, C and Plowman, L (2013) Digital technologies, play and learning. [online] Available at: https://dspace.stir.ac.uk/bitstream/1893/18240/1/Folio%20article%20Digital%20Technologies%20and%20Play.pdf (accessed 1 March 2017).

10 Expressive arts and design

CHAPTER OUTLINE AND PROFESSIONAL LINKS

The *Statutory Framework for the Early Years Foundation Stage* (DfE, 2014) defines expressive arts and design as:

> enabling children to explore and play with a wide range of media and materials, as well as providing opportunities and encouragement for sharing their thoughts, ideas and feelings through a variety of activities in art, music, movement, dance, role-play, and design and technology.

> (DfE, 2014, p 8)

The challenge in this chapter is for you to consider how technologies can be utilised to empower young children to express themselves and create a unique voice in their chosen medium. As a practitioner you are seeking to strike a balance by encouraging and developing early preferences (for example, in creating music or song) alongside building capability in a broad range of forms of expression. Working in different and varied expressive forms is very powerful for children and can create rich channels for self expression.

Critical question

» *Imagine you wanted to convey to others your experiences of a fun and busy day last week. How many different and creative ways could you do that (eg write a poem)? What would be your default approach? What approach would you find challenging? How do these varied approaches tap into different things you want to express about that day? Can technology be purposely utilised in any of your ideas?*

Exemplification from the DfE (2014) and the Standards and Testing Agency (2014a, 2014b) breaks down *expressive arts and design* in greater detail:

> **ELG 16 Exploring and using media and materials:** *children sing songs, make music and dance, and experiment with ways of changing them. They safely use and explore a variety of materials, tools and techniques, experimenting with colour, design, texture, form and function.*
>
> **ELG 17 Being imaginative:** *children use what they have learnt about media and materials in original ways, thinking about uses and purposes. They represent their own ideas, thoughts and feelings through design and technology, art, music, dance, role-play and stories.*

(DfE, 2014, p 12)

Early Learning Goals 16 and 17 offer rich opportunities for digital expression and it is important to consider both the process and the product components. The phrase '*experiment with ways of changing them*' in ELG 16 emphasises that the process stage is often reflective of key learning, especially in relation to developing a robust learning disposition. Also, digital technologies may play a part in the process of creating a product that is not necessarily digital in form. An example is given in the following case study.

CASE STUDY

Millie loves dancing and is often observed practising and creating short sequences. She sings along to herself for musical accompaniment and will repeat sections. Millie appears to particularly enjoy expressing herself kinaesthetically. She is generally a confident girl and will happily share her dancing with others by inviting them to watch. Millie asks her key worker to watch 'her show' and her key worker offers to video a few seconds on an iPad. Millie is observed watching the image of herself intently and with great fascination. She laughs out loud and asks to watch it several times.

Commentary on case study

The short recording offers Millie an opportunity to observe herself and develop a sense of how she exists in her surroundings among her peers. This intense and immediate feedback loop is very powerful to learners. Millie may subsequently adjust elements of her composition and performance. Similarly, audio playback can be a powerful tool when working with young children developing speech and language. These audio and visual technologies can be a powerful viewing lens for children to gain an external perspective of themselves; and although not necessarily being part of any finished product, they have impacted on the learning process.

The suggestion in this chapter is not that you should replace vital real-world opportunities; to paint with brushes or create music with instruments, but to enhance and extend opportunities into digital forms. For example, Figures 10.1 and 10.2 show two complementary approaches to exploring colour.

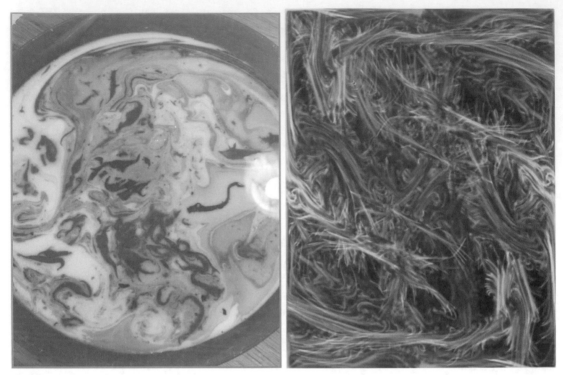

Figures 10.1 and 10.2 *Explorations of colour using paint and the* Fingerpaint *app (author's images).* Fingerpaint *is available at https://itunes.apple.com/gb/app/fingerpaint-magic/ id586165483?mt=8*

There are a wide range of content-creation apps (applications) and software designed for young children that can support interactive, imaginative and creative activities. Similarly, using technology does not imply working in isolation, or singularly for long periods; activities can be collaborative at most stages in the process. Further, the technologies can make sharing with others easier, both during and at the end of the process.

For children to make informed choices, they need a breadth of experiences. Jenkins (2006, p 47, as cited by Alper, 2011), stated that '*children must learn to sort through a range of different possible modes of expression, determine which is most effective in reaching their audience and communicating their message, and to grasp which techniques work best in conveying information through this channel*' (p 187). Through these expressions children are able to share their unique perceptions of the world and practitioners can gain essential insight by listening to and observing closely. Resnick (2012) explained why the activity of making (being an author) is so important in the learning process:

> *When you make something in the world, it becomes an external representation of the ideas in your head. It enables you to play with your ideas and gain a better understanding of the possibilities and limitations of your ideas. Why didn't it work the way I expected? I wonder what would happen if I changed this piece of it? By*

giving an external form and shape to your ideas, you also provide opportunities for other people to play with your ideas and give suggestions on your ideas. Why didn't I think of that? How can I make it more useful to people?

(Resnick, 2012, pp 50–1)

Affordances of technology and creative expression

In Chapter 2 when you were exploring the meaning and versatility of technology-enhanced learning, you were introduced to the idea of technological affordances. These affordances are very relevant to this chapter as you seek to find creative ways for the learners in your care to convey their ideas and express themselves to others. The multimodal affordance of technology means you can provide a wide variety of tools that enable children to express themselves in video, audio, photographs, animations, drawings, paintings and audio. The merits of exploring different media and approaches relate to creating personalised and inclusive learning opportunities. Your experiences to date may resonate with the research findings that adults and young learners alike process sensory input in different ways.

> *Our brains are wired to process visual input very differently from text, audio, and sound ... functional Magnetic Resonance Imaging (fMRI) scans confirm a dual coding system through which visuals and text/auditory input are processed in separate channels, presenting the potential for simultaneous augmentation of learning.*

(CISCO, 2008)

The nature of most technological tools is that children can create, revise and modify creative artefacts. The provisionality affordance means that children are free to experiment, take risks and see what happens. Mistakes are easily undone in comparison with real-world counterparts. Becta (2005a) argued that:

> *the use of digital media can unleash creativity, allowing pupils the chance to create things they have never previously been able to attempt. They can manipulate sounds, pictures and moving images in the knowledge that they can safely undo any mistakes they make. They can save different versions of their work and return to it at any time. The nature of visual and auditory media means that their work no longer relies on language skills or ability to read and write fluently. Instead, learners are free to express themselves based on ideas they can develop without the need to write them down.*

(Becta, 2005a, p 1)

Critical question

» *What synergy, or otherwise, can you detect between some of the affordances of technology and the three characteristics of effective teaching and learning when working on creative and expressive projects?*

The remix

Originality is often a concept practitioners ponder and direct reference is made to this in ELG 17 with the phrase *'in original ways'* (DfE, 2014, p 12). Are children only being creative if they are being original? You will be aware that many elements of children's play and creation involve mimicry or re-telling. This developmentally appropriate tendency carries through to digital creations also. Belshaw (2011), in defining digital literacies, referred to a *'constructive'* component that challenges practitioners to reconsider notions of originality in a digital world. This component pertains to *'creating something new, including using or remixing content from other sources to create something original'* (pp 208–9). Repurposing of digital content by using and remixing is easily accomplished digitally. The meaning of copyright will be explored in the digital literacy component of the primary computing curriculum (DfE, 2013) and with this age group, more simplistic language of borrowing or sharing is appropriate (DfE, 2013).

Aligned to the discussion of originality, Sakr et al's (2016) research findings remind us that *'ready-made content'* can be the jumping-off point for learners' imagination.

> Digital resources ... foreground the potential of narrative and art-making to be a response to the external world involving the *'remix'* of ready-made content.
>
> (Sakr et al, 2016, pp 305–6)

Visual exploration, experimentation and expression

Visual stimuli and capabilities are essential in a multisensory approach to learning. In this section you will be prompted to consider lightboxes, painting programs, photographs, animations and video. The interoperable nature of technological affordances and learning processes will be developed further.

Exploring light, colours and magnified images

Lightboxes, digital microscopes and cameras can provide rich visual opportunities for learners to explore properties of colour and form. For example, using a digital microscope to examine an object can provide a *'visual phenomenon which would otherwise be inaccessible'* (Morgan and Siraj-Blatchford, 2013, p 28). Lightboxes and sensory rooms use technologies to facilitate young learners' exploration of light and its properties.

Painting, provisionality and risk-taking

Being confident in taking risks, experimenting and trying new things are vital learning dispositions. These process steps are equally as important as the finished product. The provisionality affordance lowers the perception of risk associated with experimentation; the learner can undo if the desired effect is not achieved; redo to compare and evaluate; save different versions and move away from the perception that they have just one piece of paper – don't waste it. Hewlett and March (2015) break down the artistic composition process into four stages; from *'initial idea conception'*, through *'development and refinement'*, to *'completion'*, requiring the creator to demonstrate perseverance and determination (p 83).

> *within each phase, the decision making process makes simultaneous multiple emotive demands of the brain; exploration, experimentation, risk taking, discovery, problem solving, and continuous revaluation as the initial idea is further refined. Not all ideas culminate in a successful piece of artwork; a piece can be rejected at any stage for a variety of reasons and frequently will be. Making art, therefore, is also about mental attitude.*
>
> (Hewlett and March, 2015, p 83)

Critical question

» *How might the use of a painting app on the iPad (eg Drawing with Carl https:// itunes.apple.com/gb/app/drawing-with-carl/id480645514?mt=8) support the creative process for a young learner? Compare each stage of the process in the Hewlett and March (2015) model with the traditional approach. The suggestion is not that one is better than the other but that they are/can be different.*

Many apps for this age group can be operated by the use of a finger, removing the potential barrier of operating an intermediary device such as a stylus. Many *'mimic the physical properties and fluidity of a range of drawing and painting tools such as brushes, palette knife, pastels, pen and pencils'* (Hewlett and March, 2015, p 84). Hewlett and March (2015) go further and suggest that the technology *'allows children to work at speed and with greater spontaneity than when working with more traditional methods'*:

> *children can respond in an instant to an idea; what would happen if I did this or tried that? The undo button empowers children, giving them the freedom to make mistakes and take risks. Mistakes can quickly and easily be rectified which often leads to bolder experimentation.*
>
> (Hewlett and March, 2015, p 84)

Typical packages will reinforce children's understanding of fundamental skills; for example, colour mixing, tinting and toning. In both media you will need to encourage children to use the correct tool for the job; otherwise their pictures may not move on from being very simplistic or symbolic (eg the lollipop representation of a tree). When using technology it is just as important for you to encourage children to use a smaller brush for more precise operations as you would when using real paint brushes. You can no doubt recall a situation when a young learner wants to add eyelashes to their self portrait with a thick brush and dripping gloopy paint with frustrating results!

Additionality

Do these art packages, simulating real-life experiences, really add anything? To answer this question you need to consider what extra working digitally offers. This section explores some common additionality features that working digitally might add. There are some techniques afforded when working digitally that are not possible, or are very cumbersome to achieve, in traditional media.

Figure 10.3 *Screenshots from 2Paint, an artwork tool for children aged three and above. It is available via Purple Mash, a multi-disciplinary platform developed by 2Simple, www.2simple. com/purple-mash (reproduced by permission of 2Simple Ltd)*

- *Layering* is a technique when you can save or fix a layer of work and then create another, or multiple layers, over the top. This is not as complicated as it sounds. For this age group it could be children drawing over a photograph they have taken. Many apps and programs make this a seamless process. Annotating over aerial photographs can also contribute towards early map-making.

- *Special effects* include tools which are not available in traditional forms. Popular ones include colour effects; for example, manipulating images through the application of colour filters.

Figure 10.4 *An example of a layered graphic for role-play purposes, created using Mashcam by 2Simple, also available via Purple Mash www.2simple.com/purple-mash (reproduced by permission of 2Simple Ltd)*

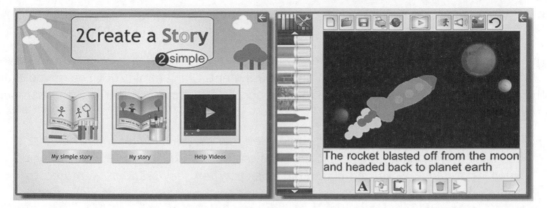

Figure 10.5 *Screenshots from* 2 Create a Story, *available via Purple Mash www.2simple.com/ purple-mash (reproduced by permission of 2Simple Ltd)*

- *Symmetry* tools where children's drawings are automatically reflected in x and or y axis.

- *Creating stamps, tiling and flipping* to create and recreate repeating and/or intricate patterns.

- *Animation* technologies are very appealing to young children for storytelling. The illustration below is from the popular *2Simple 2Create a Story*. Audio, special effects, animation, text and graphics can be incorporated following simple procedures.

- *Stop frame animation* is increasingly becoming accessible to younger children; for example, *I Can Animate* (see www.kudlian.net/products/icananimatev2/Home. html) could be used with adult support.

- *Avatar creators* can be great fun. Typically they involve importing a photo or creating a character on screen, which can then be made to move as if gesturing or speaking (Savage and Barnett, 2015, p 81). External microphones can be used to record speech. One important e-safety consideration is that creating avatars also develops young learners' understanding that '*other people can represent themselves via an avatar (and associated profile) online*' (Metcalfe et al, 2013, p 7).

Photography

Ching et al (2006) reported on a kindergarten project where children used a digital camera to document their daily activities and then created individual photo journals (p 348). The researchers posed three interesting questions for you to consider:

- *How did the children negotiate the* dual roles *of documentation of and participation in classroom activities as they took pictures?*

- *Would the* content *of children's journals ... reflect differences in how young children attend to and represent their school experiences and environment?*

- *What kinds of reflections would children exhibit when making their photo journals?*
(Ching et al, 2006, p 348)

The children were free to take pictures of what interested them, a simple and effective insight into their unique experience of the environment. Ching et al (2006) observed that children used their photographer role to *'gain access and empowerment in the classroom community'*:

> *Initially they focused primarily on people, their friends, the head teacher, and other teaching staff. After a round of pictures, they started to explore less obvious things such as friends' books and classroom objects. Then they gradually ventured to more peripheral spaces such as the calendar on the corner or a bookshelf next to the desks.*
>
> (Ching et al, 2006, p 354)

Further, Ching et al (2006) described the different approaches adopted by children, from *'wanting to be unobtrusive with candid shots of people and activities'*, to *'elaborate photo-shoots of staged events with their peers'*.

Critical question

» *Reflect on the last time you worked with a child equipped with a digital camera. What was the subject of the images recorded and what narrative did the learner provide?*

Ching et al (2006, pp 360–1) listed:

- *object-focused pictures;*
- *pictures of individual people;*
- *pictures in the classroom;*
- *playground pictures;*
- *action shots;*
- *still pictures;*
- *and pictures of teachers or other adults.*

Photography activities of this nature provide an opportunity for children to think deeply about their early childhood classroom world and to talk intimately with adults about many facets of their environment and the visual representations they created (Ching et al, 2006, p 362).

Video: visual and aural expression

The British Educational Communications and Technology Agency (Becta) recognised the potential for video to encourage creativity by enabling learners to express their ideas as a sequence of moving images rather than through language. Becta (2005b) noted that using digital video can:

- increase motivation, enthusiasm and enjoyment;

- develop 'soft' skills, including collaboration, teamwork and problem solving;

- promote and develop alternative learning styles;

- improve learners' communication skills;

- help to develop critical analysis skills and 'media literacy';

- raise learner self-esteem;

- provide instant feedback on performance, for instance in sport or drama.

(Becta, 2005b, p 1)

Reid et al suggested that making films allowed students to explore different roles and identities (Reid et al, 2002, as cited in Becta, 2003).

CASE STUDY

Utilising the research carried out by Marsh (2004, pp 496–8) with three- and four-year-olds in the UK.

An 'animation studio' was set up in one corner of the nursery on a regular basis. This consisted of one or two laptops, connected to which were webcams. There were a variety of props to hand for the animation: toy figures, artefacts and scenery. Some children planned their stories first using a storyboard, although the majority preferred not to plan them at all. The children filmed the plastic figures using webcams, ... scaffolding took the form of verbal instructions and modelling when appropriate. The majority of children were able to complete most of the activities independently....

Sofia, aged four, planned a story on paper ... it included familiar characters drawn from her experiences of family life. The storyboard outlined a narrative that focused on a girl who was 'walking and clapping'. A baby entered the plot and the baby 'crashed the cupboard'. Sofia then produced an animated film in ten frames which incorporated a soundtrack that included clapping and crashing sounds at appropriate points in the story.

Commentary on case study

Marsh explained that Sofia had observed other children's filmmaking, including their use of sound effects, before taking her turn.

Sofia suggested that the difference between her story on paper and the animated film was that one could 'hear the cupboard crashing' on her film.

(Marsh, 2004, pp 496–8)

Marsh (2004) concluded that the children demonstrated their implicit understanding of this in their creation of the films, often drawing on features of the visual mode (relationship of objects to each other in space) and aural mode (adding very specific sound effects to their films).

Music

Many aspects of aural composition (eg adding narrative or sound effects) have already been discussed. Playing ready-made music by others may contribute to creative expressions, for example, in movement and dance:

> Whilst outside playing with the scarves Georgia selects a pop CD and places it in the CD player. Charlotte says 'put on track 12, that's my favourite.' Georgia finds the song and says 'yeah I like this song, it's fast.' Together they dance with the scarves in time to the music. As the song finishes a slower song starts. Georgia stops dancing and says 'this song is too slow, let's do the other song again?' The girls repeated the dance for song 12.
>
> (Standards and Testing Agency, 2014b, p 4, ELG 17)

In relation to creating musical compositions, digital technologies can make this an accessible activity for most ages.

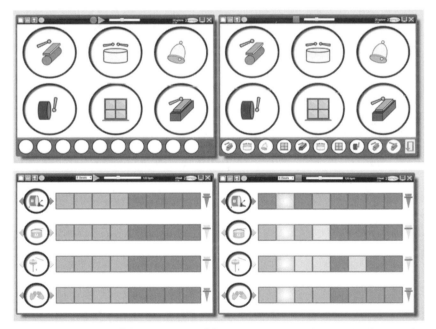

Figure 10.6 *Screenshots of* 2Explore *and* 2Beat, *available via Purple Mash, from 2Simple, www.2simple.com/purple-mash. From the product description:* 'Play and record simple melodies by clicking on the instruments! Children as young as three can make their own music with 2Explore. Once they've mastered 2Explore they can take it to the next level with 2Beat or 2Sequence', *to build up various beats with a mixture of instruments and sounds (reproduced by permission of 2Simple Ltd)*

International perspective: Italy

Many of you will have encountered the Reggio approach developed from the work of the psychologist Loris Malaguzzi, in and around the Italian city of Reggio Emilia. In the Reggio tradition it is believed that all children are naturally creative and that they should have opportunities to develop their creative skills and expression (Thornton and Brunton, 2010, p 30). Malaguzzi introduced the notion of the hundred languages of children and recognised that children have many different ways of expressing themselves, including talking, singing, dancing, painting, drawing and performing (as cited by Thornton and Brunton, 2010, p 30). At the time of his research and writing, in the post-WW2 era, Malaguzzi did not have access to digital technologies. However, some contemporary practitioners in this tradition have incorporated digital tools and consider experimentation and media manipulation part of the full ecology of digital and non-digital languages (Alper, 2011, p 185).

> In the Reggio classroom, digital tools are not isolated from non-digital tools in a computer lab; rather, they are available among other tools in the classroom environment and used within larger projects. As young children and adults fluidly interact with digital and nondigital media, they may be reshaping the boundaries for the impact of information technologies both on play and as play.
>
> (Alper, 2011, p 185)

Research in digital technology and the Reggio approach makes reference to the notion of transmedia, which resonates with the earlier discussion of multimodality in learning and expression.

> Each medium ... orients children to different aspects of the subject matter. Each medium makes certain questions more askable than other questions. And in order to eventually find the solution to any problem, children have to ask of the event many different types of questions. Thus by using a variety of media to represent a single phenomenon, we are helping children ask better questions.
>
> (Forman, 1996, p 57, cited in Alper, 2011, p 187)

Conclusion

Throughout this chapter you have been guided through opportunities to employ digital technologies in relation to expressive arts and design. The term *media* should be expanded to include digital media in its many forms (video, photography, graphics, animation, music, ebooks etc). You were also asked to recognise that digital technologies may be part of the expressive and creative process but not necessarily be the form of the final product. Technologies provide children with new ways to communicate and share their ideas, resonating with the Reggio concept of the hundred languages of children.

Finally, in reading this chapter you will have engaged in reflection on some of the key questions commonly posed (eg by Kashin) and be confident in your pedagogical response to incorporate technology in this area. Kashin (2016) articulated some of these by asking:

- *What is the relationship of technology to children's creativity?*

- *Is there a place for children's expression of creativity through technology?*

- *Should early learning professionals assume that art and creativity can only be expressed with paint, paper, markers, and crayons? Why or why not?*

(Kashin, 2016)

Recommended further reading

- Due for publication in 2017 is a more extensive piece of writing by Sakr, discussing how digital technologies impact upon art-making:

  Sakr, M (2017) *Digital Technologies in Early Childhood Art: Enabling Playful Experiences*. Bloomsbury.

- Barnaby, B and Burghardt, V (2016) Creativity in a Digital Age, in Kaye, L (ed) *Young Children in a Digital Age: Supporting Learning and Development with Technology in Early Years*. London: Routledge. This chapter explores how technology can be used to scaffold children's creativity.

References

Alper, M (2011) Developmentally Appropriate New Media Literacies: Supporting Cultural Competencies and Social Skills in Early Childhood Education. *Journal of Early Childhood Literacy*, 13(2): 175–96.

Barnaby, B and Burghardt, V (2016) Creativity in a Digital Age, in Kaye, L (ed) *Young Children in a Digital Age: Supporting Learning and Development with Technology in Early Years*. London: Routledge.

Belshaw, D (2011) What is 'digital literacy'? [online] Available at: http://neverendingthesis.com/doug-belshaw-edd-thesis-final.pdf (accessed 1 March 2017).

British Educational Communications and Technology Agency (Becta) (2003) Becta ICT research: what the research says about digital video in teaching and learning. [online] Available at: http://miran-danet.ac.uk/wp-content/uploads/2016/04/wtrs_15_digital_video.pdf (accessed 13 March 2017).

British Educational Communications and Technology Agency (Becta) (2005a) *Creativity and Digital Video*.

British Educational Communications and Technology Agency (Becta) (2005b) *Benefits for Students*.

Ching, C, Wang, X, Shih, M and Kedem, Y (2006) Digital Photography and Journals in a Kindergarten-First-Grade Classroom: Toward Meaningful Technology Integration in Early Childhood Education. *Early Education and Development*, 17(3): 347–71.

CISCO (2008) Multimodal learning through media: what the research says. [online] Available at: www.cisco.com/web/strategy/docs/education/Multimodal-Learning-Through-Media.pdf (accessed 1 March 2017).

Department for Education (DfE) (2013) National curriculum in England: computing programmes of study – Key Stages 1 and 2. [online] Available at: www.gov.uk/government/publications/national-curriculum-in-england-computing-programmes-of-study (accessed 1 March 2017).

Department for Education (DfE) (2013) The national curriculum in England framework document. [online] Available at: www.gov.uk/government/uploads/system/uploads/attachment_ data/file/425601/PRIMARY_national_curriculum.pdf (accessed 1 March 2017).

Department for Education (DfE) (2014) Statutory framework for the Early Years Foundation Stage: setting the standards for learning, development and care for children from birth to five. [online] Available at: www.gov.uk/government/uploads/system/uploads/attachment_data/file/335504/EYFS_framework_from_1_September_2014__with_clarification_note.pdf (accessed 1 March 2017).

Hewlett, C and March, C (2015) How Might the iPad Encourage Risk Taking in the Pursuit of Artistic Endeavour? in Sangster, M (ed) *Challenging Perceptions in Primary Education: Exploring Issues in Practice*. London: Bloomsbury, pp 83–5.

Kashin, D (2016) Creative and critical thinking: documentation meets the digital age. [online] Available at: https://tecribresearch.wordpress.com/2016/02/13/creative-and-critical-thinking-documentation-meets-the-digital-age/ (accessed 1 March 2017).

Marsh, J (2006) Emergent Media Literacy: Digital Animation in Early Childhood. *Language and Education*, 20(6): 496–8.

Metcalfe, J, Simpson, D, Todd, I and Toyn, M (2013) *Thinking Through New Literacies for Primary and Early Years*. London: Learning Matters.

Morgan, A and Siraj-Blatchford, J (2013) *Using ICT in the Early Years*. London: Practical Pre-School Books.

Resnick, M (2012) Lifelong Kindergarten. *Cultures of Creativity*, pp 50–2. [online] Available at: web.media.mit.edu/~mres/papers/CulturesCreativityEssay.pdf (accessed 1 March 2017).

Sakr, M (2017) *Digital Technologies in Early Childhood Art: Enabling Playful Experiences*. Bloomsbury.

Sakr, M, Connelly, V and Wild, M (2016) Narrative in Young Children's Digital Art-making. *Journal of Early Childhood Literacy*, 16(3): 289–310.

Savage, M and Barnett, A (2015) *Digital Literacy for Primary Teachers*. Northwich: Critical Publishing.

Standards and Testing Agency (2014a) EYFS profile exemplification for the level of learning and development expected at the end of the EYFS: expressive arts and design. ELG16 – exploring and using media and materials. [online] Available at: www.gov.uk/government/uploads/system/uploads/attachment_data/file/360543/ELG16___Exploring_and_ using_media_and_materials.pdf (accessed 1 March 2017).

Standards and Testing Agency (2014b) EYFS profile exemplification for the level of learning and development expected at the end of the EYFS: expressive arts and design. ELG17 – being imaginative. [online] Available at: www.gov.uk/government/uploads/system/uploads/attachment_data/file/360544/ELG17___Being_imaginative.pdf (accessed 1 March 2017).

Thornton, L and Brunton, P (2010) *Bringing the Reggio Approach to Your Early Years Practice*. Abingdon, Oxfordshire: Routledge.

082421

11 Technologies for inclusion

CHAPTER OUTLINE AND PROFESSIONAL LINKS

This chapter begins by exploring what is meant by the term *inclusion*. In the widest sense, *'inclusion in the early years is about practices which ensure that everyone "belongs": from children and their parents, to staff and any others connected with the setting in some way'* (Nutbrown, 2012, p 58).

Critical question

» *Before reading further consider how you might utilise digital technology to help ensure that* everyone *belongs.*

A key principle in the EYFS framework (DfE, 2014) is that *'every child is a "unique child", who is constantly learning and can be resilient, capable, confident and self-assured'* (p 6). Further, there is an emphasis on practitioners creating an *'enabling environment'* which is responsive to *'individual needs'* (DfE, 2014, p 6). The EYFS framework acknowledges that *'children develop and learn in different ways and at different rates'*. Therefore, inclusive provision means that *every* child is given the opportunity to thrive, *'including children with special educational needs and disabilities'* (SEND) (DfE, 2014, p 6).

Critical question

» *Critically consider the nuances of the terms* inclusion *and* SEND *provided so far. Does inclusive practice only apply to children with identified SEND?*

The SEND Code of Practice is a useful document to become familiar with and Chapter 5 (DfE & DoH, 2015, pp 78–90) is dedicated to early years educators. Key legislation in this area includes the *Children and Families Act* (2014) and the *Equality Act* (2010). Your setting should have *'a clear approach to identifying and responding to SEND'* and you may want to request access to this policy if you are not fully aware of its contents.

'The benefits of early identification are widely recognised – identifying need at the earliest point, and then making effective provision, improves long-term outcomes for children' (DfE & DoH, 2015, p 79). All approaches should be founded on ensuring dignity and respect for children.

This responsibility is articulated in both sets of Teachers' Standards (emphasis added by author):

- **Early Years Teacher Status** (National College for Teaching and Leadership, 2013)
  - Standard 1.2: *'set goals that stretch and challenge children of **all** backgrounds, **abilities** and dispositions'* (p 2);
  - Standard 4: *'plan education and care **taking account** of the **needs of all** children'* (p 3);
  - Standard 5: *'**adapt** education and care to **respond** to the strengths and needs of all children'* (p 4);
  - Standard 5.3: *'demonstrate a clear understanding of the needs of all children, including those with Special Educational Needs and Disabilities, and be able to use and evaluate **distinctive approaches** to engage and support them'* (p 4);
  - Standard 5.5: *'**know when a child is in need of additional support** and how this can be accessed, working in partnership with parents and/or carers and other professionals'* (p 4). This may involve working as part of a *'multi-agency team'* (Standard 8.7, p 5).
- **Teachers' Standards** (DfE, 2011) for the award of **Qualified Teacher Status** cover this aspect of professional practice under Standard 5: *'adapt teaching to respond to the strengths and needs of all pupils'* (p 11);
  - *'know when and how to **differentiate** appropriately, using approaches which enable pupils to be taught effectively'*;
  - *'have a secure understanding of how a range of **factors** can inhibit pupils' ability to learn, and how best to **overcome** these'*;
  - *'demonstrate an awareness of the physical, social and intellectual development of children, and know how to **adapt teaching** to support pupils' education at different stages of development'*;
  - *'have a clear understanding of the needs of all pupils, including those with special educational needs ... those with disabilities; and be able to use and evaluate distinctive **teaching approaches to engage and support them**'*.
  (DfE, 2011, p 11)

Assistive and adaptive technology

You may have encountered the terms *assistive* or *adaptive* technology and they are often used interchangeably. In principle they are different in that everyone might use *assistive* technologies (eg mind mapping software) to perform everyday tasks more efficiently; whereas *adaptive* technologies are those that have been designed or built with a particular *need* in mind (eg a head switch).

- '**assistive technology** *is any object or system that increases or maintains the capabilities of people with disabilities'*;

- '**adaptive technology** *is any object or system that is* **specifically designed** *for the purpose of increasing or maintaining the capabilities of people with disabilities'.*
  (Wikipedia, 2016, Assistive Technology https://en.wikipedia.org/wiki/ Assistive_technology, author's emphasis)

Figure 11.1 includes examples of adaptive technologies; for example, *Big Red Twist Switch* can used when a young child does not have the fine motor dexterity to click a conventional mouse. '*The Big Red offers a 125mm activation surface with tactile and auditory feedback and interchangeable red, yellow, green and blue switch tops*' (Inclusive Technology, 2016). You can also purchase toys that have been adapted to be operated by switches; for example, *Dotty Dalmation*. '*Helpikeys is a programmable membrane keyboard which replaces the traditional keyboard and mouse*' (Inclusive Technology, 2016).

Figure 11.1 *Examples from Inclusive Technology:* Big Red Twist Switch, Switch Adapted Toy – Dotty Dalmatian *and* Helpikeys *(reproduced by permission of Inclusive Technology)*

Savage's (2016) research reported on pre-service teachers' reflections on using technologies for children with SEND in both directions in the teaching and learning exchange. *Input* – where technologies, matched to learners' needs, enabled children to *access* the curriculum. And *output* – where technologies enabled children to *express* their engagement with the curriculum by, for example, offering alternative methods of recording knowledge and understanding. This might include audio recording, photography or film (pp 542–6). Figure 11.2 highlights some of the many possibilities you could explore with children in your care who have SEND. Technology can be an important enabler for young children with SEND. Careful deployment of technologies can transform a *dis*-abling environment to an enabling one.

Critical question

» *Independence,empowerment, dignity and self-respect are fundamental principles in providing an enabling environment and ethos. Consider how technology might support those principles. It may help to recall one or two children you have worked with who have SEND.*

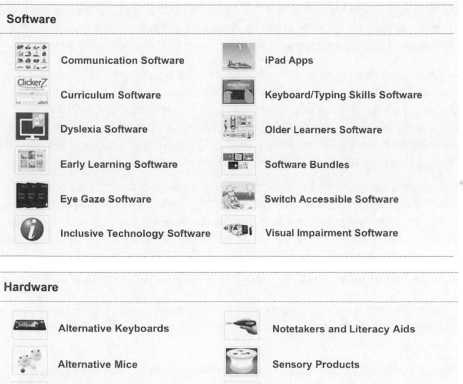

Software

Communication Software	iPad Apps
Curriculum Software	Keyboard/Typing Skills Software
Dyslexia Software	Older Learners Software
Early Learning Software	Software Bundles
Eye Gaze Software	Switch Accessible Software
Inclusive Technology Software	Visual Impairment Software

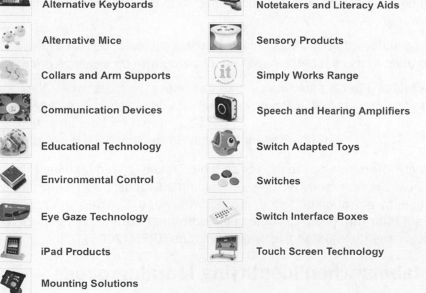

Hardware

Alternative Keyboards	Notetakers and Literacy Aids
Alternative Mice	Sensory Products
Collars and Arm Supports	Simply Works Range
Communication Devices	Speech and Hearing Amplifiers
Educational Technology	Switch Adapted Toys
Environmental Control	Switches
Eye Gaze Technology	Switch Interface Boxes
iPad Products	Touch Screen Technology
Mounting Solutions	

Figure 11.2 *A screenshot of the categories of assistive and adaptive technologies available from* Inclusive Technology *(Inclusive Technology, 2017, www.inclusive.co.uk/shop)*

Recapping technology affordances: personalisation, provisionality and multimodality

In other chapters we have introduced the idea of technology affordances and how these may enhance learning. The most relevant to this chapter are personalisation, provisionality and multimodality.

Most tablets, smart devices and PCs have accessibility options that can be set up and saved (personalised) for individual users. Detailed suggestions are given in the sections below; however, a few general resources you could begin to explore include:

- *Apple's* accessibility support webpage at www.apple.com/uk/accessibility/ covers all of their platforms. For example, iPads contain an extensive range of personalisation options; '*powerful assistive features are built into iPad to complement your vision, hearing, motor skills, learning and literacy*' (Apple, 2016, www.apple.com/uk/accessibility/ipad/). Examples are categorised and include: '*vision, hearing, physical and motor skills, and learning and literacy*'.

- *Microsoft's* Accessibility in Windows 10 at www.microsoft.com/enable/products/ windows10/default.aspx (Microsoft, 2016). Includes explanations of how to use or modify the '*Magnifier to see items on the screen*'; '*text or visual alternative to sounds*'; '*keyboard shortcuts*'; '*hear text read aloud with Narrator*' and '*speech recognition to control your PC*'.

The *provisionality* affordance can be useful to inclusive practice as it can:

- create discrete stages in a process; for example, '*recording initial ideas*' which can be developed, '*reviewed and refined*' and the '*effectiveness of choices evaluated*';

- help children to be confident making bolder choices; '*can take risks as the edit and undo tools enable them to make changes with no evidence of early drafts*';

- scaffold children's creativity as '*they can import pictures*' which they '*adapt by changing colours, pattern, tone and shape to create their own images*'.

(Department for Education and Schools,
Primary National Strategy: Key Features of ICT, 2004)

Multimodality refers to when technology enables teaching and learning to be augmented by '*diagrams, symbols, text, pictures and sound*'. Graphics can be annotated over or accompanied by narration or sound effects. With video, children can pause, restart and replay to set their own pace. Children can create their own recordings, video or audio, to communicate their understanding or observations (DfES, 2004).

Using labels when identifying learning needs

Reflect on your personal experience for a moment, focusing on stereotypes and categorising. There are probably numerous times when you've said to yourself, '*these are the less able children'* or more specifically, something such as *'Matthew's a selective mute'* or *'Jane's the computer wiz'*. But what does this really mean? Does one single ability, ie lower or higher ability, permeate all subjects and aspects of the child's behaviour and might Matthew's label colour your judgement? Bourne (2008) noted that, *'we can be so quick to label him or her that we miss out on other important information that could be helpful'*. What's more, labelling usually focuses on negative characteristics and can feed self-fulfilling prophesies, ie *'when you begin to actively seek behaviours that fit the label's definition'* (Bourne, 2008). Labelling of children, particularly very young children, may conceal as much as it identifies. Nonetheless, when approached sensitively and with a predisposition to re-evaluate in light of the ongoing accumulation of evidence, labels can provide a useful starting point for planning and responding to the individual learning needs of the unique child.

The following sections identify a range of familiar categorisations of learning needs and suggest how you might use digital technology to enhance the quality of learning.

'Children's SEN are generally thought of in the following four broad areas of need and support ...:

- *communication and interaction*
- *cognition and learning*
- *social, emotional and mental health*
- *sensory and/or physical needs'*

(DfE & DoH, 2015, p 85)

It is fundamental to remember that all children are individual and unique and there will not be one perfect solution. Importantly, it is recommended to involve parents/carers and the child when exploring technology options.

Sensory and/or physical needs

Some children may have a SEND that includes or is limited to a single sensory impairment, for example, a visual (VI) or hearing impairment (HI). Other children may have multiple sensory impairments (MSI) (DfE & DoH, 2015, p 98). There are a number of adaptive technology solutions available and suggestions are made below.

Hearing impairment

Keeping ambient noise to a minimum and ensuring your hearing-impaired child sits in an unobstructed position close to the sound source are some of the obvious non-technological strategies. Using Makaton sign language and speaking clearly while looking at the hearing-impaired child will also be useful. Within the digital domain, *assistive listening devices* (ALD) are available, eg to amplify the volume of the teacher's voice using sound loops and hearing aids. A similar type of ALD is an FM system where the teacher typically wears a small microphone and the pupil a small receiver tuned to the same frequency. ASDF (2017) found that children from six months to seven years old with mild to severe hearing loss had delayed language development and that this was exacerbated when hearing aids had not been fitted properly but was *'minimized with early and aggressive intervention'* (Gray, 2015). Other strategies include use of multimodal resources and strategies to accentuate visual and kinaesthetic approaches to teaching.

> *Individuals who are deaf or hard of hearing utilise a variety of assistive tech-nologies that provide them with improved accessibility to information in numerous environments. Most devices either provide* **amplified sound** *or alternate ways to access* **information through vision and/or vibration***. These technologies can be grouped into three general categories:* **hearing technology***,* **alerting devices***, and* **communication support***.*
>
> (Wikipedia, 2016, Assistive Technology https://en.wikipedia.org/wiki/ Assistive_technology; author's emphasis)

Visual impairment

The first port of call is to use the accessibility features of the computer such as changing colours and text size. Mouse trails, screen magnifiers and text-to-speech screen readers can also improve accessibility. You also could consider use of audio books and older chil-dren may benefit from portable electronic Braille note-takers.

> *Examples of assistive technology for visually impairment include screen read-ers, screen magnifiers, Braille embossers, desktop video magnifiers, and voice recorders.*
>
> (Wikipedia, 2016, Assistive Technology, https://en.wikipedia.org/wiki/ Assistive_technology)

With thousands of iPad apps already available, it's useful to have a website dedicated to evaluating apps for supporting visually impaired children. *Wonderbaby.org* from Perkins School for the Blind is one such website. Apps are categorised according to type and usefully include an *Education* category focusing on developing aspects of vision such as developing communication, shape recognition and fine motor skills. There are several apps performing the same function but the app *Answers: Yes/No* is essentially a simple switch with a customisable either/or type response and the children will be motivated to record their own and their friends' responses, eg *'Yeah!'*, *'I said yes'*, *'All right then'* etc. (www.wonderbaby.org/articles/answers-yes-no-app-review). The *My Talking Picture Board* app allows you to create multimodal picture-based stories where you can change the visual complexity by selecting backgrounds as well as number size and the location of displayed images (www.youtube.com/watch?v=2I4VBMeC0ww). The *EDA Play* app helps to develop visual discrimination using different levels and tasks (www.wonderbaby.org/ articles/eda-play-app-review).

Physical needs

A fundamental principle when using digital technology to support children with phys-ical disabilities is that *'the technology should be used to magnify abilities that remain, by bypassing the disabilities as much as possible'* (PDST, no date). A range of assistive technologies are available, including speech recognition software such as *Dragon Dictate* which is useful as an alternative to typing, although children need to be able to read and speak clearly (http://learningworksforkids.com/apps/dragon-dictation/); turning pages can be easier with an ebook; adapted keyboards, joysticks and rollerballs can provide support for shaky fingers (www.assist-it.org.uk/assets/content/disability.htm); devices can be controlled using head pointers and eye blinks. Figure 11.3 shows the *Eye Gaze* solution from Inclusive Technology.

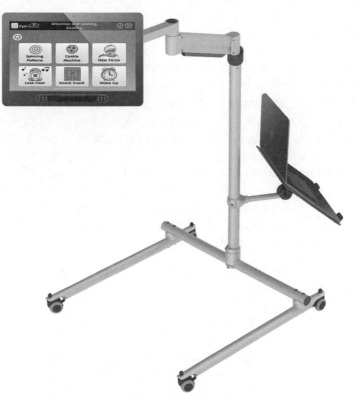

Figure 11.3 All in One Eye Gaze, *www.inclusive.co.uk/all-in-one-eyegaze-education# (repro-duced by permission of Inclusive Technology)*

Communication and interaction

Young children with '*speech, language and communication needs (SLCN) have difficulty in communicating with others*' (DfE & DoH, 2015, p 97). This group may include children with autistic spectrum disorder; Asperger's syndrome and autism. Young children '*are likely to have particular difficulties with social interaction*'; including '*difficulties with lan-guage, communication and imagination, which can impact on how they relate to others*' (DfE & DoH, 2015, p 97).

Autism

Autistic spectrum disorder (ASD) children are more likely to find it difficult to communicate, need support to develop social skills, have limited fine motor skills and a preference for one particular learning style (Edelson no date; Clicker 7, 2016; Cullen and O'Conner 2013). A range of digital technology is available, from mind mapping software such as Kidspiration (www.inspiration.com/Kidspiration) to support planning and self-management through use of humanoid robots such as *Milo*, which supports '*understanding and meaning of emotions and expressions, and demonstrates appropriate social behaviour and responses*' (www.robokindrobots.com/robots4autism-home/). The Autistic Spectrum Disorder Foundation (ASDF, 2017) identified several affordances of iPads that make this technology a useful aid to learning for autistic children: iPads are customisable, which helps meet the needs of the ASD child; as mobile technology, the iPad goes wherever the child is; it's easy to communicate using images; no need to move the eyes from keyboard to screen; and '*apps are easily organised, predictable, and accessible*'. You may find the Accessibility features useful, such as locking the orientation of the screen to prevent this changing automatically which can be distracting. And the *Guided Access* feature allows you to restrict access to different parts of an app, eg where there are several games you might select just one as active and lock the app to keep it open; *Active Touch* allows operation by just one finger as well as allowing you to create customised gestures, useful where fine motor skills are restricted (http://help.apple.com/ipad/10/). Inclusive Technology (2016) supplies a range of '*software to support communication and produce communication and symbol-based resources*'.

Figure 11.4 illustrates some of the range of communication technologies available.

Figure 11.4 Recordable Light Panel, Recordable Thought Cloud *and* Smart/Talk *available from Inclusive Technology (2017, www.inclusive.co.uk/hardware/communicators-and-controllers) (reproduced by permission of Inclusive Technology)*

Critical question

» *What apps can you find to support visual learning styles?*

Cognition and learning

Learning difficulties cover a wide range of needs, including moderate learning dif-ficulties (MLD), severe learning difficulties (SLD), where children are likely to need support in all areas of the curriculum and associated difficulties with mobility and communication, through to profound and multiple learning difficulties (PMLD), where children are likely to have severe and complex learning difficulties as well as a physical disability or sensory impairment.

(DfE & DoH, 2015, pp 97–8)

'Specific learning difficulties (SpLD), affect one or more specific aspects of learning. This encompasses a range of conditions such as dyslexia, dyscalculia and dyspraxia' (DfE & DoH, 2015, p 98).

Dyslexia

Dyslexia may begin to be evident as early as three years old so you'll need to be alert to early signs such as trailing speech development, not recognising rhyming words and non-language indicators such as putting shoes on the wrong feet and seeming to be inattentive (BDA, no date1). Crivelli (2013, p 1) suggested that *'technology can provide the necessary risk taking, patient, multi-sensory environment many Dyslexic learners need'* and provides an extensive list of affordances of dyslexia-friendly software such as clear spoken instructions when the mouse points to or clicks on the text, uncluttered screens and easy navigation. The British Dyslexia Association (BDA, no date2) extends this list using the three broad categories of *Text*, *Formats* and *Website design*. For example, when thinking about media you may need to change the colour of the background screen on PowerPoints, Word documents and interactive whiteboard screens; you may need to for-mat documents so they can be read more easily by screen-reading software; and if you need to prepare website resources, moving text is more difficult to read.

The popular Crick Software *Clicker 7* was originally developed for use with a range of special needs children but has also established a place supporting learning across the entire primary age and ability range. The software and apps are essentially a multimodal word bank that can be customised for all ages, abilities and different learning needs, including children at pre-reading and pre-writing stages. Clicker 7 provides extensive sup-port for children with dyslexia including help to *'organise and plan their writing'*, a *voice notes* tool *'giving children with dyslexia a valuable opportunity to capture their thoughts without being distracted by the mechanics of writing'*, *'realistic speech feedback'*, *'writing support grids tailored to each child's learning needs'* and a *'Dyslexia font'* specifically designed for children with dyslexia (Clicker 7, 2016).

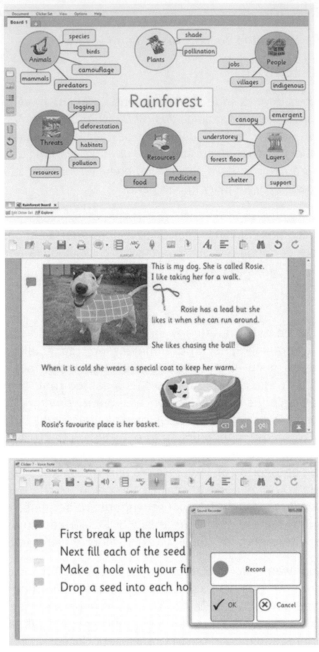

Figure 11.5 *Screenshots from* Clicker 7 *by Crick (reproduced by permission of Crick Software)*

Social, emotional and mental health difficulties

Understood is a website which aims to provide support for parents of children from pre-school and older in relation to a range of concerns including attention deficit, hyperactivity and social skills (www.understood.org/en). Technologies that help children express themselves may be particularly important. '*"Coping With Chaos" is a story based program about emotions and behaviour, suitable for children with emotional and behavioural difficulties*' (www.inclusive.co.uk/coping-with-chaos-p2173).

English as an additional language (EAL)

It is important not to confuse *language delay*, *language disorder* and *selective mutism* (ASLHA, 2016; MHS, 2016) which relate to SEND, with the *silent period* which many EAL children go through as they listen and observe before starting to risk speaking. Bligh and Drury (2015) emphasised that the silent period is '*a crucial time for self-mediated learning within the early-years community of practice*' (p 259). Open-ended and more creative activities can be very supportive during this silent period as there is no right answer and following instructions precisely is less critical to success. It's also worth noting that the Early Learning Goals (ELGs), apart from the communication and language prime area, can be assessed in any language. These considerations suggest that you provide digital technology supporting creative activities and art-based apps/software, some of which may use the child's first language, as well as video games where signs of success are intuitively easy to grasp and can be associated with words of praise repeated frequently.

They are easily overlooked but you will be able to find YouTube video versions of popular stories for children narrated in a range of different languages, such as *Little Red Riding Hood* narrated in Hindi, www.youtube.com/watch?v=haRx1BOP_NI; Spanish, www.youtube.com/watch?v=Wix_dP5kNSU; and Polish, www.youtube.com/watch?v=SyxGEz7C28M. You'll also find that numerous interactive apps are available in a variety of languages, eg *Animal Pants* for the iPad where children match clothes to animals in countries with different climates, which is available in English, Spanish, French and German (www.youtube.com/watch?v=261PObczFIU). And the *Kinder Town* search engine for apps is available in English, French, German, Italian, Japanese, Korean, Polish, Russian and Spanish.

CASE STUDY

Although the following innovative project occurred in Belgium it could equally well have happened in the UK or anywhere with a broadband internet connection and video conferencing facilities such as Skype or Windows Messenger.

> *Laura is a 6-year-old girl living in a rural town. She started her first year of primary education in the school year 2010–2011. Since the age of 3 she went to kindergarten in the same school, but then got seriously ill, which meant that she had a series of hospital and recovery periods at home. There she received instruction from her kindergarten teacher and from a teacher for temporary education at home (4 lessons per week). During her illness in the last year of kindergarten, the school management team ... decided to initiate the [streaming video] project at the start of Laura's first year of primary education, in combination with teaching at home. The necessary equipment and broadband connection were installed in Laura's home and classroom; Laura, her parents, teachers and classmates were trained in the use of ... the system and Laura started joining classes from home.*

The ... system not only allowed her to observe the teaching, but also to read and print the content of the blackboard and to participate in the teaching and learning process, as well as chatting online with her school friends after class time.

(Watkins et al, 2011, p 39)

Commentary on case study

Video conferencing is easy to set up and use and supports participation where actual presence in the classroom is not possible. In the case study, this was a positive learning experience for both Laura and the children in her class. As is to be expected, the computer screen was a slight distraction for the class to start with but soon became integrated into the daily routine. Watkins et al (2011) commented that video conferencing used in this way *'can contribute to the learner's healing by supporting a goal oriented motivation and diverting the learner's focus away from illness and its consequences, to a more 'normal' life'* (p 42).

International perspective

CALL (Communication, Access, Literacy and Learning) Scotland was founded in 1983 and is both a *'Research and Development centre'* and a *'working Service unit'* funded by the Scottish Goverment (www.callscotland.org.uk/home/). They offer a range of services including; *Specialist Information and Expert Advice* and *Assistive Technology Loans and Technical Support*, enabling users to try out devices before purchase. What is particularly impressive is the holistic support provided to the setting, child, professionals and parents/guardian; from assessment of need, to trialling of solutions matched to need and provision of technologies. There are several case studies that are thought-provoking to read and convey how well-matched technology has enabled a child to make progress and express themselves.

- Ella's story at www.callscotland.org.uk/about/case-studies/ella/. *'Ella is a 5 year old girl who communicates using a combination of vocalisation, gesture, pointing to symbols, and her own gestures/signs. However, it is very difficult to understand her communication out of context'*. A number of iPad apps are explored in partnership between Ella, her mum and experts at CALL Scotland.

Conclusion

This chapter has suggested taking a sensitive and responsive approach in order to enhance the experience of belonging. All children are unique individuals and this chapter has considered the value that digital technology can contribute to the enabling environment when used as part of an overall approach to responding to individual learning needs.

Recommended further reading

- *Abilitynet* is a charity which aims to support educators, children and families use technology. There are a number of free factsheets and they can provide individual services: www.abilitynet.org.uk.

- *Inclusive Technology* is an online retailer for inclusive technology products, software and hardware, and well worth a browse: www.inclusive.co.uk.

  Inclusive Technology provides … software, switches and computer access devices, simple communication aids, eye gaze and assistive technology for learners with a physical disability, sensory impairment or learning difficulty.

  They also produce a range of inclusive apps: www.inclusive.co.uk/apps.

  - Booth, T and Ainscow, M (2002) *Index for Inclusion*. Centre for Studies on Inclusive Education. [online] Available at: www.eenet.org.uk/resources/docs/Index%20English.pdf.

- Pinterest page for SEND and digital technology: https://uk.pinterest.com/pin/514747432383339261.

- Helen Caldwell (University of Northampton) has a detailed collection of *pins* on Pinterest including:

  - *Computing and SEND, iPads for SEND, SEN Resources* and *Technology supporting literacy difficulties* to list a few examples. https://uk.pinterest.com/helencaldwel.

- Special iApps: www.specialiapps.org/en-us/apps-for-special-needs.html.

- Watkins, A, Tokareva, N and Turner, M (2011) *ICTs for Education for People with Disabilities: Review of Innovative Practice*, UNESCO. [online] Available at: www.european-agency.org/sites/default/files/ICTs-with-cover.pdf.

References

American Speech-Language-Hearing Association (ASHA) (2016) Selective mutism. [online] Available at: www.asha.org/public/speech/disorders/SelectiveMutism.htm (accessed 1 March 2017).

ASDF (2017) Why the iPad is such a helpful learning tool for children with autism. [online] Available at: www.myasdf.org/site/media-center/articles/why-the-ipad-is-such-a-helpful-learning-tool-for-children-with-autism/ (accessed 1 March 2017).

British Dyslexia Association (BDA) (no date1) Indicators of dyslexia. [online] Available at: www.bdadyslexia.org.uk/parent/indication-of-dyslexia (accessed 1 March 2017).

British Dyslexia Association (BDA) (no date2) Dyslexia style guide. [online] Available at: www.bdadyslexia.org.uk/common/ckeditor/filemanager/userfiles/About_Us/policies/Dyslexia_Style_Guide.pdf (accessed 1 March 2017).

Bligh, C and Drury, R (2015) Perspectives on the 'Silent Period' for Emergent Bilinguals in England. *Journal of Research in Childhood*, 29(2): 259–74.

Bourne, L (2008) Is labelling kids a mistake? *Montessori for Everyone*. [online] Available at: www.blog.montessoriforeveryone.com/is-labeling-kids-a-mistake.html (accessed 1 March 2017).

Caldwell, H (2016) Helen Caldwell (Pinterest boards). [online] Available at: https://uk.pinterest.com/helencaldwel/ (accessed 1 March 2017).

Clicker 7 (2016) Support for children with dyslexia. [online] Available at: www.cricksoft.com/uk/products/clicker/special-needs/dyslexia.aspx (accessed 1 March 2017).

Crivelli, B (2013) Using Technology to support dyslexic pupils (British Dyslexia Association. Dyslexia Friendly Schools Pack. Technology Supplement.) [online] Available at: www.bdadyslexia.org.uk/common/ckeditor/filemanager/userfiles/Services/QM/Technology-for-Literacy-2013.pdf (accessed 1 March 2017).

Cullen, C and O'Conner, G (2013) Using iPads to Support Students with Autism Spectrum Disorders. *Spectronics Inclusive Learning Technologies*. [online] Available at: www.spectronics.com.au/blog/resource/using-ipads-to-support-students-with-autism-spectrum-disorders/ (accessed 1 March 2017).

Department for Education (DfE) (2011) Teachers' standards. [online] Available at: www.gov.uk/government/uploads/system/uploads/attachment_data/file/301107/Teachers__Standards.pdf (accessed 1 March 2017).

Department for Education (DfE) (2014) Statutory framework for the Early Years Foundation Stage: setting the standards for learning, development and care for children from birth to five. [online] Available at: www.gov.uk/government/uploads/system/uploads/attachment_data/file/335504/EYFS_framework_from_1_September_2014__with_clarification_note.pdf (accessed 1 March 2017).

Department for Education and Schools (2004) *Primary National Strategy: Key Features of ICT*. London.

Department for Education & Department of Health (DfE & DoH) (2015) Special educational needs and disability code of practice: 0 to 25 years – statutory guidance for organisations which work with and support children and young people who have special educational needs or disabilities. [online] Available at: www.gov.uk/government/uploads/system/uploads/attachment_data/file/398815/SEND_Code_of_Practice_January_2015.pdf (accessed 1 March 2017).

Edelson, S (no date) Learning styles and autism. *Autism Research Institute*. [online] Available at: www.autism.com/understanding_learning (accessed 1 March 2017).

Gray, L (2015) Helping children hear better. *Iowa Now*. [online] Available at: https://now.uiowa.edu/2015/10/helping-children-hear-better (accessed 1 March 2017).

Inclusive Technology (2017) Big red twist switch. [online] Available at: www.inclusive.co.uk/Index.aspx?Path= product-reviews&Params=big-red-twist-p2544 (accessed 13 April 2017).

Michigan Health Service (MHS) (2016) Speech and language delay and disorder. *University of Michigan Health System*. [online] Available at: www.med.umich.edu/yourchild/topics/speech.htm (accessed 1 March 2017).

National College for Teaching and Leadership (2013) Teachers' standards (early years). [online] Available at: www.gov.uk/government/uploads/system/uploads/attachment_data/file/211646/Early_Years_Teachers__Standards.pdf (accessed 1 March 2017).

Nutbrown, C (2012) Early years for everyone, teach nursery. [online] Available at: www.teachearlyyears.com/images/uploads/article/inclusion-in-early-years-settings.pdf (accessed 1 March 2017).

Savage, M (2016) Mapping Pre-service Teachers' Evolving Information and Communication Technologies Pedagogy. *Technology, Pedagogy and Education*, 25(5): 533–54.

12 Safeguarding and welfare

CHAPTER OUTLINE AND PROFESSIONAL LINKS

This chapter will recap and extend your professional understanding of the safeguarding issues that revolve around employing digital technologies. Practitioners and settings will hold detailed information about children digitally and you should be aware of best practice and legal requirements related to storage and access. Throughout, the rights of the child, safeguarding and confidentiality protocols are considered paramount. This chapter will provide a holistic overview of these rights and responsibilities for all parties, including children, practitioners, outside agencies, parents and guardians. Cloud-based services, for sharing progress and development with parents, are becoming increasingly popular and offer many benefits; however, their use must be accompanied by an understanding of safeguarding protocols. Are you aware of the safeguarding features built in to systems such as *Tapestry* and *2 Build a Profile*? Have you thought about whether or not personal devices should be used in your setting? In the event of iPads/tablets going missing, how safe are the stored contents? Fortunately, there is detailed advice available on recommended protocols (and requirements) from key bodies including Ofsted (2016), the National Crime Agency, the Local Safeguarding Children Board and the National Day Nurseries Association (NDNA). This chapter will focus your awareness of the requirements, within the EYFS framework and the Teachers' Standards, which have a digital safeguarding dimension. Guidance will be given to assist you in reviewing your own practice and how to respond to any concerns you may have about observed practices. Sample policies covering the use of personal devices (eg mobile phones and iPads) will be critically reviewed.

The chapter also aims to consider your personal welfare and safeguarding. Have you thought about your own professional online reputation? Have you experienced cyber-bullying or inappropriate contact from (ex)colleagues or parents? The chapter offers guidance on reviewing your personal online professional reputation and/or profile and addressing any privacy issues. As a professional it is often wise to differentiate between personal and professional digital personas.

A final point is that safeguarding concerns can, understandably, make people feel nervous about using technologies and some may feel a desire to avoid using it to be 'safe'. However, this is unhelpful and potentially can have the opposite effect. Throughout this book it is acknowledged that digital technologies are a daily part of children's lives and can enrich and enhance learning. With both adults and children, the key is about understanding. If an individual has a robust understanding of how a technology operates, they can carry out an informed risk assessment, put measures in place to negate risk and make empowered learning and teaching decisions. Are children in the EYFS too young to be learning about online safety?

Professional responsibilities and rights

Within the EYFS Framework, the Department for Education (2014) noted that the *'safeguarding and welfare requirements'* are *'designed to help providers create high quality settings which are welcoming, safe and stimulating, and where children are able to enjoy learning and grow in confidence'* (p 16). For the purposes of this chapter you should consider the *'space'* to be both the physical setting but also associated digital and online presence, whether this is administrative or communicative (ie with parents or outside agencies). Your setting, and those working within it, are required to *'take all necessary steps to keep children safe and well'* (p16).

Policies and procedures in your setting *must* cover the technologies in use, training and best practice including:

- *'the use of mobile phones and cameras in the setting'* (DfE, 2014, p 16). In reality this applies to any device or technology capable of capturing or sharing images, videos or audio recordings involving children. Nuances to be considered include day-to-day practice as well as special events or visits off-site. People to be considered include: yourself, colleagues, visitors, parents, external agencies and contractors on site.

- The *'setting'* managers or proprietors have an obligation to ensure that all staff members are aware of the safeguarding policy and receive appropriate training at induction and throughout their employment (DfE, 2014, pp 16, 20). It is important to note the continuous nature of this requirement for the setting to provide adequate training. Technologies and online services continue to evolve and policies and training need to reflect this.

- Each member of staff has a duty to report concerns about colleagues, including *'inappropriate sharing of images'* (DfE, 2014, p 16).

- Risk assessment and management of risk is a continuous process (DfE, 2014, p 28).

Both sets of Teachers' Standards also highlight the importance of safeguarding and welfare (emphasis added by author):

- The **Teachers' Standards (Early Years)** (National College for Teaching and Leadership, 2013) make reference in standard 7 to the requirement to '*safeguard and promote the welfare of children, and provide a safe learning environment*' (NCTL, 2013, p 4).

  - **Standard 7.1** *Know and act upon the **legal requirements and guidance** on health and safety, **safeguarding** and promoting the welfare of the child.*

  - **Standard 7.2** *Establish and **sustain** a safe environment and employ practices that promote children's health and safety.*

  - **Standard 7.3** *Know and understand **child protection policies and procedures,** recognise when a child is in danger or at risk of abuse, and know how to act to protect them.*

    (NCTL, 2013, p 4)

- The **Teachers' Standards (Qualified Teacher Status)** make direct reference to '**Personal and professional conduct**' (DfE, 2011, p 14, Part Two):

  - '*Teachers uphold public trust in the profession and maintain high standards of ethics and behaviour, **within and outside school**';*

  - *...at all times observing **proper boundaries** appr opriate to a teacher's professional position;*

  - *...having regard for the need to **safeguard pupils' well-being***;

  - *Teachers must have proper and professional regard for the ethos, **policies and practices** of the school...;*

  - *Teachers must have an understanding of, and always act within, the statutory frameworks which set out their **professional duties** and **responsibilities.***

    (DfE, 2011, p 14, Part Two)

The Office for Standards in Education, Children's Services and Skills (Ofsted) Inspection Guidance

Ofsted's (2016) guidance, detailed in *Inspecting Safeguarding in Early Years, Education and Skills Settings,* stated that '*safeguarding is not just about protecting children, learners and vulnerable adults from deliberate harm, neglect and failure to act. It relates to broader aspects of care and education, including: ... online safety and associated issues*' (Ofsted, 2016, pp 5–6). Further, the Ofsted inspection framework for safeguarding (2016) makes direct reference to *online bullying* (p 5), *online safety* (p 6), *e-safety education* (p 11), the *robustness of systems in place to protect children being exposed to harmful online material* (p 12) and *awareness of reporting strategies.*

Many large or local authority settings will purchase an approved, filtered internet service for their setting. However, all settings are required to demonstrate that their internet service provision includes *'appropriate filters'* and that *'monitoring systems are in place to protect learners from potentially harmful online material'* (Ofsted, 2016, p 12).

Theoretical perspectives and pedagogical links

This chapter will now address aspects from both the Teachers' Standards and Ofsted inspection guidance to ensure you have adequate knowledge and understanding to continue using technologies in a safe and responsible manner. Any policies and procedure in your setting should be aligned to best practice and inspection models at both the local and national level.

Information and records

In your daily practice you will contribute information and data, about the young children in your care, to the settings information and data storage systems. These records may be part of both administrative systems and working documents on the child's learning and development. Increasingly, a portion of, or the entirety of, these records will be digitised. These detailed records are an essential part of *'the safe and efficient management of the setting, and to help ensure the needs of all children are met'* (DfE, 2014, p 29). These records should be *'easily accessible and available'*; however, *'confidential information and records about staff and children must be held securely and only accessible and available to those who have a right or professional need to see them'* (DfE, 2014, p 29). It is equally as important to ensure the security of digital records as it is physical records and this aspect is referred to in both the *Data Protection Act (DPA) 1998* and the *Freedom of Information Act 2000* (DfE, 2014, p 29). It may be tempting to assume that responsibility for digital security, whether based in the cloud or held on devices, is the responsibility only of senior managers but *'all staff'* must *'understand the need to protect the privacy of the children in their care as well the legal requirements that exist to ensure that information relating to the child is handled in a way that ensures confidentiality'* (DfE, 2014, p 29). This responsibility also extends to a *'reasonable period of time after they have left the provision'* (DfE, 2014, p 29).

Critical question

» *Do you collect data or information about children in your care using portable devices; for example, cameras and tablet devices? Are you aware of the safeguarding protocols related to the child's digital footprint created by you and your colleagues? Are the procedures robust and do they cater for unexpected events; for example, theft? How involved are children in this process?*

Data protection

When thinking about digital data storage, it is important to identify all stages in the process; for example, from taking an image or video to it being embedded within a digital profile tool. Beyond that, how secure is the system holding the data? How do you balance cyber-security with accessibility? Do protocols and levels of access vary for external agencies, parents and colleagues? You should always follow the policy in place in your setting – if you think it is inadequate, you have a professional responsibility to bring this to the manager's or owner's attention alongside constructive suggestions for improvement.

Capturing, storing and sharing digital data

Mobile phones are often explicitly mentioned in setting policies and it is worth exploring this aspect in more depth. Remember that many of these points are equally relevant for any device capable of capturing images and recordings and/or connecting to the internet.

Personal mobile phones

Legally there is not an outright ban on personal mobile phones. However, Ofsted (2016) require '*leaders of early years settings*' to '*implement the required policies with regard to the safe use of mobile phones and cameras in settings*' (p 8). We outlined previously, in relation to the professional standards, the requirement to be aware of and to adhere to setting safeguarding policies.

CASE STUDY

The following article by Parkes (2016) was featured in *Nursery World*: 'Pre-school fights Ofsted downgrade on mobile phone use'.

> *Managers of a preschool stripped of its Outstanding status after reported failings with mobile phone safeguarding claim that they had a formal policy with which parents were happy.... XXX nursery are challenging Ofsted's Inadequate rating, which seemingly resulted from the nursery sending photos of children to parents with their signed consent. ...The contention centres around a photo of a child sent to a mother's mobile by XXX, which the nursery claimed was part of the setting's practice of reassuring parents of their children's well-being ... The inspector went on to report that the children were 'not safeguarded effectively' at the setting. This was said to be because, 'Staff use personal mobile phones to photograph children at the setting, such as for observations and sending messages to parents.*
>
> (Parkes, 2016)

Commentary on case study

This case study highlights the importance of clear and unambiguous protocols, agreed upon by managers, employees and parents, to protect all parties. The article also included a statement from Jo Baranek, NDNA's lead early years adviser:

> *childcare workers should 'never use their own mobile phones to take, store or transmit photos of children'. She added, 'If pictures are being taken for pre-determined*

purposes, with the relevant parental consent, staff should use a camera, tablet or phone that belongs to the setting and is securely kept there. Managers should be checking and monitoring what photos have been taken and any emails or social media activity undertaken. Images should not be stored on devices. Any needed for the longer term should be moved to a secure computer drive location.'

(Parkes, 2016)

In summary:

- You are advised not to use your personal devices in the setting.
- There should be clarity and agreement about why images or recordings are being made.
- Parents/guardians should be aware of procedures for taking and storing images and recordings and consent in writing should be obtained.
- Appropriately robust and agreed upon systems should be used for storing and sharing digital artefacts.
- Guidance should be explicit in regard to the further sharing of images and recordings where other children are present.

An online search will reveal a number of example policies from other settings; you may wish to review several and compare and contrast with the policy in place at your setting.

Example of a policy relating to mobile devices:

- Windmill City Farm Ltd (www.windmillhillcityfarm.org.uk/wp-content/uploads/policies/cfs/CF21 Photography-Video-Mobile-Phone-and-e-Safety-Policy.pdf).

This example offers guidance on the important question of how to manage the scenario when a recorded observation of a child features other children, either interacting with the focus child or in the periphery.

Where photos are taken of children interacting/playing with each other, these will be used in the appropriate children's learning diaries as these photos will provide evidence of their developing social skills. If this raises any concerns/issues please notify a staff member.

(www.windmillhillcityfarm.org.uk/wp-content/uploads/policies/cfs/CF21-Photography-Video-Mobile-Phone-and-e-Safety-Policy.pdf)

Cloud-based record keeping systems

Two popular online learning journals for early years are *Tapestry* and *2Build a Profile*. Typically, photos, videos and text descriptions are uploaded by practitioners on a day-to-day basis. There are procedures for parents and guardians to sign up for access records relating to their child(ren). Access can usually also be gained via associated apps. The benefits of these detailed records are typically greatly appreciated by parents.

A media-rich chronological record of a child's learning and development over time is created. Most systems can also be transferred to new settings for continuity. However, it is important to scrutinize the safeguarding features of products and services, especially as data is hosted outside of the setting and can potentially be accessed by third parties. You might want to ask who 'owns' this data, how secure is third-party storage, and what rights does the child retain in respect of their data? These are interesting and complex questions for all educators. They are not intended to be alarmist questions but reflect some cultural queries emerging relating to ethics, ownership and the rights of young children in relation to their digital footprint. If you carry out online searches on the topic of *safeguarding* and the product name, you will see that practitioners and teachers are discussing these issues and asking for advice on discussion forums. The products and services often have a range of settings that managers can select; for example, whether staff can access the system away from the setting.

- **Tapestry** is an '*online learning journal, Tapestry helps educators and parents to record, track and celebrate children's progress in early years education*' (2016, https://tapestry.info).

  - Example from Long Wittenham Pre-School: a policy relating to the use of Tapestry in a pre-school setting (www.longwittenhampreschool.co.uk/wp-content/pdfs/policies-2016-02/1-9-Online-Learning-Journals.pdf).

  - Example from Sandhurst Nursery School: a policy relating to the use of Tapestry in a nursery setting (www.sandhurstnurseryschool.co.uk/Policies/Tapestry%20On.pdf)

- **2 Build a Profile** comes from the popular 2Simple brand (www.2simple.com/2buildaprofile).

Critical questions

Figure 12.1 includes an extract from 2Simple's website relating to security and privacy (www.2simple.com/2buildaprofile) for you to read and analyse which issues are (or are not) addressed. A number of ethical *and* safeguarding *questions have been introduced into the discussion so far; for example:*

» *What security protocols are available? (safeguarding)*

» *Who has access to the records within and beyond the setting? (safeguarding)*

» *Who 'owns' the data? (ethical)*

» *What rights does the child retain in respect of their data? (ethical)*

A policy statement should robustly address all safeguarding questions. However, the ethical questions are more challenging and complex to answer. Critically reflect on your response to these ethical questions.

Security and Privacy

Privacy

- *During normal use of the app, evidence photos and attainment data is transmitted from the app to our data centres.*

- *This data is available on the Web Management Suite ONLY to users within the school or setting with the appropriate password.*

- *All staff using the app should be subject to their organisation's policy on "Acceptable use of Electronic Communications". An example policy is available on request.*

- *Children featured on evidence photos should be subject to the organisation's standard "Parental Permission for Photos" policy. An example policy is available on request.*

- *The data stored in our data centres is used for no other purpose than to provide the services available in the app and associated website (www.2buildaprofile.com).*

- *CRB-Checked 2Simple staff may access your online account to assist with support queries. This permission can be switched off in the settings area on the Web Management Suite.*

Security

- *To avoid unauthorised access, the app can be locked with a user-defined PIN code.*

- *The app can be remotely deactivated should a device be lost or stolen.*

- *All data is held securely in the app and in our datacentres within the British Isles.*

- *All email transfers use industry standard encryption. PDFs sent by email can only be read using a PIN code when you protect your app with a code.*

- *The Web Management Suite uses industry standard encryption.*

- *Website encryption is performed using a Globalsign secure certificate.*

Figure 12.1 *An extract from 2Simple's website relating to security and privacy (www.2simple. com/2buildaprofile)*

Online safety education

The introduction to this chapter ended with the question as to whether online safety education has a place in early years education. If yes, at what age and what form should it take? In January 2017, the Professional Association for Childcare and Early Years (PACEY) posed this question to its members on an online blog:

> *The Children's Commissioner for England has stated that it is time to teach online and internet safety from as young as four years old. CEOP Command (formerly the Child Exploitation and Online Protection Centre) state that half of 3- and 4-year-olds are using tablets.*

> (PACEY, 2017)

In Chapter 4 a brief overview was given of how online safety education is a requirement within the national curriculum for computing. At Key Stage 1 pupils will be taught to:

use technology safely and respectfully, keeping personal information private; iden-tify where to go for help and support when they have concerns about content or contact on the internet or other online technologies.

(DfE, 2013)

However, with careful consideration the empowerment process of equipping young learn-ers with the knowledge, understanding and skills to be digitally literate, safe and respon-sible can begin earlier. Ofsted (2016) clearly stated, '*In relation to early years, inspectors should consider how staff promote young children's understanding of how to keep them-selves safe from relevant risks and how this is monitored across the provision*' (p 35). Across educational age phases, Ofsted (2016) considered that '*the term "online safety" reflects a widening range of issues associated with technology and a user's access to content, contact with others and behavioural issues*' (p 6). Further, Ofsted will look for evidence that '*action is taken to ensure that children are taught about safeguarding risks, including online risks*' (p 11). As age appropriate, '*inspectors should include online safety in their discussions with children and learners (covering topics such as online bullying and safe use of the internet and social media)*' (p 15).

Fortunately, there are already some high-quality resources available. Well-known exam-ples include:

- The *Hector's World* cartoons are part of CEOP's (National Crime Agency – Child Exploitation and Online Protection Centre) *Thinkuknow* series and can be accessed at www.thinkuknow.co.uk/5_7/hectorsworld/. There are cartoons introducing components of online safety education in a manner accessible to young children in early years settings. Accompanying guidance notes are available for educators.

    Hector's World offers an engaging group of animated characters, with whom children 2–10 years old can form strong emotional bonds and use as positive role models. The adventures of these characters can be the 'building blocks' of cybercitizenship education, especially when viewed and discussed with the guidance of a teacher, parent, or youth group leader.
    (Hector's World Ltd, www.thinkuknow.co.uk/5_7/
    hectorsworld/Credits/)

- *Lee and Kim's Adventures: Animal Magic* is aimed at five-, six- and seven-year-olds and develops the foundational concepts of online safety further. These are also part of the *Thinkuknow* series; the cartoon and resources can be accessed at www.thinkuknow.co.uk/5_7/.

Critical question

» *After watching the* Hector's World *cartoons can you identify which online safety concepts are being introduced? Critically review the aspects that are, in your opinion, handled well or otherwise. What misconceptions could young children pick up? How would you support children discussing these aspects?*

Online safety education is a complex issue and sensitivity is needed. However, it would be difficult to argue that foundational concepts of digital literacy should not be addressed from the outset. For example, many young children will experience adopting an avatar or character in games and can be supported to develop the awareness that these personas are not exact representations of real people. This does not need to be addressed in an overwhelming or scare-tactic approach.

Digital footprints and online professional reputation

This section focuses on reviewing your personal digital footprint and considering whether this enhances or detracts from your online professional reputation. It is easy to envisage prospective employers, colleagues and possibly parents looking you up online. The Teachers' Standards make reference to conduct within and beyond the setting. Savage and Barnett (2015) detailed that *'you need to feel confident that anything publicly accessible online complements your role in a position of trust educating children'* (Savage and Barnett, 2015, p 121). Think carefully about your privacy settings and the temptation to let off steam at the end of a hard day at work! The Open University (2014) defined digital footprints as:

> *everything on the internet that is about you. This could include: a profile on Facebook or MySpace; photographs that you, your friends or family have posted online; anything you have written or that has been written about you, for instance on discussion boards, blogs, or in articles. We are all being encouraged to put aspects of ourselves and our lives online, and much of this content is freely available to view. Each time we add something about ourselves on the internet we enlarge our own digital footprint.*
>
> (Open University, 2014)

Critical question

» *Should you ever accept or initiate 'friendship' requests with parents on social media platforms? Carefully consider the potential issues that may arise and clarify for yourself what boundaries you feel should be in place.*

Auditing your profile and privacy settings

How aware are you of your digital footprint? The Careers service at the Open University suggested undertaking the following activities:

> *You should first check what others can see about you. Search for your name using Google or other search engines and see what information already exists about you. Repeat the search regularly using services such as Google Alerts which give automatic updates. Although you may not have added anything new, your friends and family might have.*
>
> (Open University, 2014)

Research projects and training assignments

If you are currently studying, training or enrolled in formal continuing professional development courses, you will often be asked to reflect on your professional practice in seminars and assignments.

Critical question

» *What rights to privacy do children, colleagues and employers have in relation to your studies or activities? Is it ethical to be critical if confidentiality is maintained?*

Savage and Barnett (2015) offer this generic guidance, but emphasise that detailed consultation should take place with managers at the setting in question:

> *On all occasions reference to school-based experiences in external documents of any form must be anonymous to respect individual privacy. The school or organisation, children, staff and parents must not be identifiable even if you are being complementary rather than giving a professional critique. If the scope of what you intend using digitally captured data for goes beyond the scope or remit of what the school has agreed with parents, specific parental consent must be sought.*
>
> (Savage and Barnett, 2015, p 131)

International perspective

The international work of Third et al (2014) reported in the publication *Children's Rights in the Digital Age* concur with the emphasis globally on empowering children. Third et al argued that *'ensuring that all children are safe online requires approaches that promote digital literacy, resilience and cyber savvy'* (2014, p 6). As educators *'it is necessary for us to examine how this changing environment impacts the wellbeing and development of children and their rights'* (2014, p 6). As educators, parents and civic members across global boundaries we must involve and listen to children about their digital experiences.

> *It is only in partnership that we can reach consensus on how to create a safe, open, accessible, affordable and secure digital world. Critically, children and young people's profound insight must help inform, shape and drive this goal – which needs to focus on equity of access, safety for all, digital literacy across generations, identity and privacy, participation and civic engagement.*
>
> (Third et al, 2014, p 6)

Third et al confirmed the importance of digital literacy education if children are truly to be heard and have the opportunity *'to both imagine and enact their rights in the digital age'* (2014, p 35).

Critical question

Third et al (2014) refer to Collier's (2012) conceptualisation of digital literacy as comprising both 'technical and higher order evaluative skills'; specifically, children having:

- *'**Technical literacy**' – 'successfully navigate technologies';*

- *'**Media literacy**' – 'make judgments about the quality and reliability of online sources';*

- *'**Social literacy**' – understand 'the social norms that apply'.*

(Collier, 2012, as cited by Third et al, 2014, p 35)

The synergy between the three forms is crucial for impact but in an an early years context the development of these capabilities might take place as bite-size chunks that are developmentally appropriate.

» *Consider each of the forms in turn and reflect on how you have recently engaged in an interaction with a child that fostered the development of these literacies. How could you extend those opportunities further?*

Conclusion

This chapter has taken a careful look at both your personal and professional use of digital technologies in relation to safeguarding and welfare in an early years context. You have been prompted to reflect on technical and ethical aspects of deploying digital technologies in day-to-day practice, whether administrative or related to teaching and learning. Critical questions have asked you to focus on the rights of children in relation to their digital footprints and to clarify your principles for respecting their rights. The focus has not been on scaremongering but on proposing an informed understanding of functionality and adopting safe practices.

Recommended further reading and product reviews

- If you would like to develop your knowledge, understanding and professional status relating to online safety you may be interested in this affordable online course offered in partnership between the National Crime Agency's CEOP Command and the NSPCC – *Keeping Children Safe Online (KCSO),* www. thinkuknow.co.uk/Teachers/KCSO/.

- Similarly, should you wish to develop your online safety knowledge beyond early years you may wish to look at the resources available on Childnet in relation to the computing curriculum Key stages 1–4 at www.childnet.com/resources/esafety-and-computing.

- Savage and Barnett (2015) in *Digital Literacy for Primary Teachers* dedicate two chapters to addressing the areas and issues introduced here and provide more detailed guidance:

  Chapter 8: Digital identity and footprints for teachers, p 119

  Chapter 9: E-safety and digital safeguarding, p 133

- Although many of the extracts from children are from six years of age, there is still a great deal offered by Third et al's work when considering digital rights and responsibilities in relation to early childhood education. Additionally, many of the research tools employed offer ideas for enabling children to articulate their rights and responsibilities in a digital world.

  Third, A, Bellerose, D, Dawkins, U, Keltie, E and Pihl, K (2014) *Children's Rights in the Digital Age: A Download from Children Around the World*. Melbourne: Young and Well Cooperative Research Centre. [online] Available at: www.unicef.org/publications/files/Childrens_Rights_in_the_Digital_Age_A_Download_from_Children_Around_the_World_FINAL.pdf (accessed 9 March 2017).

References

Department for Education (DfE) (2011) Teachers' standards: guidance for school leaders, school staff and governing bodies. [online] Available at: www.gov.uk/government/uploads/system/uploads/attachment_data/file/301107/Teachers__Standards.pdf (accessed 9 March 2017).

Department for Education (DfE) (2013) Computing programmes of study: Key Stages 1 and 2, national curriculum in England. [online] Available at: www.gov.uk/government/uploads/system/uploads/attachment_data/file/239033/PRIMARY_national_curriculum_-_Computing.pdf (accessed 9 March 2017).

Department for Education (DfE) (2014) Statutory framework for the Early Years Foundation Stage: setting the standards for learning, development and care for children from birth to five. [online] Available at: www.gov.uk/government/uploads/system/uploads/attachment_data/file/335504/EYFS_framework_from_1_September_2014__with_clarification_note.pdf (accessed 9 March 2017).

HM Government (2015) Working together to safeguard children: a guide to inter-agency working to safeguard and promote the welfare of children. [online] Available at: www.gov.uk/government/uploads/system/uploads/attachment_data/file/419595/Working_Together_to_Safeguard_Children.pdf (accessed 9 March 2017).

National College for Teaching and Leadership (NCTL) (2013) Teachers' standards (early years). [online] Available at: www.gov.uk/government/uploads/system/uploads/attachment_data/file/211646/Early_Years_Teachers__Standards.pdf (accessed 9 March 2017).

National Day Nurseries Association (NDNA) (2016a) Camera, mobile phone and recording device use – England [online] Available at: www.ndna.org.uk/NDNA/Shop/Policies_and_Procedures_page_1.aspx (accessed 12 March 2017).

National Day Nurseries Association (NDNA) (2016b) *Mobile Phone and Social Networking – England*.

Office for Standards in Education, Children's Services and Skills (Ofsted) (2016) Inspecting safeguarding in early years, education and skills settings. Guidance for inspectors undertaking inspection under the common inspection framework. [online] Available at: www.gov.uk/government/uploads/system/uploads/attachment_data/file/547327/Inspecting_safeguarding_in_early_years_education_and_skills_settings.pdf (accessed 9 March 2017).

Open University (2014) Digital footprints. [online] Available at: www2.open.ac.uk/students/help/your-online-presence (accessed 9 March 2017).

Open University (2017) Your online presence. [online] Available at: Accessed 13/3/17 at www2.open.ac.uk/students/help/your-online-presence (accessed 13 March 2017).

Professional Association for Childcare and Early Years (PACEY) (2012) Staying safe online: An early years issue? [online] Available at: www.pacey.org.uk/news-and-views/news/staying-safe-online;-an-early-years-issue/ (accessed 9 March 2017).

Parkes, J (2016) Pre-school fights Ofsted downgrade on mobile phone use. *Nursery World*. [online] Available at: www.nurseryworld.co.uk/nursery-world/news/1156040/pre-school-fights-ofsted-downgrade-on-mobile-phone-use (accessed 9 March 2017).

Savage, M and Barnett, A (2015) *Digital Literacy for Primary Teachers*. Northwich: Critical Publishing

Third, A, Bellerose, D, Dawkins, U, Keltie, E and Pihl, K (2014) *Children's Rights in the Digital Age: A Download from Children Around the World*. Melbourne: Young and Well Cooperative Research Centre. [online] Available at: www.unicef.org/publications/files/Childrens_Rights_in_the_Digital_Age_A_Download_from_Children_Around_the_World_FINAL.pdf (accessed 9 March 2017).

13 Conclusion

At the outset of the book it was acknowledged that the topic of technology in early childhood education evokes varied responses in educators. The book has offered a way to consider your implementation decisions in an informed manner in relation to the context, age of learners and their uniqueness as individuals. Care was taken to unpick the Early Learning Goals and to explore how technology may enhance the learning process and/or outcome of that learning.

Chapter 2 presented a grounded-in-practice definition of *technology-enhanced learning* related to early years education. Informed by this holistic definition, a range of typical concerns were analysed in Chapter 3 by exploring what research to date has revealed. The concept of providing young children with a broad and balanced curriculum has been maintained. Technologies should be viewed as additional and complementary tools for accessing and expressing learning, rather than replacing traditional capabilities. Everyday cultural and societal practices with technology should be reflected in early years learning opportunities. Technology can be used to enrich learning, empower and include individuals.

Chapter 4 considered how developing technological capability allows children to understand and interact in the world around them. How the themes of *computer science and computational thinking*, *digital literacy* and *information technology* can be embedded in early years practice was considered. Simultaneously, the transferable skills involved in computational thinking and creativity were articulated. Chapter 5 explored the potential contribution technology can make in the prime area of communication and language development. Specifically, the range of digital contexts children encounter was analysed and the communicative competencies required were examined. The notion of language as a culturally defined system of symbols allowed you to reflect on your early years practice. You were encouraged to critically review the role of ebooks in relation to active listening strategies.

Chapter 6 moved the discussion forward to review the enhancement possibilities technology can offer in relation to physical development. The fine motor skills and gestures required to interact with tablet technology were examined. This discussion was extended to explore the merits of gaming in respect of psychomotor development. The notion of object affordance provided a framework to guide practitioners in the selection of developmentally appropriate technologies. Chapter 7 began by tackling some of the claims that technologies can have a detrimental impact on personal, social and emotional development and instead offered an analysis of the constructive ways in which technologies can support self-esteem, interpersonal relationships and extend networks of interaction.

Chapter 8 on literacy extended the discussion of communication and language from Chapter 5 and looked at how technologies can scaffold the development of early literacy. An overview was given on how applications can support letter and sound correspondence as children develop as readers and writers. You were encouraged to explore the scope of contemporary genres and the multimodal affordances offered by digital texts. The equally important area of mathematics development was addressed in Chapter 9. A comprehensive analysis was given on the relation between technology exploration and the development of mathematical schema in key conceptual areas.

Chapter 10 delved into technology-enabled forms of expression and creativity as children share their unique voice and perspectives on their world. Technological tools are viewed as extending the repertoire and language possibilities available to young learners. The potential for technological tools to be personalised extended the discussion to further explore the unique child in Chapter 11 on inclusion. Empowerment and independence are the goals in technology-enabled learning environments and an overview was given of technologies which can improve access to the curriculum. In both Chapters 10 and 11 the importance of children having unrestricted access to and control over their technology choices is viewed as fundamental. This pedagogical question of where the locus of control is underpins a stance adopted by the book of not limiting children's choices to adult capabilities and preferences. To do so may miss the transformational, empowerment and creative power of digital exploration and expression.

Finally, Chapter 12 ensured you are aware of your professional safeguarding and welfare responsibilities in relation to digital data, e-safety and the rights of the child growing up in a digitally rich world.

Where next?

Now to the question of what next and where technological innovation is likely to take us in the next few years. Trends in technology-enabled early years practice are likely to echo and reflect cultural adoption and situated practices.

The Internet of Things (IoT)

You may have already encountered the phrase the *Internet of Things*. This term can be understood as describing; the '*development of the Internet in which everyday objects have network connectivity, allowing them to send and receive data*' (Google, 2016). Another powerful viewpoint is that the IoT is the '*infrastructure of an information society*' (Wikipedia, 2016).

The Internet of things (stylised Internet of Things or IoT) is the internetworking of physical devices, vehicles (also referred to as 'connected devices' and 'smart devices'), buildings, and other items – embedded with electronics, software, sensors, actuators, and network connectivity that enable these objects to collect and exchange data.

(Wikipedia 2016, IoT, https://en.wikipedia.org/wiki/Internet_of_things)

Most devices in our homes, workplaces, centres of learning and places of leisure will be '*smart*'; capable of monitoring, tracking and reporting activity. Issues of digital privacy and cyber security will continue to grow in importance. Technology and technological innovation are in essence neutral. It is the power relationships and uses to which technology and data are put that evoke a value-based judgment of good or bad. The young children you are working with now will grow up to shape the ethical and moral landscape, where technology can be deployed to solve world problems, empower disenfranchised groups and promote global interconnectedness.

Critical question

» *Which smart devices do you already own or have you considered purchasing for your home or workplace? How might the role-play area and associated play look a decade from now? What rights and responsibilities will you require or wish to uphold in relation to the IoT in 2027?*

Will you, and the children you care for, own a smart *Family Hub Refrigerators,* already available in the marketplace? Will you interact with your fridge via a touchscreen and associated apps while '*inventory-watching cameras on the inside*' keep track of consumption and restock in consultation with the inbuilt '*menu and recipe planner*' (Samsung's Family Hub Fridge, 2016, www.cnet.com/uk/products/samsung-family-hub-refrigerator/review/)? CNET's 2016 *best smart home devices* contains many gadgets you may already own including:

• Amazon's Echo speaker – '*central control point for your smart home gadgets*', the '*voice-activated smart speaker*' and '*virtual assistant, "Alexa"*' (CNET, 2016).

John Lewis sell smart solutions for our heating, lighting, monitoring and security devices, entertainment and well-being (see their website at www.johnlewis.com/electricals/smart-home/c7000070016?rdr=1).

Wearable(s) technology

Another trend that is emerging, when watching young children mimic adults in role play, is that of *wearable technology*, often referred to as *wearables*. Think *fitbit* and similar products.

Wearable technology, wearables, fashionable technology, wearable devices, tech togs, or fashion electronics are smart electronic devices (electronic device with microcontrollers) that can be worn on the body as implant or accessories.

(Wikipedia, 2016, https://en.wikipedia.org/wiki/Wearable_technology)

Some wearable technologies have been with us a while; for example, hearing aids and smart heart implants. '*Wearable devices are rapidly advancing in terms of technology, functionality, and size, with more real-time applications*' (Wikipedia, 2016). Popular personal devices often fulfil the function of '*fitness or sport performance tracking*'; '*synchronising data and communication from other gadgets*'; '*navigation tools*'; '*media devices*' and '*communication gadgets*' (Wikipedia, 2016).

These trends are already reflected in the children's market and devices growing in popularity include:

- VTech's *Kidizoom* Smart Watch (www.vtech.co.uk/brands/brand_page/kidizoom).

- HereO the '*smallest, coolest GPS watch for kids*' (www.hereofamily.com).

- *Orbo Kids Smartwatch with Camera and lots of learning games* (http://tracking. watch/kids-smartwatch-with-camera/).

Connectivism

Technology constantly prompts educators to examine their pedagogical approaches and their appropriateness for society as it is now. One prominent model for technology-enhanced learning is that of connectivism. Siemens' (2004) seminal work, *Connectivism: A Learning Theory for the Digital Age* poses some of the questions that are reflective of the information-rich era that young children are growing up in. Downes and Siemens' model of connectivism is often referred to in words similar to '*a learning theory for a digital age, it seeks to explain complex learning in a rapidly changing social digital world*' (Cross et al, 2010). Some of the elements pose questions and challenges for educators including the ideas that:

- *Learning and knowledge rests in diversity of opinions.*

- *Learning is a process of connecting specialized nodes or information sources.*

- *Learning may reside in non-human appliances.*

- *Capacity to know more is more critical than what is currently known.*

- *Nurturing and maintaining connections is needed to facilitate continual learning.*

- *Ability to see connections between fields, ideas, and concepts is a core skill.*

- *Decision-making is itself a learning process. Choosing what to learn and the meaning of incoming information is seen through the lens of a shifting reality.*

(Cross et al, 2010)

Some aspects listed above already reflect elements of established early years practice; for example, the fundamental importance of fostering a disposition for learning in young children. Your practice seeks to enable young children to see patterns and make connections as they form and re-form mental schemas. Whatever your personal attitudes and values held about technology and our digital society, you will probably agree that it has never been more important to enable learners to be selective, probing, critical and adept purveyors of digital information and services.

Bloom's digital taxonomy

Another popular approach adopted by educators is re-envisaging Bloom's taxonomy of *thinking behaviours* in a digital context reflective of today's world (Cross et al, 2010). One site worth browsing is Churches' (2016) wiki, *Educational Origami*, found at http://edori-gami.wikispaces.com/home, where there is a wealth of information to ponder.

International Society for Technology in Education

The US-based *International Society for Technology in Education* (ISTE) set professional standards for educators which embody the '*new skills and pedagogical insights educators need to teach, work and learn in the digital age*' (ISTE, 2016). Aligned to these are aspirational standards for learners, '*enabling them to engage and thrive in a connected, digital world*' (ISTE, 2016):

- *empowered learner;*
- *digital citizen;*
- *knowledge constructor;*
- *global collaborator;*
- *innovative designer;*
- *computational thinker;*
- *creative communicator.*

(www.iste.org)

The principle of '*every child is a unique child*' underpins the ethos and pedagogical approaches suggested in this book (DfE, 2014, p 5). Technologies can be personalised and used to scaffold learning for individuals. The repertoire of digital tools means there are multiple opportunities for children to express and share their unique perspective. The provisionality affordance of technology can constructively support children to be experimental, and to develop '*resilient*', '*capable*' and '*confident*' dispositions (DfE, 2014, p 5). The authors have argued that technological tools should form a complementary part of the physical and virtual '*enabling environment*' and contribute to building and sustaining '*positive relationships*' and networks within and beyond the setting (DfE, 2014, p 5). Technologies can engender a '*playful*' approach to learning with tools to explore and investigate, creating transformational viewpoints that may not be possible otherwise (eg microscope) (DfE, 2014, p 9). Many young children will find using technology is motivational and enjoyable, replicating practices of parents and siblings. Technology is not a barrier to '*creating and thinking critically*'; it opens up greater possibilities and demands a discerning approach by users (DfE, 2014, p 9).

To conclude, let us reflect on where in this book examples have been suggested that embody the aspiration of enabling learners.

Table 13.1 Mapping the ISTE Standards for Students *across TEL in EYFS chapters*

ISTE Standards for Students (2016)	Exemplification of how technologies can enhance learning in this book
Empowered learner	TEL has at its core the principle of empowering learners and we have underscored the principle of children having autonomous control and access to technologies in their setting throughout the book. **Chapter 11: Technologies for inclusion** provides numerous examples of where technology can empower children by overcoming barriers related to SEND.
Digital citizen	**Chapter 4: Understanding the world** explored the aligned concepts of digital literacy and digital citizenship.
Knowledge constructor	In relation to knowledge construction, the book's structure reflects the *'seven areas of learning and development'* (DfE, 2014, pp 7–8): • *communication and language* – **Chapter 5**; • *physical development* – **Chapter 6**; • *personal, social and emotional development* – **Chapter 7**; • *literacy* – **Chapter 8**; • *mathematics* – **Chapter 9**; • *understanding the world* – **Chapter 4**; • *expressive arts and design* – **Chapter 10**.
Global collaborator	**Chapter 4** directly addresses the notion of digital citizenship. However, from **Chapter 3** onwards the authors sought to challenge the notion of technology as a *'static activity, carried out in isolation'*. Collaborative technology tools and approaches are given in each chapter.
Innovative designer	In relation to creativity and innovative design, **Chapter 4** explores creative approaches in the design process. Similarly, **Chapter 10** explores art and design processes using technology.
Computational thinker	**Chapter 4: Understanding the world** robustly tackled the links between computational thinking and pedagogical approaches including; *'tinkering, creating, debugging, persevering and collaborating'* (Barefoot Computing, 2016).
Creative communicator	Several chapters make a contribution to enabling children to be creative communicators. **Chapter 5: Communication and language** and **Chapter 8: Literacy** focused on how technology can equip learners with the means to communicate digitally. **Chapter 10** extends this to include **expressive arts and design**.

Recommended further reading

- Donohue, C (2014) *Technology and Digital Media in the Early Years: Tools for Teaching and Learning*. Abingdon: Routledge.

- Donohue, C (2017) *Family Engagement in the Digital Age: Early Childhood Educators as Media Mentors*. Abingdon: Routledge.

- Garvis, S (2016) *Understanding Digital Technologies and Young Children*. Abingdon: Routledge.

- Kaye, L (2016) *Young Children in a Digital Age: Supporting Learning and Development with Technology in Early Years.* Abingdon: Routledge.

- Kucirkova, K and Falloon, G (2016) *Apps, Technology and Younger Learners: International Evidence for Teaching*. Abingdon: Routledge.

- Savin-Baden, M (2015) *Rethinking Learning in an Age of Digital Fluency: Is Being Digitally Tethered a New Learning Nexus?* Abingdon: Routledge.

References

Barefoot Computing (2016) [online] Available at: http://barefootcas.org.uk (accessed 9 March 2017).

CBS Interactive Inc (CNET) (2016) Samsung Family Hub Refrigerator review: Finally, a smart fridge that feels smart. Available at: [online] www.cnet.com/uk/products/samsung-family-hub-refrigerator/review/ (accessed 13 March 2017).

Churches, A (2016) Educational origami. [online] Available at: http://edorigami.wikispaces.com (accessed 9 March 2017).

Cross, C, Hamilton, K, Plested, D and Rezk, M (2010) *Connectivism*. EduCitizenship 2020 wiki. [online] Available at: http://education-2020.wikispaces.com/Connectivism (accessed 9 March 2017).

Department for Education (DfE) (2014) Statutory framework for the Early Years Foundation Stage: setting the standards for learning, development and care for children from birth to five. [online] Available at: www.gov.uk/government/uploads/system/uploads/attachment_data/file/335504/EYFS_framework_from_1_September_2014__with_clarification_note.pdf (accessed 9 March 2017).

Donohue, C (2014) *Technology and Digital Media in the Early Years: Tools for Teaching and Learning*. Oxon: Routledge.

Donohue, C (2017) *Family Engagement in the Digital Age: Early Childhood Educators as Media Mentors*. Oxon: Routledge.

Garvis, S (2016) *Understanding Digital Technologies and Young Children*. Oxon: Routledge.

Google (2016) The Internet of Things (as searched for on Google) [online] Available at: www.google.co.uk (accessed 13 March 2017).

International Society for Technology in Education (ISTE) (2016) ISTE Standards: Education technology standards to transform learning and teaching. [online] Available at: www.iste.org/standards/standards (accessed 9 March 2017).

Kaye, L (2016) *Young Children in a Digital Age: Supporting Learning and Development with Technology in Early Years.* Oxon: Routledge.

Kucirkova, K and Falloon, G (2016) *Apps, Technology and Younger Learners: International Evidence for Teaching*. Oxon: Routledge.

Savin-Baden, M (2015) *Rethinking Learning in an Age of Digital Fluency: Is Being Digitally Tethered a New Learning Nexus?* Oxon: Routledge.

Siemens, G (2004) Connectivism: a learning theory for the digital age. [online] Available at: www.elearnspace.org/Articles/connectivism.htm (accessed 9 March 2017).

Wikipedia (2016) The Internet of Things. [online] Available at: https://en.wikipedia.org/wiki/Internet_of_things (accessed 13 March 2017).

Index